The Guide to Creating Dazzling Graphics for Your

PAINT SHOP PRO
Web Graphics

Third Edition

Written By

Andy Shafran & Lori J. Davis

with Sarah Arnott

Paint Shop Pro Web Graphics

Library of Congress Catalog Number 00-106697

ISBN 1-929685-13-0

5   4   3   2   1

Educational facilities, companies, and organizations interested in multiple copies or licensing of this book should contact the publisher for quantity discount information. Training manuals, CD-ROMs, and portions of this book are also available individually or can be tailored for specific needs.

MUSKA&LIPMAN

Muska & Lipman Publishing
2645 Erie Avenue, Suite 41
Cincinnati, Ohio 45208
www.muskalipman.com
publisher@muskalipman.com

This book is composed in Melior, Columbia, Helvetica, and Courier typefaces using QuarkXpress 4.1.1, Adobe PhotoShop 6.0, and Adobe Illustrator 9.0.

Created in Cincinnati, Ohio, in the United States of America

Credits

Publisher
Andy Shafran

Managing Editor
Hope Stephan

Copy Editing
Hope Stephan
Molly Flynn

Technical Editor
Sarah Arnott

Proofreader
Molly Flynn

Cover Designer
John Windhorst

Production Manager
Cathie Tibbetts

Production Team
DOV Graphics
  Michelle Frey

Indexer
Dawn Spencer

Printer
C.J. Krehbiel

About the Authors

Andy Shafran

Chapters 6, 7, 12, and 13
andy@shafran.com
http://www.shafran.com

Andy Shafran is a Paint Shop Pro expert and the author of more than a dozen books. A graduate of Ohio State, he now lives in Cincinnati. He has personally taught several thousand users how to get more out of Paint Shop Pro at SmartPlanet. He is an avid fan of the Cincinnati Reds and the Ohio State Buckeyes. When he's not writing, you can often finding him watching or listening to a baseball game.

He lives with his wife, Liz, and their two cats, Cary Grant Shafran and Audrey Hepburn Shafran, in a small house that has a lot of hedges, always in need of a trim. His favorite color is red.

Acknowledgments

Muska & Lipman Publishing was started three years ago, and the first book was the previous edition of this title. Because publishing a book is such a collaborative process, there are many people I'd like to thank. Most importantly, I'd like to thank my wife, Liz, for being so supportive, patient, and understanding as we have gone down the path towards starting and running a publishing company.

Next, I'd like to thank the great staff at Muska & Lipman. Without them, this book wouldn't be here. Thank you to Lori and Sarah for being great collaborators on this project. You are both very knowledgeable about Paint Shop Pro and were a great team. You kept my sections honest and succinct with gentle prodding. This book is so great because of your dedication.

Finally, I'd like to thank the many supporting companies and partners who have made this book and Muska & Lipman successful. Thanks to Jasc for writing great software and helping us out whenever they could. Thanks to book retailers who took a chance that this title would be well received, and thanks to SmartPlanet for their unwavering support of our classes.

Lori Davis

Chapters 1, 2, 3, 4, 5, 8, 9, and 14

An art lover all her life and a Net fanatic since the early 1980s, Lori Davis found that Web graphics provided a wonderful melding of two of her longtime interests. She started out with Paint Shop Pro, and even though she's since used many different graphics programs as well, Lori still finds PSP to be the ideal tool for creating Web graphics. You can see this at her PSP tutorial Web site, Lori's Web Graphics, at **http://loriweb.pair.com/**.

The author of *Paint Shop Pro 6 Power!*, Lori is a former college teacher who has also had a stint as a computer manual writer and editor. She continues to write, both in her current day job and on her own projects. When she isn't writing or experimenting with graphics, Lori enjoys walks on the beach, photography, knitting, gardening, and drinking good but inexpensive wine. She lives with her husband, Larry, and their two cats in New Jersey, the Garden State.

Dedication

To Miss Feldman and Sr. Jeanne LaFreniere. Thanks for the crayons, clay, chisels, and encouragement!

Acknowledgments

I can't begin to list all the fun-loving and creative people in the online graphics community who I've had the pleasure to interact with. For fear of inadvertently leaving someone out, I won't even try to thank you all by name here, but do know how much I appreciate your sharing and your friendship.

Thanks to my fellow instructors at ElementK and SmartPlanet, Pat Kalbaugh and Nancy Dixon, and to the great people who have served as our teaching assistants. Thanks, too, to all the private beta testers for Paint Shop Pro 5, 6, and 7—you folks are wild.

Thanks to everyone who helped make this book possible, especially Andy Shafran, Sarah Arnott, and Hope Stephan. Besides their admirable talent, Andy, Sarah, and Hope all have incredible energy and a marvelous sense of humor—qualities that are essential for making a project like this one become a reality. These guys have made working on this book a joy, despite the inevitable rough spots.

An extra special thank you to my husband, Larry Synal, who had to endure my hours and hours at the computer as I typed away and worked on examples. Thanks for your patience, wacky commentary, and helpful suggestions, Lar! (Not to mention your never *really* hitting the power button while I was working.)

Sarah Arnott

Chapter 11
http://www.bysarah.com/mg

Sarah Arnott is a computer professional who spends most of her time working in a character-based world. When she's not working, she enjoys creating Web pages, working with digital photography, and, of course, graphics. Sarah started making simple Web graphics with Paint Shop Pro several years ago and was instantly hooked.

Sarah has worked with Lori as a teaching assistant for Paint Shop Pro classes at ZDU/Smart Planet and provided technical editing for Lori's book, *PSP Power*! She enjoys helping others learn this program and has created a series of tutorials at her site, Making Graphics.

Dedication

To Diane who really got me started with graphics and who has been a source of limitless encouragement, inspiration and friendship *whw*.

Acknowledgments

I would like to thank Andy and Lori for inviting me to write for this book and Hope for making sure it all came together. Thanks to the PSP gang for lots of fun and challenges that have helped me learn more about Paint Shop Pro: Mary, Sherry, Jade, Jen, Diane, Laura, Rollie, Deb, and so many others.

Contents

7—Optimizing Web Graphics   133

8—Coordinating Web Graphics   157

9—Making the Best Backgrounds   183

Part III Accelerating Your Images

Part IV Powerful Web Tools

Introduction

Welcome to *Paint Shop Pro Web Graphics, Third Edition*. This book has been completely revised for the latest version of Paint Shop Pro and is the best way for you to learn how to create great-looking graphics for your Web site.

Graphics are the heart and soul of the World Wide Web. Nearly every page you visit, every site you bookmark, and every hour you spend browsing focuses on Web sites built around exciting and innovative Web graphics.

This book teaches you to master Paint Shop Pro, one of the world's leading graphics packages. This introduction is meant to give you an overview of the book and help you get the most out of it.

What You'll Find in This Book

This book will step you through the techniques needed to create eye-catching graphics suitable for your Web site. Paint Shop Pro is a multifaceted tool, but it has many features available to optimize, edit, and publish graphics specifically for the Web. We've included numerous tutorials, dozens of practical tips, and fourteen chapters of solution-oriented text.

You'll learn how to use impressive tools and techniques to create great graphics for your Web sites with Paint Shop Pro. This award-winning software is all you'll need to create graphics from scratch. Every image presented, every example used, and every graphic on this book's companion Web site has been created and edited within Paint Shop Pro. We not only *explain* how to use this excellent product, but we show you as well.

Here are several important concepts that you will learn. Keep these concepts in mind as you read; they are the guiding principles of this book:

▶ **Graphics can make, or break, a decent Web page.**

▶ **Paint Shop Pro has all the necessary tools built in to create great Web graphics.**

▶ **Expert-looking graphics can come from non-graphics experts who have the right knowledge of Paint Shop Pro.**

▶ *Paint Shop Pro Web Graphics* **is all about optimizing colors, shapes, and photos so they look good and download fast when placed on Web pages.**

As you read this book, you'll find we don't gloss over difficult subjects nor do we assume you understand all sorts of new terminology. Instead, we give you complete explanations, step-by-step techniques, and comprehensive coverage of the features found within Paint Shop Pro.

This is meant to be a practical guide to making Web graphics. You'll find help in achieving all your image-related goals in these easy-to-understand and fun-to-read chapters. You'll enjoy seeing entertaining examples and building graphics that can complement a variety of different Web pages.

Who This Book is For

This book is for graphics hobbyists and Paint Shop Pro users who want to build the best images for their Web site. New users to Paint Shop Pro will appreciate the early chapters introducing the software and basic features, while experienced users can get up to speed quickly on the new features in Paint Shop Pro 7.

This book assumes you are comfortable with Windows, have Paint Shop Pro installed, and are interested in Web graphics, but you don't know where to start or how to use the built-in specialized tools of Paint Shop Pro.

Here are a few other assumptions we made about you and your skill level:

▶ **You're a Web User**—You should already be connected to the Web at home, work, or school, and understand how to use Netscape or Internet Explorer to comfortably surf from one site to another.

▶ **You Can Build Web Pages**—This book focuses on creating and using graphics on a Web page and only glosses over some HTML techniques that specifically pertain to using graphics effectively. If you don't know anything about HTML or building simple Web pages, go to your local bookstore and grab a solid reference on the subject. I recommend *Creating Your Own Web Pages, Second Edition* or *Teach Yourself HTML 4 in 24 Hours*.

▶ **You Want to Learn**—This book has been carefully planned and laid out to be most useful and efficient for those learning Web graphics. Working with graphics can sometimes be challenging—particularly when working with advanced options and features. However, your desire to learn graphics will make understanding even the trickiest tasks a breeze.

▶ **You're Running Windows 95, 98, or NT 4, or above**—Paint Shop Pro is only available for the PC platform. Other graphics software products are available for Mac users, but they are not covered here. Additionally, you should be familiar with installing and running programs on your own computer.

How This Book is Organized

In general, this book is intended to be read from beginning to end, as the easiest subjects tend to be presented first, with the hardest last. We start off with basics that everyone should know when using graphics on the Web, then focus on specific advanced Paint Shop Pro subject areas.

Feel free, however, to use this book as a reference. Remember that some chapters do build on previous ones; but many subjects are self-contained and organized logically in the order that you're likely to need them.

For your convenience, we've divided the book into four sections. Here they are, along with a brief description of the chapters they contain:

Part I: Making Great Images

▶ Chapter 1, "Paint Shop Pro Basics." Learn the nuances of the Paint Shop Pro interface and see what's new in version 7.

▶ Chapter 2, "Acquiring Images." This chapter teaches you how to find images to start with for your Web site. Learn how to build images from scratch, integrate images from a digital camera, or scan an image directly into Paint Shop Pro.

▶ Chapter 3, "Editing Images." Delve into the Paint Shop Pro image editing tools to make simple adjustments that vastly improve the quality of your graphics.

▶ Chapter 4, "Making Images By Hand." An entire chapter that teaches you the specific Paint Shop Pro tools useful for building Web graphics, icons, and illustrations from scratch.

Part II: Marrying PSP to the Web

▶ Chapter 5, "Web Graphics Basics." Learn the specific image formats and Web particulars when creating and saving graphics for your Web site.

▶ Chapter 6, "Creating Transparent Images." Master image transparency, a useful technique for placing images on colored backgrounds.

▶ Chapter 7, "Optimizing Web Graphics." Paint Shop Pro comes with an advanced set of optimization tools that let you adjust the appearance and file size of your Web graphics. Learn about these tools and related techniques here.

▶ Chapter 8, "Coordinating Web Graphics." This chapter teaches you how to create a set of graphics for your site that are coordinated and follow good Web-design principles.

▶ Chapter 9, "Making the Best Backgrounds." Background images add texture and flair to your site. Learn how to create small background images that integrate into your site's background.

Part III: Accelerating Your Images

▶ Chapter 10, "Using Layers." Layers let you build images that have multiple parts in easier fashion. Learn about using layers effectively.

▶ Chapter 11, "Drawing with Vectors." Vectors are a new functionality that enables you to edit text and objects added to your image. Learn how to add a vector object to make future edits easier when building web images.

Part IV: Powerful Web Tools

▶ Chapter 12, "Image Mapping and Slicing." When building large Web graphics and navigation bars, you'll often need to take advantage of two new Paint Shop Pro tools—the Image Mapper and Image Slicer. Learn how these tools work and when to use them on your Web site.

▶ Chapter 13, "Animation on the Web." This chapter introduces you to Animation Shop, the powerful tool that comes with Paint Shop Pro used to make animated images for Web sites.

▶ Chapter 14, "Creating Rollovers."' Rollover effects allow you to add pizzazz to your Web site without using animation or other advanced tools. Learn the basics behind rollovers, how to create the images, and how to use them in your site.

Conventions Used in This Book

The following conventions are used in this book:

All HTML conventions and tags appear in FULL MONOSPACE CAPS. This will enable you to tell the difference between the text that appears on-screen and text that tells your Web browser what to do. Web browsers don't care whether your HTML is in full caps.

Commands, actions, and hot keys are shown in **bold** type. When you are giving a choice of commands to achieve the result you want, the commands are shown in ***bold italic*** type.

All Web page URLs mentioned in the book appear in **boldface**, as in **www.jasc.com.**

Besides these terminological and typographic conventions, the book also features the following special displays for different types of important text:

TIP

Text formatted like this offers a helpful tip relevant to the topic being discussed in the main text.

NOTE

Text formatted like this highlights other interesting or useful information that relates to the topic under discussion.

CAUTION

Cautions highlight actions or commands that can make irreversible changes to your files or potentially cause problems in the future. Read them carefully, because they contain important information that can make the difference between keeping your files, software and hardware safe and your losing a huge amount of work.

Keeping the Book's Content Current

You made a long-term investment when you purchased this book. To keep your investment paying off, We've developed a comprehensive companion Web site for you. The site contains:

- ▶ Up-to-date information on the world of graphics
- ▶ Special offers on software and products just for readers
- ▶ Corrections or clarifications to the book's text and images
- ▶ New resources you can use to stay on the cutting edge
- ▶ URLs of readers like you who submit their Web site
- ▶ Much more!

Make sure you visit **http://www.muskalipman.com/webgraphics** to stay current on any important updates to this book. In addition, all of the examples used and mentioned throughout the book can be downloaded, for free, from this Web site. We are committed to providing you with the best and most up-to-date information possible on using Paint Shop Pro to build Web graphics.

Part I
Making Great Images

1
Paint Shop Pro Basics

You've purchased and installed Paint Shop Pro. What's next? The first thing to do is to get comfortable with the program. Here's what you'll look at in this chapter:

▶ **Getting Acquainted with Paint Shop Pro's Interface**
Discover the unique and versatile features of this robust graphics computer program. The award-wining Paint Shop Pro lets you do everything from creating and editing images to designing complete Web pages and animations.

▶ **Configuring Paint Shop Pro to Better Suit Your Needs**
Learn about the powerful tools PSP puts at your fingertips and how to set them up to best serve you.

What is Paint Shop Pro?

Paint Shop Pro (PSP) is an easy-to-use yet powerful bitmap graphics editor developed and released by Jasc Software, Inc. (**http://www.jasc.com/**). Jasc, founded in 1991 and located in Minneapolis, Minnesota, specializes in producing graphics and graphics management software for Windows-based computers. Besides Paint Shop Pro, Jasc Software's products include Jasc Media Center Plus, Quick View Plus, and Image Robot, among others.

Paint Shop Pro is comparable to much higher priced painting and photo editing programs, enabling you to create new images, edit existing images, add interesting deformations and effects, and convert more than thirty different image formats into graphics that are perfect for Web pages, print, or multimedia presentations.

In addition to its painting and photo-enhancing tools, Paint Shop Pro includes vector-based drawing tools. Vector graphics, unlike bitmap graphics, aren't made by painting pixels on a computer screen. Instead, vector graphics are produced from instructions to the computer on how to draw a shape. Vectors allow you to create graphics that are readily resizeable without distortion.

Paint Shop Pro also includes some very handy tools for creating Web graphics.

A visit to Jasc's home page gives you easy access to all its products and support features (see Figure 1.1).

Figure 1.1
The Jasc Software home page is the clearinghouse for everything pertaining to Paint Shop Pro.

The PSP Workspace and Interface

When you first load Paint Shop Pro, you'll see the splash page followed by a window containing a tip. As you'll quickly notice, most of the Paint Shop Pro window is blank—wide open for you to start creating your own Web graphics, shown in Figure 1.2. This is the PSP workspace.

Figure 1.2
Paint Shop Pro's Workspace, major palettes, and menus.

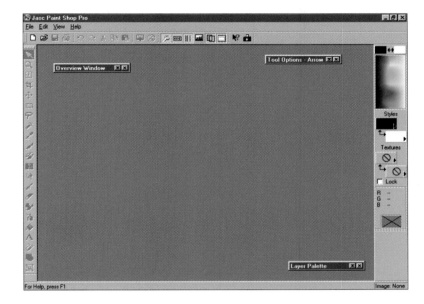

Paint Shop Pro's workspace is surrounded by PSP's major palettes and toolbars: the Tool Palette, Color Palette, the Tool Bar and the Menu Bar. And at the bottom of the workspace is PSP's Status Bar.

The Tool Palette

The Tool Palette, which appears by default along the left edge of the workspace, contains all of PSP's image editing and selection tools. Figure 1.3 shows the Tool Palette displayed horizontally.

Figure 1.3
The Tool Palette.

To select a tool, click its icon on the Tool Palette. We'll look at some of the most commonly used tools in later chapters.

Part I Making Great Images

The Color Palette

On the right-hand side of the workspace, you'll notice the Color Palette (Figure 1.4).

Figure 1.4
The Color Palette.

From the Color Palette, you can choose the colors to use for painting on your image canvas, drawing lines and shapes, or adding text. Move your mouse over the spectrum-like array of colors towards the top of the Color Palette and notice how the mouse cursor changes shape, looking like an eye dropper. Click on any of the colors of this section—called the Available Colors panel—and you'll select that color as the current foreground/stroke color. Right-click on any of the colors in the Available Colors panel and you'll select that color as the current background/ fill color.

Right below the Available Colors panel is a set of two overlapping blocks of color labeled "Styles." When a painting tool is active, these two color blocks represent the current foreground and background painting colors. You can click with a painting tool on either one of these blocks to bring up the Color dialog box (Figure 1.5).

Figure 1.5
The Color dialog box.

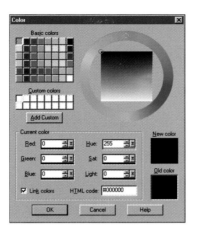

NOTE
If the color depth of the image you're editing is less than 16.7 million colors, the Color dialog box will show your image's limited color palette rather than the color selection controls you see in Figure 1.5.

When a drawing tool is active, the Styles blocks represent the Stroke (that is, the outline) and the Fill of your drawn shapes and curves.

We'll take a closer look at the painting and drawing tools and the Color Palette in Chapter 4, "Drawing Images by Hand."

The Tool Bar

The Tool Bar, which by default appears toward the top of the workspace, enables you to access the most commonly used PSP commands and palettes (see Figure 1.6).

Figure 1.6
The Tool Bar.

TIP
You can customize the Tool Bar by adding or removing icons for the various operations and palettes. To customize the Tool Bar, choose **View > ToolBars**. In the Toolbars dialog box, highlight ***Standard Toolbar*** and then click the **Customize** button. You can then select from the available icons to add to the Tool Bar, and you can also choose to remove any of the icons currently displayed on the Tool Bar.

NOTE

Paint Shop Pro includes three other toolbars that you can also display: the Web Toolbar, the Photo Toolbar, and the Effects Toolbar. You can display any or all of these toolbars by choosing **View > ToolBars** and, in the Toolbars dialog box, checking the toolbars that you want to be displayed.

You can customize the Web toolbar, Photo toolbar, and Effects toolbar in the same way that you customize the Standard toolbar. Just highlight the name of the relevant toolbar in the Toolbars dialog box, click **Customize**, and then **Add/Remove** icons for that toolbar.

Floatable Palettes

Each of these palettes—the Tool Palette, the Color Palette, and the Tool Bar—is floatable and dockable. To float the Tool Palette or Tool Bar, drag the handle on the palette's left or top. (The handle appears on the left when the palette is currently docked and horizontal. The handle appears on the top when the palette is currently docked and vertical.) To float the Color Palette, drag on an empty area of the palette.

You can reposition a floating palette on the workspace by dragging its title bar. To redock one of these floating palettes, just drag it to one of the side edges or top of the workspace or double-click on the palette's title bar.

The Menu Bar

The Menu Bar, which appears at the very top of the workspace, contains menus for accessing PSP commands and operations. As Figure 1.7 shows, the Menu Bar includes menus labeled **F**ile, **E**dit, **V**iew, **I**mage, Effects, **C**olors, **L**ayers, **O**bjects, **S**elections, **M**asks, **W**indow, and **H**elp.

Figure 1.7
The Menu Bar.

TIP

Paint Shop Pro's tools and palettes, along with most of its commands and operations, can be accessed with keyboard shortcuts. See Appendix B, "PSP Keyboard Shortcuts" for listings.

The Status Bar

At the very bottom of the PSP workspace is the Status Bar, which
displays information of various sorts:

▶ When you mouse-over a tool's icon on the Tool Palette, a description
of the tool is displayed.

▶ When you mouse-over an icon on the Tool Bar, a description of the
PSP command or operation accessed by the icon is displayed.

▶ When you mouse-over areas of the Color Palette, the Status Bar
indicates what the various parts of the palette are for.

▶ When you position the mouse cursor in an image canvas, the Status
Bar displays the coordinates of the cursor. Other useful information
may also be displayed, depending on which tool is active.

Using the Tool Options Palette

One of the most important palettes to understand and master is the Tool
Options palette, the palette you use to set the majority of options for
PSP's tools. Each tool on the Tool Palette has its own version of the Tool
Options palette. Depending on the tool, you'll find either two or three
tabs on the Tool Options palette. The leftmost tab is the tool's main tab.
Figure 1.8 shows the tool tab for the Selection tool. Notice that this tab is
labeled with the tool's icon as it appears on the Tool Palette.

Figure 1.8
The tool tab of the
Tool Options palette for
the Selection tool.

TIP

When you have an image open and the Tool Options palette is not displayed,
you can toggle the palette on by pressing the letter O key on your keyboard or
by clicking the Tool Options palette icon on the Tool Bar.

To toggle the Tool Options palette off, press the letter O or click the palette's
icon on the Tool Bar again.

The Tool Options Tab

Some tools have more controls than can fit on a single tab. For these tools, there's also an Options tab. Figure 1.9 shows the Tool Options tab for the Retouch tool.

Figure 1.9
The Tool Options tab on the Tool Options palette for the Retouch tool.

The Cursor and Tablet Tab

All tools have a Cursor and Tablet tab, shown in Figure 1.10.

Figure 1.10
The Cursor and Tablet tab on the Tool Options palette.

This tab contains controls for setting options for the cursor and for pressure-sensitive tablets (the tablet controls being active only if you have a pressure-sensitive tablet). If you make a change to the options on this tab, the settings remain in effect—even if you switch to a different tool—until you change the settings again.

The Tool Selection Button

Something else that's available on any Tool Options palette is the Tool Selection button, on the upper right of the palette. Press this button to get a drop-down menu of all the tools available on the Tool Palette. This handy feature makes it possible to access the tools even if you have the Tool Palette turned off. When you want to select a tool, just press the Tool Selection button and make your selection.

Auto Rollup

Besides being able to toggle the Tool Options palette on and off, you can make use of Auto Rollup. When Auto Rollup is on, the palette will "roll up" like a window shade when the cursor is used in another window (such as an image canvas). If you'd prefer to have the palette locked in its open position, click the arrow-labeled button on the palette's title bar.

NOTE

Auto Rollup is also available for the Layer Palette, Overview Window, and the Histogram Window.

The Layer Palette

Paint Shop Pro makes available to you a very powerful feature—layers. Layers let you separate your image into different levels so you can edit and modify pieces of a graphic independently. Think of a layer as a clear sheet of plastic on which you paint. Like painted sheets of plastic, layers can be stacked one on top of another, allowing solid areas on lower layers to show through transparent areas of higher layers.

The Layer Palette, shown in Figure 1.11, is the control center for creating and editing individual layers in your PSP images.

Figure 1.11
The Layer Palette.

On the Layer Palette, each layer has its own labeled Layer button and set of controls. We'll be examining the Layer Palette more closely in Chapter 10, "Using Layers."

Part I Making Great Images

The Histogram Window

The Histogram Window (Figure 1.12) is a handy PSP interface feature to get familiar with if a lot of the work you do involves editing digital photos.

Figure 1.12
The Histogram Window.

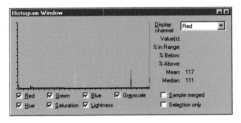

Used with advanced color adjustment operations, the Histogram Window is a graphical representation of the color and brightness values used in your image. Many designers use the Histogram Window to check contrast and color distribution in their digital photos. We'll look at this feature a bit in Chapter 3, "Editing Images."

The Overview Window

Paint Shop Pro provides you with a handy way to get an overview of your image: the Overview Window. As shown in Figure 1.13, the Overview Window lets you get a look at your entire image even when the image is too big to fit on the screen.

Figure 1.13
The Overview Window.

Toggling the Toolbars and Palettes

Each set of tools can be toggled on or off by clicking its icon on the main PSP Tool Bar or by choosing **View** > **ToolBars** from the Menu Bar to bring up the Toolbars dialog box (Figure 1.14).

Figure 1.14
Toggle on and off the various Paint Shop Pro toolbars from here.

Use the Toolbars dialog box to select all the toolbars that you want to see, then click on Close to continue editing your images.

You can also toggle some of the palettes and windows on and off using keyboard shortcuts:

Histogram Window	**H**
Layer Palette	**L**
Tool Options palette	**O** (the letter)
Tool Bar(s)	**T**
Overview Window	**W**

Using Paint Shop Pro's Help System

Paint Shop Pro comes with a comprehensive and extremely useful interactive help system. Nearly any topic you can think of that relates to making images or configuring PSP is presented, along with many useful tips for using PSP.

To access the interactive help, choose **Help** > **Help** Topics from the Menu Bar. Figure 1.15 shows the Help Topics in action.

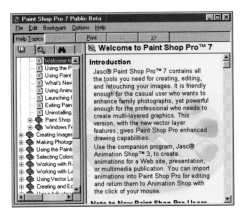

The PSP Help window has two panes: on the left is the navigation pane
and on the right is the contents pane. In the navigation pane, you can
choose the Contents tab, the Index tab, or the Search tab. This provides
you three different ways of locating the information you want.

Make liberal use of the PSP Help system. And take some time to browse
it even before you have a specific problem. You're bound to find useful
nuggets of information!

Configuring Paint Shop Pro

We've already seen that you can customize PSP's toolbars with **V**iew >
ToolBars. Under **F**ile > **P**references, you'll also find an option called
General Program Preferences. Select this menu option to open the
General Program Preferences dialog box (Figure 1.16). Here you can
modify the settings for such things as grid spacing, undo limits, and
aspects of the appearance of dialog boxes and palettes.

Figure 1.16
The General Program
Preferences dialog box.

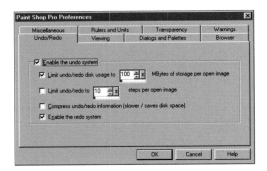

You can also tell Paint Shop Pro where to look for various support files, such as Patterns, Gradients, Picture Tubes, and so on. You open the File Locations dialog box (figure 1.17) with **F**ile > Preferences > File Locations. There you click on the tab you want and specify paths for the relevant files.

Figure 1.17
The File Locations dialog box.

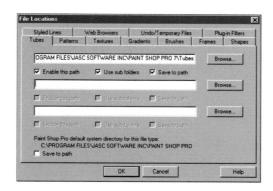

2
Acquiring Images

In this chapter, you'll learn how to find and work with existing images, either ones from digital image collections or ones that you've scanned or taken with a digital camera yourself. You'll learn how to adjust the images for your own Web pages and will discover a number of handy techniques for customizing existing images.

▶ **Finding Graphics on the Internet or CD-ROM**
A world of images is waiting for you to explore and use when you get permission from the original artists or choose stock images and photographs.

▶ **Using Scanners and Digital Cameras with PSP**
Scan images and offload photos from your digital camera directly to PSP.

▶ **Capturing Screen Shots**
Sometimes the graphics you need are right in front of you. Paint Shop Pro makes grabbing and using them a snap.

Finding Existing Graphics to Use

Sometimes the best way to get the graphic files you need is to find them ready-made. Literally millions and millions of photos, drawings, animations, and Web graphics are available for you to use. This section describes several different popular and common methods for obtaining great images to start with.

Searching the Web for Images

With millions of drawings, photos, and icons available, you are virtually guaranteed to find useful images through a little exploration on the Web. Hundreds of sites have collections of images for free download. You can download these images and edit them with Paint Shop Pro or use them without making any changes.

Keep in mind that, although it's easy to grab almost any graphic you see on the Web, you can legally use only those images that the copyright holder grants (or sells) to you. Many sites offer collections of free-to-use graphics. But if the owner hasn't indicated that his or her images can be used for free, without any restrictions, you should not assume that the images are yours for the taking. When in doubt, contact the owner. Figure 2.1 shows the ArtToday Web site, an affordable subscription-based service where you can find great images.

Figure 2.1
ArtToday is one source of free graphics.

Here are a few popular sites for innovative and free graphics:

▶ **ArtToday**
   http://www.arttoday.com/

▶ **Free Stuff**
   http://webweaverxxi.com/freestuff/

▶ **Iconz**
   http://www.geocities.com/Heartland/1448/

▶ **Jim's Cool Icons**
   http://snaught.com/JimsCoolIcons/

▶ **NBCi.com - Clip Art**
   http://wwwx.nbci.com/images/

Also try visiting Yahoo! (**http://www.yahoo.com**) or any other search site. Search for Free Graphics or Icons or Clip Art. You'll find many Internet sites that have free images, along with sites that offer images for sale.

Getting the Graphics You Find

As you probably know, grabbing an image from a Web page is as simple as right-clicking the image, then picking Save Image As in Netscape Navigator or Save Picture As in Microsoft Explorer. Figure 2.2 shows an image being saved with Netscape.

Figure 2.2
Browsers let you save images from a Web site.

Saving an Image to your Computer

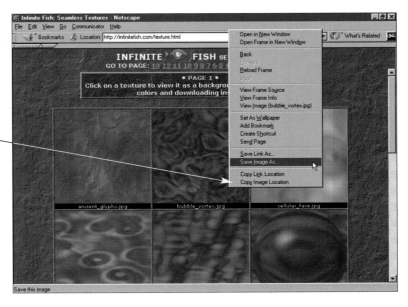

You can also save background images from Web pages with your browser. Just move your mouse over an empty part of the Web page, click the right mouse button, and choose Save Background As. Figure 2.3 shows a background graphic being saved with Netscape Navigator.

Figure 2.3
Save a background
image to your computer.

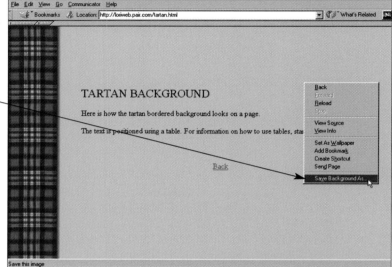

Saving a
Background
Image

NOTE

Netscape Navigator version 4.6 was used in the examples above. If you have a different browser or a different version, the process for saving images might be slightly different.

Note, too, that right-click might be disabled on some Web pages. If it is, this is a good indication that the author does not want anyone else to use the graphics.

Graphics from a CD-ROM

Because so many images are available on the Web, sorting through them to find the exact photo, icon, or image that you want can be a slow and grueling process.

If you're like most folks, you probably don't want to spend hours finding images online. There are many other ways to find great images besides searching the Web. Probably the best method is purchasing a collection of images on CD-ROM that you can browse at your leisure. Then you don't have to stay online while browsing, or wait for large HTML pages to download.

Your favorite computer store probably has dozens of different clip-art and Web-art collections. Most have tens of thousands of images or more and are priced between $15 and $100, depending on the quality, quantity, and subject of the images.

Creating Your Own Digital Photos

Generic photos and clip art are useful only to a point. Often, the images you need to work with are digitized versions of personal photos, custom logos, and other original artwork.

Paint Shop Pro makes it easy for you to manipulate and modify digital images, but first you have to get your art into digital form. Among the many popular ways for getting images from real life into your computer are scanning, using a digital camera, and using a personal video camera.

This section introduces you to several ways to bring images into your computer with Paint Shop Pro.

Using a Scanner

Scanners are affordable tools that let you transfer an image from any book, paper, or photograph and then store it electronically on your computer. Color scanners start at about $69 and are priced based on their resolution and color quality.

Scanners are especially good for digitizing business logos and photographs. Once the images are scanned, you can customize them to fit your needs. Figure 2.4 shows the logo of the company that published this book, after it was scanned into Paint Shop Pro. This scan was made using a Microtek 600×1200 color scanner.

Figure 2.4
This scan can be used for stationery, Web pages, or electronic documents.

TIP

Just because you want to scan a photo or logo doesn't mean you have to purchase your own scanner. Many public libraries and universities have public workstations with scanners attached, to use without charge. Alternatively, local copy shops such as Kinko's let you use a scanner for a nominal fee.

If you decide to buy a scanner yourself, make sure you understand the quality of images you can expect to see. Don't forget to test your scanner immediately after getting it home or to your office to make sure it is adequate for your anticipated usage.

Scanning in PSP

Once you've identified an image to scan, the next step is to scan, or acquire, the image into PSP. Paint Shop Pro handles virtually any scanner imaginable, as long as the scanner is TWAIN-compliant. TWAIN is a scanning standard that allows software programs and scanners to communicate with each other in a standard fashion. Paint Shop Pro includes the standard TWAIN interface for scanners, so you can scan images without leaving the program.

CAUTION

This chapter assumes that you have successfully obtained and installed a scanner for your computer. There are literally thousands of different scanners, each with its own installation and configuration routines. Paint Shop Pro can work with just about any of them once they are properly installed.

If you have problems using or installing your scanner, your best bet is to call the manufacturer's technical support phone number or contact tech support online at the manufacturer's Web site.

To scan an image, select **File** > **Import** > **TWAIN** > **Acquire**, from the PSP menu bar. Paint Shop Pro launches your scanning software for you automatically. Figure 2.5 shows the scanning software for this HP scanner.

Figure 2.5
Ready to scan!

The dialog box that you see when you select the Ac**q**uire command might very well look different from this one, because each scanner manufacturer provides its own dialog box. The exact interface will depend on which scanner you use and on the software drivers you installed when you connected the scanner to your computer.

Even though Figure 2.5 shows the elements for a particular scanner interface, your options are likely to be similar. Basically, you'll be able to choose settings for scanning either a color photo or a black-and-white image. Then you'll make sure the paper or photo is loaded into the scanner, and you'll click on the **Scan Now** button (or its equivalent). After a few seconds of the scanner's whirrings, the image gets sent to PSP, where you can then edit it as you like. Figure 2.6 shows a scan in progress.

Figure 2.6
The scan in progress.

NOTE

If you get an error message or if nothing happens when you select **F**ile > Import > **TWAIN** > Ac**q**uire, check to make sure your scanner was turned on before you started your computer. Many scanners need to be on before the computer starts so they can be recognized and accessible.

If you still have problems, try using the vanilla scanning software that comes with your scanner. Then save the images you scanned individually and load them into PSP, instead of scanning them directly into PSP.

You will want to add the Acquire Image button to your toolbar if you plan to scan images often. To do so, select **V**iew > **T**oolBars to bring up the Toolbars dialog box, then highlight **Toolbar** in the list of toolbars and click the **C**ustomize button (Figure 2.7).

Figure 2.7
It's easy to customize PSP's toolbar.

Highlight the **Acquire Twain Image** icon from the left list and click on the **A**dd button (Figure 2.8). While you're at it, you also might want to add to your Tool Bar the icons for some of the color adjustment operations—such as Brightness/Contrast and Adjust RGB—and/or some of the photo-correction effects, all of which are useful tools for editing scanned images, as you'll see in Chapter 3, "Editing Images."

Figure 2.8
If you scan and correct images frequently, you'll want to add the Acquire and color adjustment buttons to PSP's Tool Bar.

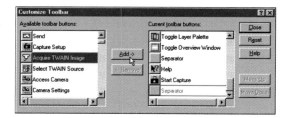

TIP

An alternative method for getting to the Customize Toolbar dialog box is to right-click on any icon on the Tool Bar and then select Customize from the resulting menu.

Getting More Scanner Information

You can find many books and magazines to teach you about scanners, scanning, and advanced color optimization and enhancement techniques. One good scanning resource is Winston Steward's *Scanner Solutions* (Muska & Lipman, 1999, ISBN 1-9662889-7-1). Here is a set of URLs that can also provide you with more information on scanning:

▶ **http://www.pandi.hp.com/pandi-db/home_page.show**
   Home of HP printing and imaging products

▶ **http://www.microtekusa.com/**
   Home of Microtek scanners and accessories

▶ **http://www.hsdesign.com/scanning/**
   Sullivan's On-line Scanning Resources and Tips—a great place to learn some advanced scanning techniques

▶ **http://www.scantips.com/**
   Wayne Fulton's entertaining and enlightening site devoted to scanning basics and tips

Using a Digital Camera

Besides scanners, digital cameras are another way to get an image into your computer. Rapidly gaining momentum, digital cameras are becoming affordable and easy to use for the nonprofessional photographer.

Digital cameras work pretty much like standard cameras except that they store images digitally rather than on film. You take pictures with your camera, attach the camera to your computer, and save the images directly to your hard drive.

Instead of film, pictures are stored in memory in the camera; so the more memory your camera has, the more pictures you can take before hooking the digital camera to your computer to transfer the images. In most cases, you can augment the camera's memory with some sort of storage medium (usually a CompactFlash or SmartMedia memory card). Most digital cameras also let you take photos at varying quality (varying either in terms of number of pixels or in terms of compression level). The lower the resolution you select, the more photos you'll be able to store for later download.

Using a digital camera is perfect if you need to take a lot of pictures for Web pages or to store on your computer (for example, Realtors and insurance agents commonly use digital cameras). And with today's high-resolution cameras and photo-quality ink-jet printers, it's also easy to get good print photos with a digital camera.

Image quality for digital photos has been more than acceptable for quite a while now. For example, Figure 2.9 shows a picture taken with a consumer-grade digital camera from a couple years ago, a Kodak DC120Zoom Digital Camera. With today's mid-priced digital cameras, picture quality is truly excellent—and as new models become available, image quality keeps improving while prices continue to go down.

Figure 2.9
A digital camera is easy for almost anyone to use.

Like scanners, digital cameras come with special software to transfer images from the camera to your computer. Paint Shop Pro also has built-in support for many popular brands and models of digital camera. If you have one of the supported cameras, you can directly import and manipulate images on your digital camera in PSP, instead of using the separate software program that came with the camera. (If your camera is not supported but is TWAIN-compliant, you can still import your images directly into PSP, using **F**ile > **I**mport > **T**WAIN > Ac**q**uire.)

After you've acquired your photos, Paint Shop Pro enables you to edit and touch up your photos. For example, Paint Shop Pro lets you easily remove red-eye, reduce a shadowing effect, eliminate a color cast, or crop your image.

Acquiring Images into PSP with Digital Cameras

If you have a supported digital camera, the first step is to connect it to your computer via its special cable. Once your cable is connected, and you have pictures on your camera that have been taken, the next step is configuring PSP to work with your camera.

Choose **F**ile > **I**mport > **D**igital Camera > **C**onfigure from the menu bar to bring up the Digital Camera Configuration dialog box (see Figure 2.10).

Figure 2.10
You must tell PSP which digital camera you are using.

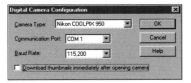

NOTE
Support for the KODAK DC120 and DC2XX models is installed automatically with PSP. If you have any other brand or camera model, you'll have to install special support drivers which enable PSP to communicate directly with your digital camera. To install extra camera support after you've installed PSP, Run the **Jasc Digital Camera Support** program from your Windows program bar (**Start** > **P**rograms > Jasc Software > Utilities > **Jasc Digital Camera Support**). This option is available only if you installed PSP from CD-ROM. Otherwise you'll have to download this program from the Jasc web site (**www.jasc.com**).

Once you launch the Digital Camera Support program, a list of supported cameras is displayed. Pick your digital camera from the list and have the appropriate files installed automatically for you.

The most important step here is to designate which camera you are using, since PSP will give you an error message if you select the wrong type of camera. Specify your digital camera in the **C**amera Type drop-down box and click **OK** to continue.

Once your camera is configured in PSP, choose **F**ile > **I**mport > **D**igital Camera > **A**ccess from the menu bar to bring up the Digital Camera dialog box (Figure 2.11).

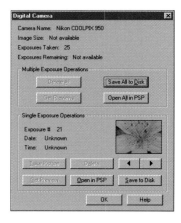

Figure 2.11 shows a lot of information. First, in the top part of the dialog box, you see information about your camera and photographs, as well as how many exposures are available to be downloaded and/or viewed.

The rest of the Digital Camera dialog box is split into ways to access your pictures. The Multiple Exposure Operations section lets you download, delete, open, or preview all the exposures in PSP.

You can open all of your images directly into PSP or save them all directly onto your computer. Your best bet is to click on the **Open All** button. Paint Shop Pro will download all your images and open them up for you to view. Then you can save the good images yourself.

When you're sure you are finished with the current set of photos, click on the D**e**lete button to erase the set of images in the camera.

CAUTION

When you click the D**e**lete button, your digital photographs are permanently removed from your camera's memory. Make sure that you have the images you want saved on your hard drive before you delete them from your camera!

You can do similar tasks one exposure at a time, using the controls in the bottom of the Digital Camera dialog box. If you have any free exposures left, you can even take a picture from this dialog box—a good technique if your camera is on a tripod.

Once you've imported the photos into PSP, you can re-colorize them, crop them, or edit them however you like. As the example in Figure 2.12 shows, even fairly nice images can use a little retouching. We'll look at how to edit digital images in Chapter 3, "Editing Images."

Figure 2.12
A snapshot in need of some editing.

There are quite a few good books available on digital cameras and editing digital photos, including *Digital Camera Solutions* by Gregory Georges (Muska & Lipman, 2000, ISBN 0-9662889-6-3). Here are a few online sources of information, too:

▶ **http://www.kodak.com**
Besides providing information on its own products, Kodak has quite a bit of general digital imaging information, including its Digital Learning Center.

▶ **http://www.nikonusa.com**
For info on Nikon's digital cameras, follow the Products link.

▶ **http://www.sony.com**
Sony's Digital Imaging center.

Other Technologies

Besides scanners and digital cameras, you can get custom digital images into Paint Shop Pro in several other ways. These are not the best means of acquiring images for print work, but they might provide a workable solution for your Web pages or digital presentations. Here are just a few of the alternatives:

▶ **QuickCam**
For $49-$100 (depending on model), you can purchase a medium-quality camera that hooks up to your computer and can take video clips or still photos. An example of this is Logitech's QuickCam, which you can use for photos or video-conferencing. You can't carry the QuickCam with you and the quality is quite limited, but the price is right for many people. You can find out more about the QuickCam at **http://www.logitech.com**.

▶ **Video Blaster WebCam Go**
Like the QuickCam, the WebCam Go attaches to your computer and takes video clips or still photos. The twist here is that the WebCam Go really does go—you can take it with you, take some photos, and then download the photos to your PC. At about $150 (or less, if you shop around), this is a pretty affordable digital photo option. Keep in mind, though, that the image quality will not be as high as that of a good mid-range digital still camera. For more information, head out to **http://www.creativelabs.com**.

▶ **Snappy**
The Snappy Video Capture unit lets you digitize still shots from any videocassette tape. You simply hook up the Snappy and a VCR to your computer. The Snappy costs about $99. Quality might not be as good as that of a mid-priced digital camera, but it should be fine for Web graphics. Anyone with a camcorder can digitize photos from their tapes with a Snappy, making this an affordable way for folks who already have a camcorder to get images into their computers. You can find out more about Snappy at **http://www.play.com**.

TIP
Paint Shop Pro 7 includes a tool for eliminating (or at least minimizing) the interlaced scan lines on your video-capture images: Effects > Enhance **P**hoto > **D**einterlace.

If neither a digital camera nor any of the alternatives mentioned above are within your budget, you might instead want to check out a service like Kodak PhotoNet Online (**http://kodak.photonet.com**), shown in Figure 2.13. This service and others like it let you submit conventional photographs to be developed, and you not only get your prints back, but you get a private Web page that has digital versions of your photos, too. For a monthly fee, you can save your images, order reprints, examine the negatives, and more.

Figure 2.13
Kodak PhotoNet Online is an affordable way to get your pictures in electronic format.

And even if you do have a means of creating digital photos, you might want to check out an online service such as Jasc's StudioAvenue, which lets you store your digital photos, share them with your friends, and maybe even use them to create your own decorated items. StudioAvenue gives any PSP user free and easy access to online digital album storage. To send your images to StudioAvenue (Figure 2.14) direct from within PSP, choose **F**ile > Expor**t** > Studio**A**venue.com.

Figure 2.14
Store your images
and share them with
your friends at
StudioAvenue.

Capturing Screen Shots

Do you produce teaching aids for using computer programs? If so, you'd probably find it handy to be able to easily create images of what you see on your computer screen.

For example, maybe you want to take a snapshot of a program's dialog box or some other feature in action. The way to do this is by taking a screenshot, or computer-screen snapshot.

You can do this in either of two easy ways:

▶ Use Window's built-in screen capture capabilities by pressing the **Print Screen** button to capture the entire screen or Alt+**Print Screen** to capture the active window. Then select **E**dit > **P**aste > As **N**ew Image in Paint Shop Pro to paste the image from the clipboard. (Or simply right-click in an empty area of the PSP workspace and select Paste As **N**ew Image.)

▶ Use Paint Shop Pro's Capture menu to grab the image directly. This gives you a number of options that Windows' built-in screen capture doesn't provide.

To capture a computer screenshot, choose **F**ile > **I**mport > Screen Capture > **S**etup from the menu bar. Figure 2.15 shows the Capture Setup dialog box.

Figure 2.15
Paint Shop Pro offers
a number of options
for screen captures that
the Print Screen key
doesn't provide.

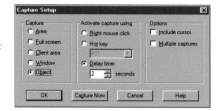

You can save the entire screen or just parts of the computer window. In addition, Paint Shop Pro has a built-in Delay timer, which lets you prepare for a screenshot to be taken.

Once your settings are established, click on the Capture Now button. If you selected to capture an Area and set the right mouse button as the activation option, Paint Shop Pro waits until you click your *right* mouse button to start the capturing process. Then you use your *left* mouse button to select the area you want to capture. Figure 2.16 shows a screen capture in action.

Figure 2.16
Here's a screen capture
of a screen capture in
action.

Screen Capture
starting point
dimensions
ending point

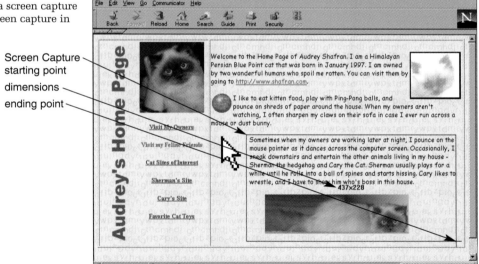

If you had selected Full Screen, Client Area, Window, or Object instead of Area in the Capture Setup dialog box, only the single right-mouse click would have been needed to capture the image. Once you've defined the area to be captured, Paint Shop Pro copies the selected area as an image and let's you edit or manipulate it.

Once you have your screen capture options set, you can later make other screen captures using the same settings by choosing **File** > **Import** > Screen **Capture** > **Start** (or by simply pressing **Shift+C**). Whenever you're ready for another screen capture, PSP is also ready.

TIP

If you have other graphics software, such as CorelDRAW, Adobe Illustrator, or a 3D-rendering program, it is probably capable of exporting some file format that Paint Shop Pro can open.

However, the graphics files that your applications save may be at a resolution better for paper printing or video production than for Web pages. This often results in significant difference between the colors you see on the screen and the colors you'll see when you open the resulting graphics file.

You may often find it faster and more reliable to simply capture images straight from the screen while a graphics application is running. That way you know the image will appear on your Web page exactly as you see it when you do the capture.

Keep in mind, too, that you can use screen captures to grab still shots from moving video clips, as well as animations as they play.

3

Editing Images

Now that you've looked at some ways to acquire photorealistic images, let's see how you can use PSP to edit your digital photos. In this chapter, you'll learn how to use PSP tools to:

▶ **Correct Color and Tone in Your Digital Photos**
Most digital photos and scans can use a little tweaking to make them look their best, and PSP makes image adjustment easy.

▶ **Repair Damaged Photos**
Dust spots on a negative or a torn area on a print can mar a scanned image. Paint Shop Pro has several tools you can use to correct these problems.

▶ **Rotate, Resize, and Crop Your Images**
If a scan is askew, or an image is too large, or a background detracts from the main figure in your photo, you can use PSP to set things right.

Red-Eye Removal

Scanning images is great, but it's not the end of the story. Usually you'll want to touch up your digital photographs. For example, many times photos are marred by "red-eye," which occurs when your subject stares directly into the camera as the flash goes off. With Paint Shop Pro, fixing red-eye is a snap.

Figure 3.1 shows a sample picture that includes a bad case of red-eye. This photo was taken with a Nikon CoolPix 950 digital camera.

Figure 3.1
A nice guy who has a
bad case of red-eye.

To correct the red-eye in this photo, choose Effects > Enhance **P**hoto >
Red-eye Removal. This opens up the Red-eye Removal dialog box shown
in Figure 3.2.

Figure 3.2
The Red-eye Removal
photo effect makes red-
eye removal a breeze!

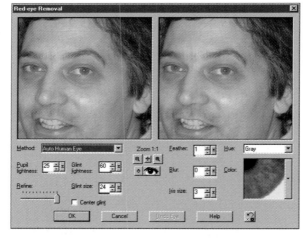

The first thing you'll usually want to do is zoom in a bit and position the
image in the preview window. Use the right zoom button, located
between the two image windows in the top half of the dialog box. Then
click the positioning button located between the two zoom buttons and
drag the preview box to where you want it, as shown in Figure 3.3.

Figure 3.3
You can adjust the position of the preview area.

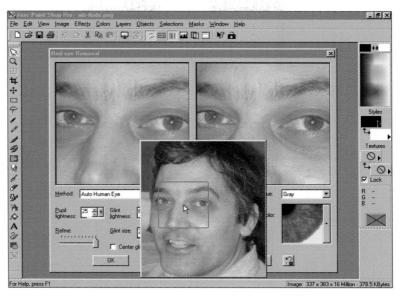

Now, pick the method to use. Since we're working on an image of a person, **Auto Human Eye** is the best place to begin. Then, choose the appropriate eye color. We'll use Aqua here.

Next, in the left image window, click on a spot in the area of one of the eyes that shows red-eye. This automatically places a control box around that red-eye area (Figure 3.4).

Figure 3.4
Select one of the affected pupils by clicking on it.

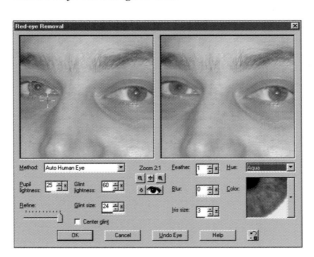

Notice the change in the right preview window. The selected pupil now looks dark, feathering to aqua along its edge. At this point, you can use any of the various settings to adjust the appearance of that pupil. Or you can adjust the size of the pupil by dragging on the control handles of the control box or by pressing **Alt+Page Up** (to increase the size) or **Alt+Page Down** (to decrease the size). You can also adjust the position of the pupil by dragging inside the control box or by pressing Alt with the arrow keys.

In this example, the image would look a lot better if the size of the pupils were increased. This could be accomplished by resizing the control box, but another option is to decrease the amount of the control area occupied by the iris. To do this, lower the setting for Iris. Figure 3.5 shows the result here with Iris set to 0.

Figure 3.5
Resize the pupil directly or by reducing the Iris setting.

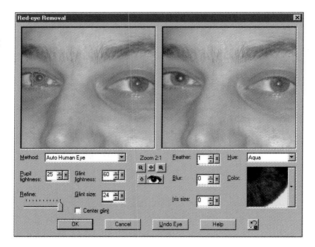

For the other eye, just repeat the same procedure: Click on the red-eye area and make adjustments as needed. The result will be something like Figure 3.6.

Figure 3.6
Repeat the procedure
for the next eye in the
photo.

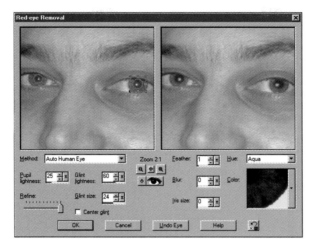

TIP
If you've made some adjustments and then wish you'd left well enough alone,
you can start over with a selected pupil by clicking the Undo Eye button.
This will undo all the adjustments you've made on a particular eye and will
also get rid of the control box around that eye's pupil.

Click **OK** once you've made all the corrections you need in your photo.
You'll then have a much improved image, like the one in Figure 3.7.

Figure 3.7
Now this photo is ready
to be used!

Automatic red-eye removal is also available for animal photos. And don't be fooled by the term "red-eye"—this method is fine for eliminating those ghostly silvery green pupils you sometimes get with photos of your pets. For your animal portraits, use **Auto Animal Eye** for the Method setting in the Red-eye Removal dialog box.

Auto Animal Eye is particularly useful for animal photos because it allows you to modify the shape as well as the size of the pupil by adjusting the control handles. The side handles squeeze or expand the pupil horizontally, while the top and bottom handles squeeze or expand the pupil vertically, as demonstrated in Figure 3.8.

Figure 3.8
Auto Animal Eye lets you adjust the shape of the pupil.

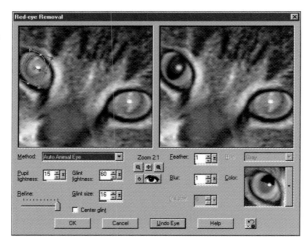

Here's a brief summary of the various Red-eye Removal settings:

▶ **Method**
Choose from Auto Human Eye or Auto Animal Eye when you want PSP to define the control area. Choose Freehand Pupil Outline or Point-to-Point Pupil Outline when you want more control about how the control area is defined.

▶ **Pupil lightness**
If the new pupil looks too dark, you can lighten it by increasing the value of this setting.

▶ **Refine**
Adjust the shape of the pupil to take into account an overlapping lid.

▶ **Glint lightness**
Adjust the lightness of the glint from 0 (dark grey) to 100 (white).

▶ **Glint size**
Adjust the size of the glint.

▶ **Center glint**
Move the glint to the center of the pupil. Use this setting only if the original glint doesn't look right in the corrected eye.

▶ **Feather**
Feather the edge of the corrected area

▶ **Blur**
Blur the entire corrected area.

▶ **Iris size**
Determine how much, if any, of the corrected area is taken up by the iris color rather than by the pupil.

▶ **Hue**
Available only with Auto Human Eye. Lets you select the general hue for the iris.

▶ **Color**
When Auto Human Eye is the selected Method and Hue is therefore active, Color allows you to select a precise color for the iris, within a range of values for the selected Hue. When Auto Animal Eye is selected, it lets you select from a small range of animal eye colors.

Color Correction Techniques

We worked through a little color correction when we eliminated red-eye. But there are also other situations in which your images would benefit from more radical color correction. The quick-and-dirty rundown that follows isn't going to qualify you for a degree in graphic arts, but it will show you the basics of how to use PSP to polish up your digital photos.

Almost all photographs and many computer-generated pictures will benefit from color correction. An image designed to be printed on paper will almost always look bleak and washed-out when viewed on a monitor. Even photos you take yourself with a digital camera will sometimes benefit from a little color correction.

Automatic Color and Contrast Correction

Let's begin with the photo in Figure 3.9, where the whole image has a reddish cast.

Figure 3.9
A photo in need of a little color correction.

You can easily remove the color cast with Automatic Color Balance, available under Effects > Enhance Photo. Check Remove color cast and set Temperature for the type of light in which the photo was taken (Figure 3.10). Since this example was taken in daylight, 6500K is appropriate.

Figure 3.10
Removing a color cast with Automatic Color Balance.

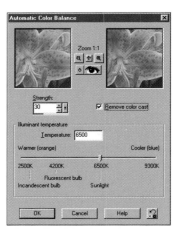

The result is shown in Figure 3.11.

Figure 3.11
A more natural-looking image achieved with little effort!

The automatic adjustments available under Effects > Enhance **P**hoto are useful in other instances, too. Let's see what they can do for the dark, flat image in Figure 3.12.

Figure 3.12
This photo is too dark and too flat.

Begin by taking care of the contrast with Effects > Enhance **P**hoto > Automatic **C**ontrast Enhancement (Figure 3.13). In many cases, the default settings work just fine, but in this case the default **Strength** of *Normal* makes the image too bright, washing it out, so we used *Mild* instead.

Figure 3.13
Adjusting the contrast
with Automatic Contrast
Enhancement.

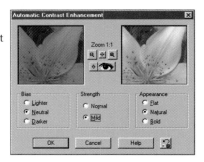

Next, use Automatic C**o**lor Balance, this time with **R**emove color cast unselected. This photo was taken in sunlight, so 6500K is again appropriate (Figure 3.14).

Figure 3.14
Adjusting the color
with Automatic
Color Balance.

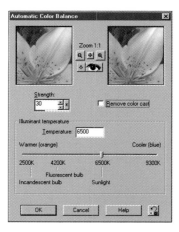

Finally, apply Effects > Enhance **P**hoto > Automatic Saturation Enhancement. We used the default settings here (Figure 3.15). The result is a brighter image with improved color and depth (Figure 3.16).

Figure 3.15
Adjusting the saturation with Automatic Saturation Enhancement.

Figure 3.16
The corrected image.

NOTE

Saturation is the purity of a color. The lower the saturation, the more grey there is in the colors. Too high a level of saturation can make your image look unnatural, so be careful with saturation adjustments.

Keep in mind that when you make brightness adjustments, you might also need to tweak the saturation.

Part I Making Great Images

Color Correction by Hand

The automatic photo enhancement operations are certainly handy and easy to use. Sometimes, though, you'll want to have more control in correcting your digital photos. In these cases, you'll use some of the other operations available under Effects > Enhance **P**hoto or the adjustment operations available under the **C**olors menu. Let's take a quick look at a few of these now. You should also experiment further with these operations later on, with your own images.

Brightness and Contrast Enhancement

Maybe the most noticeable problem with the yellow lily photo is that it's a bit dark. In PSP, the **C**olors > **A**djust submenu gives several options for correcting this problem. Starting with the original image, the first thing you might try is **B**rightness/Contrast, which certainly could do this image some good, as Figure 3.17 shows. But you should consider a few other choices as well. For example, again starting with the original dark image, Figure 3.18 shows the result of adjusting Highlight/Midtone/Shadow (Linear Adjustment Method), increasing the brightness of the Highlights (set to 62) and the Midtones (set to 54) while leaving the Shadows alone (that is, leaving the setting at 0). And Figure 3.19 shows an example of what can be done with Curves.

Figure 3.17
Using Brightness/
Contrast.

Figure 3.18
Using Highlight/
Midtone/Shadow.

Figure 3.19
Using Curves.

Adjusting Color

Now let's return to the image with a red cast. There are quite a few operations available under **C**olors > **A**djust that can help us out here. One of the easiest to understand is Red/Green/Blue, shown in Figure 3.20. By reducing the **R**ed while bumping up the **G**reen and **B**lue, you can counteract the cast.

Figure 3.20
Eliminating a color cast with Red/Green/Blue.

Another operation that you can use to eliminate a color cast is **Gamma Correction**, shown in Figure 3.21. When the Red, Green, and Blue settings are linked, Gamma Correction can be useful for adjusting the brightness of an image. When *Linked* is unchecked, you can adjust each of the color channel settings separately, reducing or increasing a particular overall color. In this example, the color cast was reduced by slightly decreasing the setting for **R**ed and slightly increasing the settings for **G**reen and **B**lue.

Figure 3.21
Eliminating a color
cast with Gamma
Correction.

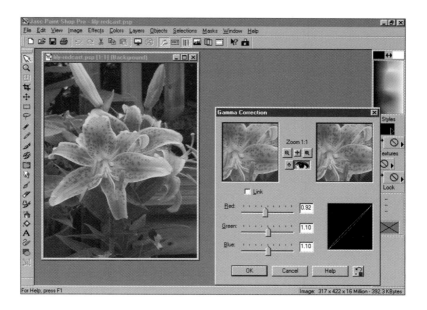

Yet another means of reducing a color cast is to adjust Color Balance,
which lets you adjust the color in three different tonal ranges: shadows,
midtones, and highlights. Don't rush into Color Balance without first
checking the image's Histogram, though. The Histogram will show you
the distribution of color throughout the image's tonal range.

To see the Histogram window for an image, click the **Histogram** button
on the standard Tool Bar, or press **H** on the keyboard. Figure 3.22 shows
the lily image with its Histogram.

TIP

When you first display the Histogram Window, you will see several separate
colored graphs, all displayed at once. These represent the amount of Red,
Green, and Blue light in the image; the Greyscale values; and the values for
the Hue, Saturation, and Lightness channels. It will be easier to correct the
color of an image destined for the Web if you display only the Red, Green,
and Blue graphs. When you want to correct the brightness and contrast of an
image, you'll probably want to display only the Greyscale graph.

Figure 3.22
Analyze an image's
color distribution by
examining the image's
Histogram.

The left side of the Histogram represents the shadows, the middle the
midtones, and the right the highlights. The Histogram for our example
indicates that there's too much red in the midtones and highlights and
not enough red in the shadows.

With this information, you can now make well-informed use of Color
Balance. Choose **C**olors > **A**djust > C**o**lor Balance to open the Color
Balance dialog box, shown in Figure 3.23. For this example, we first
selected **Mid**tones and adjusted the **C**yan-Red setting to -23. Then we
selected **H**ighlights and adjusted the Cyan-Red setting to -14. No
adjustment was made to the **S**hadows.

Figure 3.23
Eliminating a color cast with Color Balance.

Part I Making Great Images

Experiment with these and the other operations available under **C**olors > **A**djust. And keep in mind that each of these operations can be used on a selection as well as on an entire image.

Other Photo Retouching Techniques

Paint Shop Pro provides you with three other handy tools for correcting photos: the Clone Brush, the Retouch tool, and the Scratch Remover. Use the Clone Brush to remove blemishes and specks from your photos. Use the Retouch tool to make local corrections exactly where they're needed. And use the Scratch Remover to quickly erase scratches in your photos.

The Clone Brush

To "clone" areas from one part of your image to another, use the Clone Brush in its Aligned mode. Simply right-click on the area you want to pick up color from and then dab that color onto the area you want to correct by clicking on that area with the left mouse button.

Use the Clone Brush to remove a blemish or to eliminate intrusive elements in a photo, such as phone lines or rubble.

The Retouch Tool

The Retouch tool has several different modes that you can use for touching up specific areas of your photos. Soften, Sharpen, Lightness Up, Lightness Down, Dodge, and Burn are especially useful for correcting photos. For examples of using Dodge and Burn, head over to **http://loriweb.pair.com/dodge.html**.

TIP

When using the Retouch tool, set the brush Hardness rather low, so that your brush has a soft edge. Be aware that many of the Retouch modes, including Dodge and Burn, work best with the Opacity value set quite low—sometimes as low as 10 percent or less.

The Scratch Remover

The Clone Brush is great for removing scratches, but it's even easier to use the Scratch Remover. Simply set the **Width** and the brush shape and then drag along the scratch to blend the scratch into the surrounding colors of your photo.

Keep in mind, though, that although the Clone Brush and Retouch tool can be used on layers, the Scratch Remover is available only on a flat image or on the Background of a layered image.

Rotating Your Images

Color adjustment and photo retouching aren't the only image editing operations you're likely to use. Another handy operation is **R**otate, available under the **I**mage menu. This operation is useful for handmade images as well as digital photos.

Figure 3.24 shows a text headline created for a Web page. Normally, this headline would be fine; but for this page, we'll run the text up and down the left-hand side of the screen.

Figure 3.24
A simple text-only GIF.

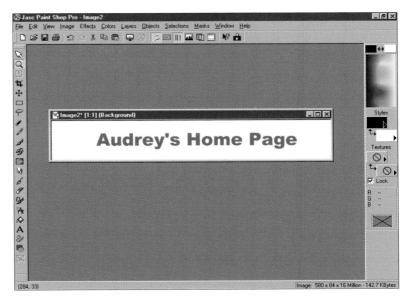

To turn this image, choose **I**mage > **R**otate from the PSP Menu Bar. The Rotate dialog box shown in Figure 3.25 appears. Paint Shop Pro gives you a few standard rotation values or lets you select very precise turning coordinates. In addition, you can rotate the entire image or just a single layer.

Figure 3.25
You can turn this image in any direction.

To figure out the right angle to turn your image, remember what you learned back in geometry class that circles are a total of 360 degrees around. So, to turn your image upside-down, you'd rotate it 180 degrees.

For this example, we want to rotate the image 90 degrees to the left. (Rotating *right* means turning the image clockwise, while rotating *left* means turning the image counter-clockwise. Thus 90 degrees left is the same as 270 degrees right.) Figure 3.26 shows the rotated image.

Figure 3.26
This rotation is complete.

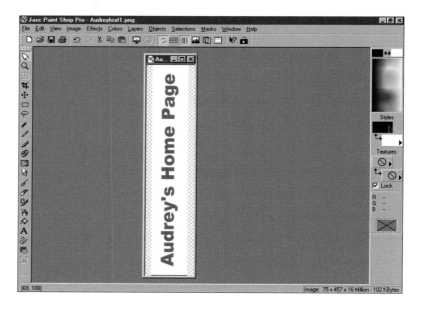

TIP

Besides the Rotate operation, PSP also has the Flip and Mirror operations. The Flip operation makes a vertically mirrored copy of your image, while the Mirror operation makes a horizontally mirrored copy of your image. This is different from rotating because the image is actually flipped around instead of turned.

Resizing and Cropping Images

The final common techniques you'll use when editing images are resizing and cropping. It's probably obvious that you'd want to use resizing and cropping for your print work, to make your images fit correctly on the printed page. But Web designers will also find resizing and cropping particularly useful, since photos are often so big that they take too long to download on a Web page. If you're using photos on the Web, you'll want to use PSP to reduce them to a manageable size.

For example, Figure 3.27 shows a sample photograph that you might want to use for a Web page. Notice that the file is very large—the lower-right corner of the Paint Shop Pro window indicates that the image of the cat is 682×212 pixels. You'll also notice that the full-sized rendition doesn't add much detail or value to the image.

Figure 3.27
This image could benefit from resizing and cropping.

Image size in pixels

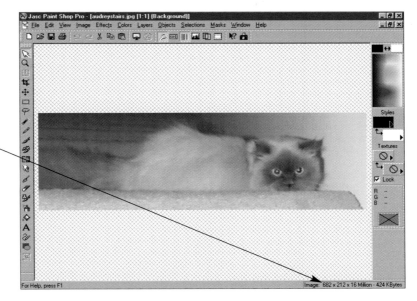

To resize this image, pick **I**mage > **R**esize from the menu bar. The Resize dialog box appears and lets you decide how to change the height and width of this image (Figure 3.28).

Figure 3.28
Images can be resized to any height or width.

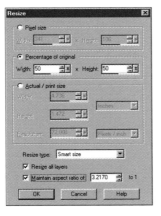

Paint Shop Pro lets you resize by exact pixel coordinates, percentage of the original image, or optimized to be printed out on paper. Table 3.1 compares these options:

Table 3.1
Image Resize Options

Options	Explanation
Pixel Size	Lets you assign a specific Pixel Height and Width to a resized image. This setting is often used to make an image conform to a specific size for your page. For example, if you create a set of buttons for your page, you will want them all to be the same Width. So you'd resize them by Pixel Size and type in the exact coordinates for the image.
Percentage of Original	Lets you specify a percentage of how the new height and width of an image will appear.
Actual/Print Size	Lets you have very specific control over the final image dimensions for printing purposes.
Maintain Aspect Ratio	Calculates the correct height in relation to the width once the original height or width has been modified. Enabling this setting will protect the image from becoming distorted once resized.

NOTE

In the Resize dialog box, there's also a control for Resize type. Your best bet here is to always use **_Smart size_**, which tells PSP to determine which resizing method is appropriate for your image type.

If you prefer to have control over the Resize type, click the Help button at the bottom right of the Resize dialog box and read the detailed descriptions and advice on when to use each type.

For this example, we'll select **P**ercentage of Original and type in 50 percent. Once the image is resized, save it and you'll notice a significant file-size savings. For this example, the photo went from 45K down to 5K—about a 90 percent savings in file size!

We can save a little more in file size, and make the image a more interesting one, by cropping away some of the background. There are two basic ways to crop in Paint Shop Pro. One way is to define a selection with the selection with the Selection tool, as in Figure 3.29, and then choose **I**mage > **C**rop to Selection.

Figure 3.29
You can crop to a selection.

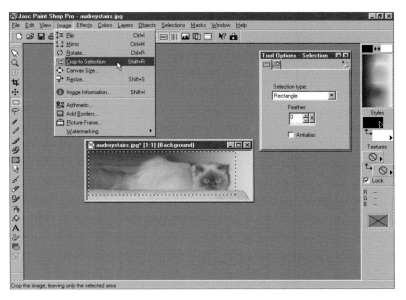

Part I Making Great Images

Alternatively, you can define a crop area by dragging with the Crop tool, as in Figure 3.30. To crop to the defined area, either double-click with the Crop tool anywhere inside the image canvas or click the Crop button on the Crop tool's Tool Options palette.

Figure 3.30
Or crop with the Crop tool.

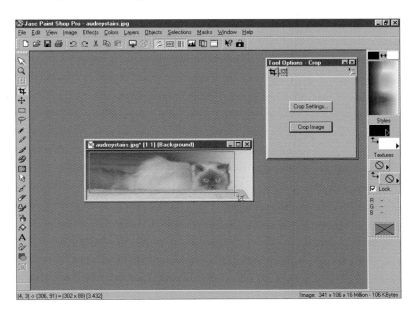

Figure 3.31 shows the final image as part of a completed Web page.

Figure 3.31
A final Web page with
the cropped, resized
photo.

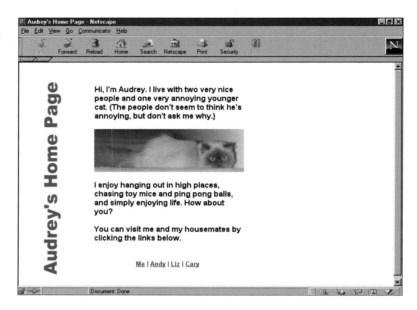

NOTE

It is important to note that resizing an image 50 percent means that both the
Height and Width of the graphic are cut in half, and the original image is
rescaled to fit that new size. This has the cumulative effect of creating an
image file that is one-fourth of the original file size.

TIP

Here's another trick you should know to squeeze the absolute best out of
images when you reduce their size. Always try to resize to exactly one-half,
one-quarter, or one-eighth the original size if possible. The mathematical
reasons for this are beyond what can be explained in this little tip—just take
it on faith that it works! Basically, Paint Shop Pro uses a complex algorithm
to figure out which pixels to keep and which ones to throw out. Using a
standard resize value lets PSP work at its optimal levels.

4

Making Images by Hand

Creating Web graphics is like doing any complicated task—you've got to learn how to walk before you can run. This chapter introduces you to many basic but important techniques for creating handmade graphics using Paint Shop Pro 7. In this chapter you'll learn how to:

▶ **Create and Save New Images**
Learn how to get started on an image and how to save your finished product.

▶ **Design Your Graphics for Proper Pixel Height and Width**
The pixel size of your Web image affects how large your image will appear on computer screens. We'll give you some rules of thumb for choosing the dimensions of your Web images.

▶ **Draw Precise Shapes and Lines**
You don't need a steady hand to draw precise shapes and lines. Let PSP handle that for you!

▶ **Paint Freehand Shapes and Lines**
And when you want to do all the drawing yourself, PSP lets you paint as you please.

Making a New Image

At this point, you've already installed or upgraded to Paint Shop Pro 7 and toured PSP, using several toolbars and palettes that enable you to control the drawing and painting tools. You've even seen some of PSP's image editing tools and operations.

Now it's time to thoroughly describe each step required to build a graphic from scratch. In this section, you'll create and then save a simple image with PSP.

Your first step in learning how to create and save a new file is to start up Paint Shop Pro. Once Paint Shop Pro is loaded, choose **F**ile > **N**ew from the menu bar to bring up the **New Image** dialog box (see Figure 4.1). This dialog box is divided into two main panels—**Image dimensions** and **Image characteristics**, with several settings in each panel. It is important that you understand exactly what these options are for. Below, you'll find a description of each option, along with a summary of the issues surrounding the option.

Figure 4.1
All new images start from this dialog box.

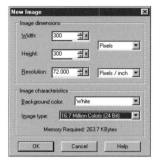

Understanding Image Dimensions

The first thing you need to decide when building a new image is how large you want it to be. Determining height and width is extremely important, because image size affects how Web browsers display your image and directly correlates with your image's file size. Thus, your image's height and width affect the time required for visitors to download and view your image on a Web page, an important metric in Web usability. In general, you want graphics to be as small as is practical, so Web browsers can load them quickly.

Your computer screen's height and width is measured in pixels—which is short for *picture element*. For example, a standard VGA monitor can display 640 pixels across and 480 pixels vertically (640×480). Super VGA (SVGA) resolution offers 800×600 pixel resolution, and Enhanced SVGA offers 1024×768 resolution and better.

Pixels are little dots of light going across your screen that make up the images displayed on the screen. Usually you can't see individual pixels, but you do see the text and images that are made up of thousands of pixels.

The higher the resolution (number of pixels), the more information a user can fit on one screen. Thus, creating a new image that has 320×240 pixel coordinates takes up approximately half a VGA screen, and about one-third of an Enhanced SVGA screen. Figure 4.2 shows how these three resolutions compare with one another.

> **NOTE**
>
> In this section, we'll look primarily at screen resolution characteristics for PC-compatible computers. Remember, though, that all sorts of computers will have access to the images on your Web page. Some Macintoshes and high-powered Sun or Hewlett-Packard workstations might have significantly higher screen resolutions available. In general, though, the PC pixel sizings can be used as a guide when creating your Web images.

Figure 4.2
Compare the three popular screen resolutions.

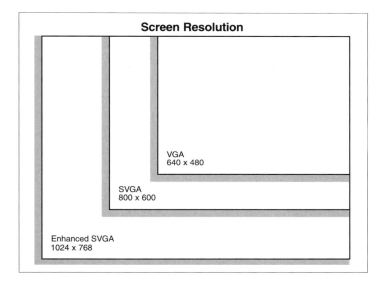

As a general rule, always design your Web page (and, consequently, your Web images) for the lowest screen resolution that your visitors are likely to use. Currently, most Web users have their screen resolutions set at 800×600. It's not a bad idea to design your Web pages for the even smaller 640×480 resolution, which quite a few folks still use. Doing so ensures that your images can be seen by anyone who surfs the Web conveniently and easily. In fact, to ensure that your images can always be seen on a Web page, no image should ever be more than 600 pixels wide and 440 pixels tall, which would provide a 20-pixel border around the image in a 640×480 pixel display area.

Figures 4.3 and 4.4 below show a sample headline image that is 300 pixels tall but 700 pixels wide. Although the two images look similar, they are taken in two different screen resolutions. Figure 4.4 shows this image on a monitor whose resolution is 800×600. The image looks fine here. However, in Figure 4.3, the image doesn't fit on my Web page with a 640×480 screen resolution. As a result, the image looks good only to those using higher screen resolutions. One solution is to re-size the headline image to fit on the smaller screen resolution, thus making it work for all visitors who stop by. Like most images, this headline would easily fit within a 600×440 limit by changing the text size or spacing. What you should do is simply be aware of and stay within the upper limits to ensure that anyone who visits your site will be able to see the graphic as intended.

Figure 4.3
This headline image at VGA resolution requires viewers to scroll to the right to see the entire image.

Figure 4.4
The same image, but at SVGA resolution.

TIP

When using images that fit smaller screen resolutions, many Web developers follow the strategy of centering their images on the screen. By adding `<DIV ALIGN="CENTER">` and `</DIV>` around the HTML that displays the image, the Web graphic looks fine on higher screen resolution monitors because the white space flanking the image doesn't look like wasted space off to the right of the image.

Other Web developers use HTML tables to lay out images on their pages to make sure that all visitors get a similar experience when they stop by.

Now that you are familiar with pixels and screen resolution, it's time to return to the New Image dialog box in Paint Shop Pro and figure out how big your image should be. Different types of images require different height and width coordinates. Table 4.1 gives general guidelines for the pixel dimensions you should choose when creating specific types of Web graphics.

Table 4.1
Dimension Guidelines for Web Images

Image Type	Height and Width Coordinates (in pixels)
Small Icon/Button	25×25
Medium Icon/Button	40×40
Large Icon/Button	60×60
Horizontal Bar	10×500
Headline Graphic	150×600
Common Web Ad Size	300×72
Logo or Photograph	300×400

In the New Image dialog box (refer to Figure 4.1), type in the appropriate Width and Height in each labeled box. The default sizing in Paint Shop Pro is pixels, so typing in 300 for height and 300 for width will create a 300×300–pixel blank image. However, you can also size your image in inches and centimeters. To the right of the Height and Width boxes is a drop-down list that lets you select the units to which your Height and Width values correspond. Changing the units for a new image to inches or centimeters is useful only if you intend to create graphics to print, such as for a flyer or brochure. On a computer screen, your image will always be displayed in terms of pixels. Since this book focuses on Web graphics, we'll always create graphics according to pixel size, not inches or centimeters.

NOTE

Below the Height and **W**idth settings, in the Image Dimension section of the New Image dialog box, are two more available options. These two settings also relate to creating images for printing, instead of for the Web.

By default, the standard resolution for an image is 72 pixels per inch (ppi), which is standard for computer monitors and so is appropriate for Web images. You can change both the quantity and units of resolution for creating printed images. When you want to create images to print, often you'll change this value to something like 300 or 600 ppi. The higher the resolution, the more detailed your printout appears.

For your image to print properly, you must also have a printer capable of printing at your image's resolution.

Note that the size of your image in pixels is roughly proportional to file size. Although not always true, images that have a larger number of pixels will also be larger in terms of file size (count your pixels by multiplying Height and Width). However, file size is even more dependent on the number of colors used in the picture, the file type you choose (GIF or JPEG), and how "busy" (full of different shapes and designs) your image actually is. Chapter 7, "Optimizing Web Graphics," focuses on this specific issue and offers tips to help you keep your final image file size down.

Understanding Background Color

Now that you've decided how big your image should appear on screen, the next choices in the New Image dialog box relate to color. You have to set the background color of the new image and decide how many different colors will be available when you work with Paint Shop Pro.

The **B**ackground color option simply refers to the default color of the image canvas of your new image. You can choose from several options, including white, black, red, green, and blue. In addition, you can set the background color to whatever is currently set as your foreground or background color in the **Color Palette**. This lets you choose from more than 16.7 million different colors.

You can also choose Transparent as your background, but we'll put off discussion of transparency until Chapter 10, "Using Layers." For now, choose a real color as your image's background color.

Before creating a new image, you can use your mouse to set foreground and background colors from the Color Palette's **Available Colors** panel. Set the color for either the foreground (using the left mouse button) or the background (using the right mouse button) by clicking anywhere within the Available Colors panel. Then, when you create a new image, you can choose from the Background Color drop-down box either your *Foreground Color* or *Background Color* instead of the handful of standard ones listed. For now, though, simply choose White as your new image's background color.

NOTE

Throughout the book, you'll see references to commands that require you to click one of your mouse buttons. For convenience, we use the terms "click" or "left-click" to mean clicking with the primary mouse button, and "right-click" to mean clicking with the secondary mouse button. Keep in mind, though, that Windows allows you to switch the mouse buttons for left-handed users, making the right button the primary mouse button and the left button the secondary mouse button.

Choosing the Correct Number of Colors

The last choice available in the New Image dialog box is the Image type, which determines the maximum number of colors available for your new image. From this drop-down box, you have five options. Table 4.2 below lists each option and explains when you want to use each of them for your own graphics.

The number of available colors has a direct impact on how your image appears and on its file size. Because file size can increase as the number of colors increases, you should choose an Image type that has a lot of colors available only when you really need many colors (for example, when you want to use PSP's Effects).

Table 4.2
Image Type Explanation

Image Type	When you want to use this Option
2 Colors (1 bit)	In general, this image type is useful only for *very* simple and plain-looking graphics. It allows only two colors—black and white; not even shades of gray are permitted. Images in this format, however, are extremely small and efficient.
16 Colors (4 bit)	Sixteen colors are useful when you create simple drawings or line art (scanned hand-drawn images). Windows originally supported only 16 colors, and these colors became the defaults for many applications and graphics. Many impressive images can be created with 16 colors. Only the GIF and PNG formats support the limited palette of 16 colors. The JPEG and PSP formats automatically allow 16.7 million colors regardless of the number selected.
Greyscale (8 bit)	Offering the maximum number of shades that GIFs can support, this option allows more flexibility than just black and white by offering 256 different shades of grey. Because there is no performance incentive to using 256 shades of gray instead of 256 varied colors, you'll find yourself using this format sparingly.
256 Colors (8 bit)	This is the maximum number of colors that GIFs can support. It represents a compromise between the millions of colors you could never even name and a reasonable number of colors with which to paint. Unfortunately, many of the cool PSP features don't support the 256-color option, so you'll use this format only when you know you have fewer than 256 colors in your image and when you don't need to use the features that require higher color depth. The default 256 colors used are the same ones you'll find at the default VGA setting for most monitors.
16.7 Million Colors (24 bit)	With 16.7 million colors available, you never have to use a single color twice. This option is used when you plan to save your image in JPEG form or need to use some of PSP's advanced features. Many of these features require that you have 16.7 million colors available because PSP mixes and matches thousands of colors for you automatically. GIF images cannot be saved in 16.7 million color (24 bit) format. Paint Shop Pro will reduce the number of colors used in an image to only 256 when you save a 24-bit image in the GIF file format.

NOTE

Here's how computer programs such as Netscape, Internet Explorer (IE), and Paint Shop Pro know how many colors are available in an image. Computer files are saved in a format called binary, a bunch of ones and zeros strung together. Each of these ones and zeros is called a *bit* (a *b*inary un*it*). Large strings of binary numbers saved together are interpreted by your computer and then displayed as your image.

In Table 4.2 above, each format is followed by a value within parentheses that lists how many bits are needed for that format. You can figure out how many colors are available for a format by multiplying 2 to the nth power, where n is the number of bits listed. So for 2 colors (1 bit), multiply 2 to the 1st power, for a total value of 2. For 256 colors (8 bits), multiply 2 to the 8th power, which is 256. And for 16.7 million colors (24 bits), multiply 2 to the 24th power—which results in 16,777,216 different colors available. Wow!

A 16.7-million color file requires 24 bits to recognize each color you refer to. However, when you use only 256 colors, it takes just 8 bits to recognize a specified color. Therefore, three different colors can be defined in the 256-color file in the same amount of space it takes to define just one color in the 16.7 million-color file. As you can imagine, the lower the number of colors you choose, the smaller your file size could be, because Paint Shop Pro doesn't have to waste 24 bits defining a single color when it saves your image. If your image is simply black and white, only one bit is needed to save each color, representing a savings of 95 percent in file size.

In general, you'll probably want to choose 16.7 million colors, since many of PSP's operations are available only with 24-bit color. You can always reduce the number of colors used when saving your image as a GIF, if that's the appropriate file type for the image you've created. You can also temporarily increase a GIF's color depth to 16.7 million colors and then reduce the color depth again later.

Now, select an **Im**age type—let's use ***16.7 Million Colors*** for this example—and click the **OK** button. Paint Shop Pro makes your new image canvas appear on the screen. Figure 4.5 shows a freshly created white image canvas.

Figure 4.5
So far, this 300×300 pixel image is pretty boring.

Dithering, the Web, and You

Just because you select 16.7 million colors for your image doesn't mean that everyone in the world will get to enjoy the images you create to their fullest extent. That's because many people still have computer display settings that only support 256 colors instead of all 16.7 million colors.

So what happens when someone with a 256-color monitor sees a full color image? That's when a process called *dithering* kicks in. Dithering is the process of your computer interpolating how each color should appear by mixing together pixels from the limited palette it has available. For example, if the 16.7-million color palette contains a color that is bright green, the 256-color monitor might alternate the pixels on the screen between yellow and blue. Your brain "mixes" the yellow and blue pixels together and fools you into seeing green.

While dithering is useful, the resulting image is rarely as detailed as the original, and you have no control over what your visitors actually see when they stop by your page. Depending on how their computer or browser is set up, all your hard work on a full 16.7-million color image might be wasted if that image dithers poorly.

Fortunately, many computer systems nowadays either support 16.7 million colors or dither images rather well. But this is an important issue to consider when creating and publishing graphics to the Web. Paint Shop Pro has many advanced techniques that allow you to reduce the color depth of an image down to 256 colors. Then you can save that image in 256-color mode to use on your Web page so that all visitors will see the same image when they stop by.

If you want to know how many colors your monitor supports, go to the Windows 95/98 desktop and click the *right* mouse button. Choose Properties from the pop-up window to bring up the Display Properties dialog box. Click on the tab labeled Settings and you'll see your current system color and screen resolution settings. Figure 4.6 shows an example—notice how the color depth is set at 24-bit color, with a 800×600 resolution.

Figure 4.6
See how you can change your color and resolution system settings.

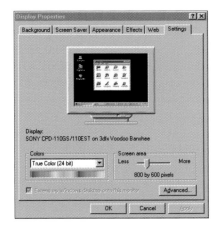

Saving Your Graphic

This section will show you how to save your newly made image so you can use it on your Web page or edit it again at a later date. You'll want to save often when creating Web graphics so your enhancements are permanently stored as a file.

Saving your images in Paint Shop Pro is rather easy. Choose **F**ile > Save **A**s from the menu bar to bring up the Save As dialog box (Figure 4.7).

Figure 4.7
The Save As dialog box.

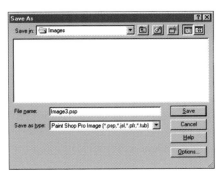

Name your file and tell Paint Shop Pro which image type to use. Two steps are required to save your file, both of which are explained in detail below. First you choose a file name; then you select an Image Type.

Naming your Web graphic file is easy. Simply type in a short but descriptive name in the box labeled File **n**ame. Although Windows 95/98 allows a name to be any length and to contain spaces and punctuation, try to keep your name short and sweet. You may have to enter that file name by hand when you create your Web page in HTML, and a short name will be easier to type.

CAUTION

Some Web servers and browsers have problems with file names that use spaces, commas, slashes, and the tilde (~) character. Unless you are sure your Web server can handle the extended characters in file names, avoid using them in your file name to prevent problems when adding Web graphics to your site.

After naming your file, the next step is to select an Image type from the Save as **t**ype drop-down box. Although Paint Shop Pro allows you to pick from more than two dozen different image types, your first choice is to use the PSP image format. The PSP image format is the ideal place to store all your images as you work on them, saving them in Web-readable format only when you're ready to publish them to the Web.

Don't forget to save your image in the proper subdirectory on your computer. Once you are ready, click on the **S**ave button and, voilà, your image is saved!

When you're working on a graphics project, you should always edit and save your image in the PSP format, since this format supports a full 16.7 million colors, uses lossless compression, and supports advanced PSP features (such as layering and vectors). But the PSP file format isn't a format that is supported by Web browsers. So when you are ready to publish a graphic to your Web site, you'll need to make a Web-ready copy by choosing either the GIF, JPEG, or PNG image formats instead. This process lets you keep a master set of images set apart from the images on your Web site. You'll find this makes it much easier to manage and work with your images, especially as you start using advanced PSP features such as layering, masks, and Effects.

TIP

To save a copy of your image with a different file name or file type, choose either File > Save **A**s or File > Save **C**opy As from the Menu Bar.

Alternatively, you can make JPEG, GIF, or PNG versions of your graphics with Paint Shop Pro's export operations available under File > Export. These export operations are discussed in Chapter 7.

Publishing Images to the Web

Once you are finished editing or creating your images in Paint Shop Pro, you'll need to convert them from the PSP file format into a GIF, JPEG, or PNG.

Chapter 5, "Web Graphics Basics," describes these three formats and suggests when you'll want to use each of them. Chapter 7 describes in detail how to save your Web images so that they are of acceptable quality yet load quickly. Here in this section we'll take a quick look at the various options available when you choose each image type from the Save As dialog box.

GIF Format

To save your graphic in GIF format, choose CompuServe Graphics Interchange (*.gif) from the drop-down box. Paint Shop Pro automatically adds the proper file extension to the file you name you typed.

Once you select GIF, click on the Options button to bring up the Save Options dialog box for GIFs (Figure 4.8).

Figure 4.8
There are several different ways to save a GIF.

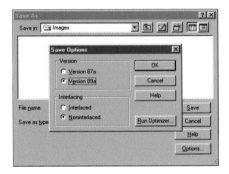

In general, you'll want to accept the default settings from here—Version 89a and Noninterlaced. The Version number designates the year ("89" is 1989) in which the standard was adopted. Version 87a and 89a are very similar and all Web browsers (and PSP) support both types. Version 89a also enables you to take advantage of GIF animation (see Chapter 13, "Animation on the Web").

The Interlacing option is more interesting. When an image is saved with interlacing turned on, Web browsers display the image in several passes, with each pass bringing the image into more detail. Displaying an interlaced image is similar to visiting an optometry office and having a few adjustments made to your glasses so that fuzzy letters become clear. Using interlaced images slightly increases your file size, but this is an excellent option for Web developers who are creating large images. Such images give your visitors a feeling for how the image will look as it downloads from the Internet.

Interlacing is good for large GIFs, but it is not needed for small icons, graphics, and buttons. Chapter 7 covers interlacing in more detail.

JPEG Format

Another available image type is JPEG. Save your graphic in JPEG format by choosing **JPEG—JFIF Compliant** from the Save as type drop-down list box (refer to Figure 4.7). Remember that the JPEG image type uses 16.7 million colors but is often more efficient when you are compressing large images that use many colors—such as photographs. PSP adds the .jpg extension to your file name automatically.

As with GIF, the JPEG file type also has a few options from which to select. Click the **O**ptions button to see the Save Options dialog box for JPG images (Figure 4.9).

Figure 4.9
JPEG also has a few options from which to choose.

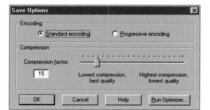

You can choose between *Standard* or *Progressive* JPEGs and select the amount of compression you want to use for this file. Standard and Progressive JPEGs are similar to Noninterlaced and Interlaced GIFs, respectively. Progressive JPEGs appear in several passes, while a standard JPEG downloads one line at a time from top to bottom. Progressive JPEGs also offer a 5 percent savings in file size from the standard JPEG file type.

JPEG Compression lets you trade off file size with image quality, another topic covered in Chapter 7. JPEG compression can be manipulated if you need to shrink your image size and don't mind losing some detail.

PNG Format

The final Web graphics type you might use is the PNG format. Choose **Portable Network Graphics** from the Save as **t**ype, and Paint Shop Pro will add the .png file extension for you.

Be careful when using this image type; only the most recent Web browsers support PNG images and the thousands of people stopping by your site might not have the latest and greatest software. And even folks with one of the latest browsers might not be able to view your PNGs correctly, since standards for PNG have not yet been universally adopted.

Drawing and Painting

Opening and saving images is only the first part of creating Web graphics. Once you have these two fundamentals down, it's time to start adding some shapes, text, and color to your actual graphics. Thus far, you've been working with boring graphics that are only a rectangular block of a single color.

Although Paint Shop Pro offers tremendous flexibility in saving and converting graphics of all types and formats, PSP originally got its start as a robust drawing and paint package. Whether you are a graphics artist or a new user, anyone can create great looking Web graphics with PSP's built-in tools.

This section shows you how to draw several different types of shapes and objects when you build your graphics from scratch. Most Web graphics are simple combinations of these basic shapes and objects.

Using the Grid, Ruler, and Guides

Two important tools will help you in your quest to create great-looking Web Graphics—the **G**rid and the **R**uler.

The Grid is a set of lines that PSP displays on top of your image (they don't get saved with your graphic) to help you line up your cursor when drawing. To toggle the PSP grid on and off, select **V**iew > **G**rid from the menu bar.

Another feature you'll find handy is the Ruler. The ruler gives you an idea of image size (in pixels, inches, or centimeters); this can be useful when you are centering and drawing on your image. Toggle the Ruler on and off by choosing **V**iew > **R**ulers from the PSP Menu Bar.

Figure 4.10 shows an image with the grid and ruler activated.

Figure 4.10
The **G**rid and **R**uler are useful tools for building all graphics.

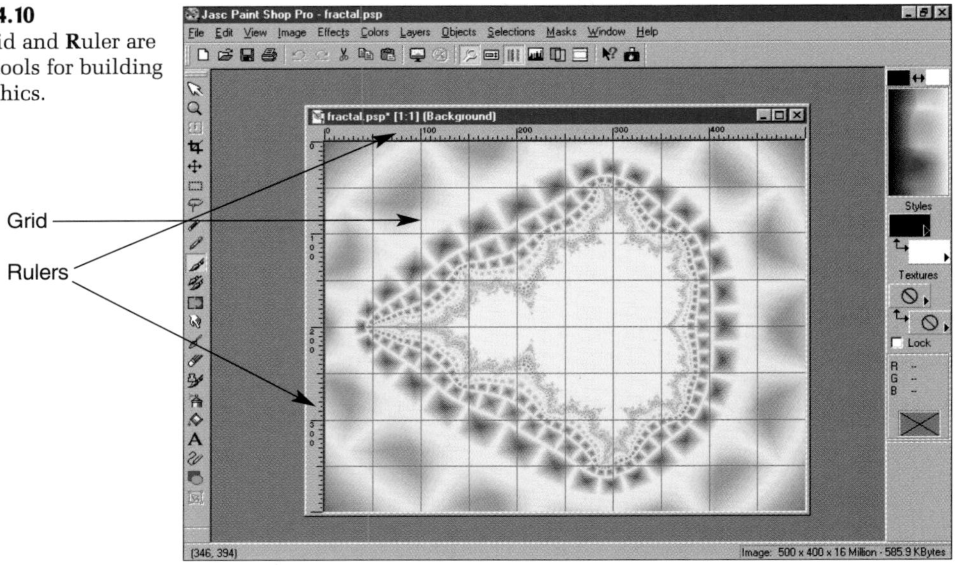

Grid

Rulers

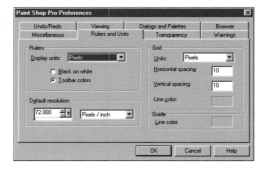

You can set and change the units and width of the grid and ruler by choosing **F**ile > Preferences > **G**eneral Program Preferences from the menu bar to bring up the Paint Shop Pro Preferences dialog box. Select the tab labeled **Rulers and Units** (Figure 4.11a). When you want to affect the grid settings for only the current image, you can right-click on the image's title bar to call up the **Grid and Guide Properties** dialog box (Figure 4.11b).

Figure 4.11a
Change the default grid spacing or ruler units from General Program Preferences.

Figure 4.11b
Change the current image's grid characteristics from the Grid and Guide Properties dialog box.

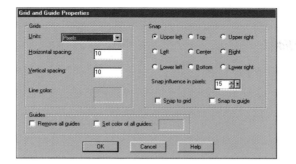

Choosing Colors

Before you can draw an object, you must choose the active colors for your drawing tools. Use the Color Palette on the right-hand side of the screen to select the different colors for your image.

Notice the two swatches labeled **Styles** in the Color Palette. When you're using the painting tools (such as the Paint Brush and Airbrush), these represent your current foreground and background colors. When you're using the drawing tools (such as the Draw tool and the Preset Shapes tool), these represent the Stroke and Fill of your line or shape.

With the painting tools, the foreground color is applied by clicking or dragging with your *left* (or primary) mouse button and the background color is applied with the *right* (or secondary) mouse button. Foreground and background colors have several different additional uses. For example, they can be used when you choose to add a gradient color to your image or when you buttonize a graphic.

You can change the current foreground/stroke or background/fill colors in three ways. The easiest way is to click your left or right mouse button in the rainbow of colors known as the Available Colors panel, directly above the overlapping color swatches labeled Styles on the Color Palette. Your color is set according to whichever color you click in the rainbow.

Often, it is hard to click in the Available Colors panel on the exact color you want to use. Another way to set your colors is by clicking on the foreground or background color swatches, labeled Styles in the Color Palette. Paint Shop Pro then brings up the Color dialog box as shown in Figure 4.12.

Figure 4.12
Millions of colors are available.

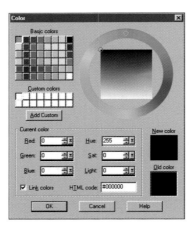

You can choose from one of the 48 basic colors or from the larger **Color Picker** on the right-hand side. Click the **OK** button to set your colors.

> **TIP**
> You can quickly switch your foreground and background colors with each other by clicking on the double-headed arrow between the two color swatches at the very top of the Color Palette.

You can also set your colors by right-clicking on the foreground/stroke or background/fill color squares. This brings up a small palette of recently used colors.

Gradients and Patterns

We've just looked at how to choose solid colors for your foreground/stroke and background/fill. Besides *Solid Color*, Paint Shop Pro's Color Palette allows you to choose two other drawing/painting modes: *Gradient* and *Pattern*. In Gradient mode, you paint with a gradient instead of a solid color, and in Pattern mode, you paint with a pattern.

To change the drawing/painting mode, click the small arrow on the right of one of the color swatches below the Available Colors panel on the Color Palette. (Alternatively, you can click and hold on any part of the color swatch.) You'll then see the flyout menu shown in Figure 4.13.

Figure 4.13
Choose a drawing/mode:
Solid Color, Gradient,
Pattern, or None.

Choose the paintbrush icon for Solid Color mode, the gradient icon for Gradient mode, the pattern icon (which looks like a pattern of dots) for Pattern mode, and the Null icon to turn the painting mode off completely.

To choose a gradient, set the drawing/painting mode to Gradient and then click on the swatch on the Color Palette. You'll then see the **Gradient Picker**, shown in Figure 4.14.

Figure 4.14
Choose a gradient with
the Gradient Picker.

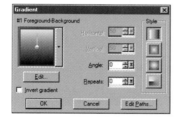

Click on the swatch that shows the current gradient and you'll be presented with a menu showing all available gradients. Select the gradient you want by clicking it, and then click **OK**.

To choose a pattern, set the drawing/painting mode to Pattern and then click on the swatch on the Color Palette. You'll then see the **Pattern Picker**, shown in Figure 4.15.

Figure 4.15
Choose a pattern with
the Pattern Picker.

Click on the swatch that shows the current pattern and you'll be presented with a menu showing all available patterns. Select the pattern you want by clicking it, and then click **OK**.

Drawing Lines

A line is the most basic object you can create on an image. Paint Shop Pro allows you to create a line by simply clicking the **Draw** icon from the Tool Palette at the top of the screen and then drawing a simple line on your image. Your line will be drawn in the color set as the foreground/stroke color in the Color Palette.

Once you click the Draw icon, the Tool Options palette lets you modify the Width and Line Type options, which allow you to specify the thickness (in pixels) of the lines you want to draw and the type of line you wish to create. You can specify any whole number between 1 and 255 to select how thick your line will be. Four line types are available: Single Line, Bezier Curve, Freehand Line, and Point to Point Line. **Single Line** allows you to simply create a straight line between two points (or a series of connected straight lines). **Bezier Curve** lets you create curved lines on your image. Bezier lines require you to first draw the line, then add curve to it with your mouse. **Freehand Line** is for drawing freehand curves, and **Point to Point Line** (which takes some practice to master) lets you make curves by defining a series of nodes (control points that let you modify the curvature of the line at each specific point).

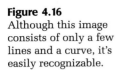

> **NOTE**
>
> For now, be sure **not** to choose the **Create as vector** option when you draw your lines. We'll look at vectors closely in Chapter 11, "Drawing with Vectors."

When drawing, make sure you use a thickness that isn't too thin and difficult to see. Figure 4.16 shows a simple drawing created from four straight lines and one Bezier curve, each with a thickness of 10 pixels.

Figure 4.16
Although this image consists of only a few lines and a curve, it's easily recognizable.

TIP

Practice using the powerful Bezier option of the Draw tool. First you draw the line, then once the endpoints are fixed, you can add curvature to the line by clicking away from the line and dragging to make further adjustments. Click and drag a second time to further refine the curve. Paint Shop Pro automatically builds a perfectly smooth curve for you.

Drawing Shapes

Paint Shop Pro also enables you to create rectangular, elliptical, and basic polygonal shapes in any size and color. All you need to do is choose the **Preset Shapes** tool, tell Paint Shop Pro which shape you want to draw in the Tool Options palette, and then click and draw the shape on your image with the mouse. You can select whether you want the shape to appear filled in (**Filled**) or just as an outline (**Stroked**) or both filled in and outlined (**Stroked & Filled**). For no stroke, set the foreground/fill swatch in the Color Palette to Null by holding down with the left mouse button on the swatch and then choosing the rightmost icon on the flyout menu. For no fill, set the background/fill swatch to Null by doing the same thing on that swatch. (Of course, you won't ever want to set both of these to Null, since that would give you nothing at all!)

On the main tool tab of the Tool Options palette for the Preset Shapes tool, you have several options. First, you can pick which of the available shapes you want to draw, then whether to **Retain style** (that is, to draw the shape just as it appears in the preview window, rather than with the fill and stroke set in the Color Palette). You can set **Antialias** on or off, and you can choose whether or not to create your shape as a vector. (For now, be sure that **Create as vector** is off.) You can also select the thickness of the shape's stroke and whether the line will be solid or have some custom style. (We won't discuss Custom Line Styles here.)

NOTE

For now, be sure **not** to choose the **Create as vector** option when you draw your shapes. We'll look at vectors closely in Chapter 11, "Drawing with Vectors".

Rectangles

Any math major will tell you that a square is simply a special kind of rectangle in which all four sides are the same length. So, to draw either a square or a rectangle, choose **Rectangle**. You can also choose **Rounded Rectangle**, which draws a square or rectangle with rounded corners.

Choose **Rectangle** from the Tool Options palette, then select a drawing color, and you are ready to start drawing. Figure 4.17 shows a handmade drawing created with only filled in squares. For each part of the pyramid, choose a different color or fill mode with the Styles swatches on the PSP Color Palette.

Figure 4.17
Rectangles are the building blocks of most images.

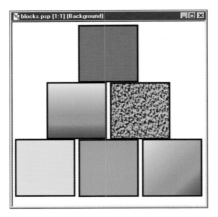

Ellipses

Using the same general procedure as you do when creating rectangles and squares, you can easily build ellipses and circles. Ellipses and circles have the same available control options discussed above, and you can draw any kind of ellipse or circle with the Preset Shapes tool.

First click the Preset Shapes icon, and choose **Ellipse** on the Tool Options palette. Then choose whether you want your shape filled in, or drawn as an outline shape, or both filled in and outlined. If you choose to have an outline, select the width of the outline. Once you have selected your options, use your mouse to draw as many shapes as you need. Of course, you can also change colors for each new circle or ellipse you draw. Figure 4.18 shows a face made completely of ellipses.

Figure 4.18
Using elliptical shapes, you can draw almost anything.

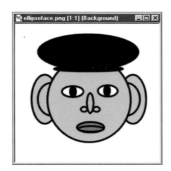

TIP

If you accidentally draw a shape or line of the wrong size, shape, or color, you can always choose Edit > Undo from the menu bar (or hit Ctrl+Z from the keyboard), and Paint Shop Pro will retract the last change made to your Web graphic. In fact, PSP lets you undo the last few commands, not just the most recent one issued.

Other Preset Shapes

Paint Shop Pro 7 includes quite a few other Preset Shapes, including polygons, stars, icons, and various shapes with a 3D look. You draw these shapes just as you do rectangles and ellipses.

One handy tip to remember is that you can constrain any of these shapes to a fixed aspect ratio by holding down the Shift key while dragging to draw the shape. Another thing to keep in mind is that if you draw your shape by dragging with the left mouse button, your shape will be drawn from corner to corner. Drag with the right mouse button to draw your shape from the mid-point out to the edges.

Using the Paint Brush

Now that you are familiar with drawing shapes and lines for new Web graphics, it's time to look at some other important tools available with Paint Shop Pro. Leading that list of tools is the Paint Brush, a virtual marker that lets you draw freehand any shape, color, or pattern on your Web graphic.

You can draw literally any shape or design imaginable with the PSP Paint Brush. It's just like drawing on a piece of paper with a marker, but you use your mouse and screen instead. You can draw a line, erase a smudge, change colors, accentuate a shape, save your changes, and choose different tools (chalk, marker, pen, and so on) with which to paint.

Out of all the available PSP tools, you'll probably use the Paint Brush most often. It can be used to add small touch-up details to a Web graphic, to create colorful and interesting patterns and backgrounds, and to paint shapes of all sorts on your screen. In fact, unless you are creating a specific line or shape, the Paint Brush is likely to be your tool of choice when you create Web graphics.

Click the Paint Brush icon from the Paint Shop Pro Tool Palette. Immediately, several options are available in the main tab of the Tool Options palette. These controls give you flexibility over how your paint brush performs when you draw on the screen. They are tremendously useful and effective when you design graphics from scratch.

Setting the Brush Tip on the Tool Options Palette

The Tool Options palette is the center where you can control most of the options that the Paint Brush has to offer. Figure 4.19 shows the main Paint Brush tab on the Tool Options palette.

Figure 4.19
You can configure your Paint Brush in several different ways.

Paint Shop Pro always shows a preview of how your brush will appear when you start painting with it. The top part of the Tool Options palette lets you select the **Size** and **Shape** of your Brush while the bottom section gives you flexibility in setting four important characteristics of your Paint Brush.

Brush Size

Size, the easiest option to decide on, is measured in pixels. You can type a number in directly or drag the size bar left or right. Brush size ranges from 1–255 pixels.

Brush Shape

When you paint your graphics, sometimes you may want to use a paint brush that has a particular shape to it. With the Paint Brush tool, Paint Shop Pro provides six different brush shapes you can choose to paint with.

You can use any of the different shapes available from the Shape drop-down box in the Tool Options palette. Figure 4.20 shows you a sample of all six shapes and how they all appear using a standard paint brush.

Figure 4.20
All six Paint Brushes are useful when building and editing images.

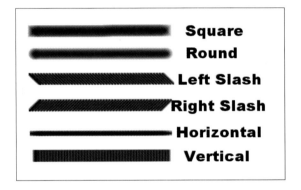

Brush Type

The easiest cool effect you can create will probably result from the Brush Type you select. Usually, you'll select the Normal paint brush, which paints as you would expect.

Additionally, Paint Shop Pro lets you select from among seven other preset brush types, each of which emulate a different type of drawing utensil. Instead of the Normal paint brush, you can choose from Charcoal, Crayon, Pen, Pencil, Marker, or Chalk.

Each brush type has its own unique flavor and style, which will allow you to add different appearances and textures to drawings by simply working with multiple brush types. For example, if you are creating a graphic for a Web page about or for children, you might choose the Crayon brush type to draw your image because it would create an appearance commonly associated with kids. Figure 4.21 lists all seven brush types along with an example of how each appears when used.

Figure 4.21
Customizing your brush
type lets you add
unique personality to
your images.

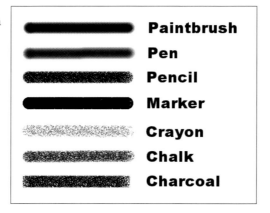

NOTE

In case you're interested, creating the graphic in Figure 4.21 didn't require
painting straight lines across the screen with a steady hand.

You can very easily paint a straight line with the Paint Brush: Click where
you want the line to begin, then hold down the Shift key and click where you
want the line to end. Voilà! A perfectly straight line.

Setting Brush Characteristics

At the bottom of the main tab of the Tool Options palette for the Paint
Brush, you'll find four settings besides Size that control different
characteristics of your paint brush. These options affect how dark your
paint brush appears, how well it integrates with the rest of the image, and
other characteristics. Table 4.3 defines each of these characteristics.

Table 4.3
The Brush options

Characteristic	Explanation
Opacity	Controls how much of the background you can see through the paint brush stroke.
Density	Designates the number of pixels with which the Paint Brush paints, evenly spread across the whole brushstroke.
Hardness	Controls how hard the brushstroke will be. The lower the hardness settings, the softer around the edges your paint brushstroke appears, making it flow more smoothly into your background.
Step	Defines the distance between overlapping brushstrokes.

Figure 4.22 shows several example settings for each characteristic to give you a good idea of the flexibility you have when using the Paint Brush.

Figure 4.22
Don't be afraid to mix and match settings across multiple characteristics.

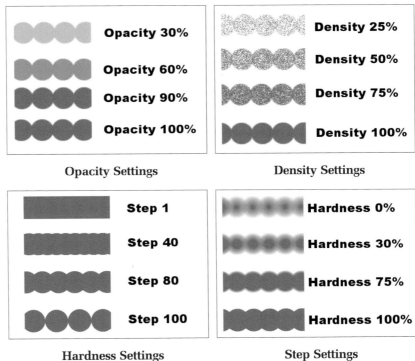

Opacity Settings

Density Settings

Hardness Settings

Step Settings

Changing Textures

The final and most impressive option the Paint Brush tool gives you is the ability to select a particular Paper Texture.

Paint Shop Pro gives you many texture options, each texture creating its own unique effect. Textures are selected from the Texture swatches on the Color Palette (below the Styles swatches). Like the Styles swatches, there's a texture swatch for foreground/stroke and one for background/fill. You set a texture on or off by clicking the arrow on a swatch and choosing either the Texture icon (on) or the Null icon (off). When the Texture icon is selected, you click the swatch to bring up the **Texture Picker**, where you select the texture you want.

Figure 4.23 shows a small sampling of the various textures.

Figure 4.23
With many different textures available, you'll never run out of options when painting and making new images.

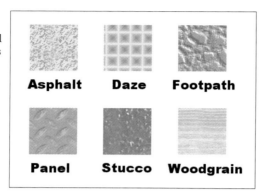

Other Painting Options

Paint Shop Pro is a truly robust graphics package. Artists and amateurs alike can create their own customized images from scratch using the tools provided. In this chapter you learned how to use Paint Shop Pro's general image drawing tools such as drawing Shapes and working with the Paint Brush. These two tools are critical functions that you will consistently use when creating your graphics with PSP.

In addition, several other tools may prove useful when you create new graphics from scratch. Some of the more popular Paint Shop Pro tools are listed below with a detailed explanation of when to use each.

▶ **Airbrush**—This tool paints as if you are using spray paint. Instead of drawing a crisp, solid line across the screen, the airbrush enables you to paint more indefinite patterns that aren't solid. You can use the airbrush tool when you paint the background of your Web graphics or when you want to add some texture and personality to an otherwise boring image. Some people refer to the airbrush as the "graffiti" tool, because the resulting graphics often look like they were spray-painted on an image.

▶ **Flood Fill**—Another useful tool, flood fill allows you to paint an entire section of your image one color, gradient, or pattern. The Flood Fill tool is often used to paint an entire canvas one color. Figure 4.24 shows a gradient flood fill added to large headline letters for a butterfly page.

Figure 4.24
Text flood filled with
a gradient.

Note that in this example the Flood Fill tool was used with a Match
Mode of None. This fills all the text with a single gradient, as if the text
were used as a cookie cutter on one large gradient. This gives a different
effect than using a gradient as the fill of the text (Figure 4.25), where each
letter is filled with its own instance of the gradient.

Figure 4.25
Text with its fill set to
a gradient.

> ► **Eraser**—Everyone makes mistakes. Even if you are a master artisan,
> eventually you'll color a square the wrong color or make some
> graphical equivalent to a typo. That's why you'll quickly want to get
> familiar with the built-in eraser, which erases the section you mark
> and replaces it with the current background color, according to the
> Color Palette.

> ► **Retouch**—This one is sure to become one of your favorite tools!
> Retouch lets you add neat special effects to your image, such as
> smudging, embossing, or softening the lines of your image. These
> tools are great for blending images together or making modifications
> to existing images.

Part II

Marrying PSP to the Web

5

Web Graphics Basics

You're sure to want to add some graphical elements to your Web site. Navigation buttons, decorative headers, and separator bars are just some of the possibilities. You might also want to add photographs to enhance your site and inform your visitors.

In this chapter, we'll look at some of the basics of Web graphics:

▶ **Coding HTML for Embedding Images and Setting the Background**
Learn the basics of how to display images and set background colors on your Web pages.

▶ **Choosing the Right File Format for Your Web Images**
Only certain file formats can be read by Web browsers, and some formats are appropriate for certain images and not others. Learn how to tell when to use what format.

▶ **Using Tables and Frames to Display Images Online**
Tables and frames give you lots of flexibility in displaying your images online.

After mastering the basics in this chapter, we'll start looking at how to create your own Web elements in Chapter 6, "Creating Transparent Images"; Chapter 8, "Coordinating Web Graphics"; and Chapter 9, "Making the Best Backgrounds." And in Chapter 7, "Optimizing Web Graphics," you'll explore the dilemma that every Web designer must face: how to balance image quality and download time.

Part II Marrying PSP to the Web

HTML Coding for Web Images

You embed images in your Web page with the IMG tag. Suppose you have an image called `MyCat.jpg` that you want to display on your page. If `MyCat.jpg` is uploaded to your Web host's server in the same directory as the HTML file for your page, you'd enter this HTML code to embed the image:

```
<IMG SRC="MyCat.jpg">
```

The SRC attribute of the IMG tag tells the browser what image to load and where to find it. Suppose `MyCat.jpg` actually is located in a directory called Pictures, and that directory is a subdirectory of the one that contains your HTML file. Then for SRC you'd enter the relative path along with the image's filename:

```
<img src="Pictures/MyCat.jpg">
```

And if your image resided on a totally different server, you'd specify the whole URL for the image. For example, if the image is located in the root directory at **loriweb.pair.com**, here's what you'd enter:

```
<img src="http://loriweb.pair.com/MyCat.jpg">
```

CAUTION

Many Web servers are Unix based, and Unix is case-sensitive. So when you enter the value for SRC, be sure that the case exactly matches the case of the filename and path spec, as they appear on the server.

Using Images Located on Other Web Sites

Using images from other Web sites has some advantages. For example, if you're an affiliate of an online store that uses standard images for its advertised products, the store may require you to link to the standard image. This saves you from taking up your own server space, and it allows the store to update the graphic whenever necessary.

Another situation in which you'd use a graphic on another site is when your page uses a graphical hit counter that is maintained by another site, as illustrated in Figure 5.1.

Figure 5.1
Using a graphical hit
counter created and
maintained on another
Web site.

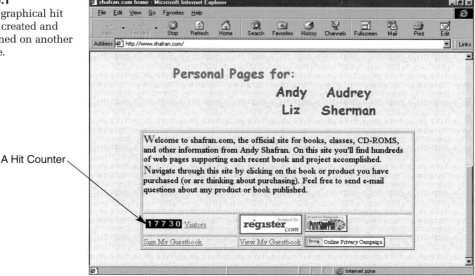

A Hit Counter

The counter used in this example is incremented by a Web server elsewhere on the Internet. For example, every time someone stops by Andy's home page, their Web browser goes out to **http://www.digits.com** and downloads a simple GIF that displays the visitor number.

Linking to images elsewhere on the Web has several drawbacks, however:

▶ **Performance**—When you link to an image at another site, visitors who stop by your site must first download your entire page of HTML and graphics, then wait for the Web browser to connect to the other site and download the images stored there. Often, this creates a real bottleneck that can significantly increase the time it takes visitors to view your Web page.

▶ **Files change**—Every so often, Web sites are updated and changed by replacing old graphics and files with new ones. When you link to another site, you are at the mercy of that Web developer to maintain the particular image you are using. If the image changes or is deleted, it no longer appears on your Web page—a real bummer!

▶ **Server consideration**—When linking to an image at another site, you place an increased workload on the second Web server. Although it isn't a big deal when a few people link to the image on someone's site, imagine if thousands of people had Web pages that used that site's images. That person's poor Web server would be swamped! This sort of "bandwidth stealing" is inconsiderate at best and may lead to serious repercussions.

▶ **Legal issues**—A hot topic among Web developers is the issue of copyright. Images that are on another page are not necessarily yours for the taking. They are almost certain to be copyrighted. The best bet is never to link to a graphic from another Web site unless the owner requests that you do so.

▶ For more information on copyright as it pertains to Web graphics, see "Purloining and Pilfering" by Linda Cole at **http://wdvl.internet.com/ Authoring/Graphics/Theft/.**

Besides linking to images on another site, browsers make it easy to download images from other Web sites. Downloading images from other people's Web sites without their permission and then using the images yourself could definitely create legal problems. While linking to images on another site might lie in a legal gray area, representing other people's images as your own is as clear as black and white: it's illegal.

In general, never download a graphic unless you have the copyright holder's permission or the image is clearly identified as being in the public domain. When you want to use an image from another Web site and there's no indication of whether the owner is willing to make the image available, it's best to e-mail the owner and ask for permission to use the image. Many individuals don't mind sharing their graphics, particularly if you agree to link back to their sites. If you obtain permission, simply save the image to your personal Web site and use it like any other GIF or JPEG.

Fixing a Broken Image Pointer

Earlier in this chapter, you saw several ways to define the SRC for the IMG tag. The exact file reference to use depends on where your image is located: in the same directory as your HTML file, on the same server but in another directory, or on a different server altogether. If you're confused as to how the many file references work, relax— you're in good company. Using an incorrect path when attempting to add images to their Web pages is among the most common problems experienced by Web developers for all sites, large and small.

When you point to the wrong place for an image file, Web browsers display a simple "broken image" icon on the page where the correct image would have appeared. Figure 5.2 shows how the "broken image" icon appears in Netscape.

Figure 5.2
The broken image icon tells visitors the file can't be found by the Web browser.

The broken image icon

When you see this icon on your Web page, you know that either the Web browser simply couldn't find and download the image or that the Web server didn't send the image to your computer within the allotted time. Most likely, there is a typo in the image's file name or the HTML file has mistakenly set the image's path to the wrong location. If you see this icon while browsing the Web, try reloading that particular page to see whether it is a server problem or an incorrect image path.

Don't let all the hard work you put into creating great Web graphics go to waste. If you see this icon on your pages, track down the problem immediately so visitors can experience all the glory of your Web graphics.

Important Attributes of the IMG tag

Besides SRC, the IMG tag has several other attributes. One of the most important of these is ALT. Use ALT to specify a string of text that will display when your visitor's browser is not displaying graphics. For example, for MyCat.jpg, you could have something like this:

```
<img src="MyCat.jpg" alt="A beautiful brown tabby cat">
```

Two other very important attributes of the IMG tag are HEIGHT and WIDTH. When you use these attributes to specify the exact height and width of your image, you tell the browser how much space to set aside for the image. This saves on load time, because the browser doesn't have to calculate how much space to set aside for the image. It also lets the browser start displaying the rest of your page before the image loads completely, thus giving your visitors the opportunity to start getting the benefit of your page right away.

CAUTION

Resist the temptation to resize your images with HEIGHT and WIDTH. Although there are a few special circumstances where this is a reasonable technique to use, it's almost always a bad idea. Resizing with HEIGHT and WIDTH will *increase* download time, since the browser must load the full-size image and then calculate how to display it at the changed dimensions.

If you want to resize a Web image, your best bet is to do so in Paint Shop Pro.

Two other attributes of the IMG tag that you'll sometimes find useful are HSPACE and VSPACE. These attributes specify horizontal and vertical buffer space between your image and any surrounding text or nearby images. Figures 5.3a and 5.3b show an example.

Figure 5.3a
A Web graphic surrounded by text, with no buffer space.

Figure 5.3b
The same graphic with
10 pixels of horizontal
buffer space.

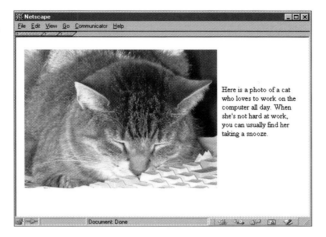

Here's the HTML code for this example:

```
<img src="MyCat.jpg" height="300" width="400" hspace="10"
align="left">
```

Notice that besides HSPACE, this example also uses the ALIGN attribute of
the IMG tag. Use ALIGN to place your image to the left or right of your block
of text. (Several other values of ALIGN are also available. See a general
HTML reference guide for more information.)

Background Colors and Images

The simplest way to add a bit of color to your Web page is to set a
background color. To do so, you add the BGCOLOR attribute to the BODY
tag of your page. You specify BGCOLOR by its hex code or by one of the
sixteen standard named colors. For example, you could specify a blue
background like this:

```
<body bgcolor="blue">
```

or like this:

```
<body bgcolor="#0000FF">
```

A hex code for specifying a background color is a string of three pairs of
hexademical numbers, beginning first with #. Hexadecimal numbers
range from 0 to F. The decimal equivalent of A is 10, of B is 11, and so on
up to 15 for F. The first pair of hexadecimal numbers specify the amount
of red in the color, the second pair specifies the amount of green, and the
third specifies the amount of blue.

Table 5.1, which displays the 16 named colors and their hex codes, will give you an idea of how the hex codes map to specific colors.

Table 5.1
The sixteen named colors and their HEX code equivalents

Named Color	HEX Code	Color Swatch
Aqua	00FFFF	
Black	000000	
Blue	0000FF	
Fuchsia	FF00FF	
Grey	808080	
Green	008000	
Lime	00FF00	
Maroon	800000	
Navy	000080	
Olive	808000	
Purple	800080	
Red	FF0000	
Silver	C0C0C0	
Teal	008080	
White	FFFFFF	
Yellow	FFFF00	

You can also use a repeating tile as wallpaper for your Web page. Figure 5.4 shows an example.

Figure 5.4
A Web page with
background wallpaper.

The image used for this wallpaper is shown in Figure 5.5.

Figure 5.5
The tileable image used
for the example Web
page's wallpaper.

To use a background tile on your page, use the BACKGROUND attribute of the
BODY tag. For a tile called concrete.gif, here's what you'd enter:

```
<body background="concrete.gif">
```

You'll see how to make your own background tiles in the Chapter 9,
"Making the Best Backgrounds."

TIP

When you use a background tile as wallpaper on your Web page, it's a good
idea to also specify a matching background color, like this:

```
<body background="concrete.gif" bgcolor="gray">
```

This ensures that text on your page will display correctly even before your
background image loads, and it also gives your visitors a nice transition into
your page.

Part II Marrying PSP to the Web

File Formats for Web Images

There are currently two standard file formats for Web images: GIF (pronounced "jif") and JPEG (pronounced "jay-peg"). A third format, PNG (pronounced "ping"), is slowly gaining ground but is still not fully supported.

Each of these file formats has its strengthens and weaknesses:

▶ **GIF** supports a maximum of 256 colors. You might think that this limited color range would make GIF a seldom-used format, but in fact GIF has also has several advantages over the other Web formats:

    — GIF compression is "lossless," which means that none of the original image's data is lost after compression.

    — GIF supports Web-based transparency, which allows you to create images that let your page's background show through parts of the image, making the image seem to be nonrectangular. You'll learn how to make transparent GIFs in Chapter 6.

    — GIFs can be used to create animations that run in a Web page without any extra plug-ins. We'll look at animation in Chapter 13, "Animation on the Web."

GIF is best used with simple graphics that contain sharp color changes and blocks of solid color.

▶ **JPEG** supports a maximum of 16.7 million colors. It is best used for photorealistic images or for other images that include subtle gradations of color.

JPEG compression is "lossy," which means that any time you save a compressed JPEG you lose some of the image's data. With images that include subtle color changes, this loss of data might not be perceptible. With simple graphics, though, JPEG compression can produce murky splotches called "artifacts."

▶ **PNG** is seen by many folks as the perfect alternative to both GIF and JPEG. PNG supports 16.7 million colors, like JPEG, and has lossless compression, like GIF. GIF also supports multiple levels of transparency, and a related format—MNG—can be used to create animations. Unfortunately, as of this writing there is still no universally accepted standard for implementing all of the features of PNG in Web browsers. You'll probably be safe nowadays, though, using simple PNGs (that is, PNGs with either no transparency or paletted transparency—the type of transparency supported by GIF).

NOTE

Two new Web graphics formats are under development as this book is going to press: JPEG 2000 and SVG (Scalable Vector Graphics). You can experiment with SVG using Jasc's Trajectory Pro. Head over to **http://www.jasc.com** to find out more about Trajectory Pro and SVG.

Using Tables to Display Web Images

The ALIGN, HSPACE, and VSPACE attributes of the IMG tag are all fine for simple formatting of your images on your Web page. You'll often find, though, that you need a little more control of the placement of images on your pages. Tables might very well be the answer!

Every table has an opening and closing tag, <TABLE> and </TABLE>. A row in a table is defined with a <TR> tag, and good style dictates that you close each table row with </TR>. Each column in a row is defined with a <TD> tag (think of "TD" as "table data"), and good style dictates that you close each table column with </TD>.

Here's an example of a simple table:

```
<table>
<tr>
<td>Row1/Col1</td>
<td>Row1/Col2</td>
</tr>
<tr>
<td>Row2/Col1</td>
<td>Row2/Col2</td>
</tr>
</table>
```

Figure 5.6 shows this table displayed on a Web page.

Figure 5.6
A simple table displayed on a Web page.

The TABLE tag has several attributes that affect its appearance. One of these is BORDER, which defines a border around the table. The default value for BORDER is 0, which displays no border at all, as in Figure 5.6. For this same table, the result is quite different if you specify BORDER="5", as Figure 5.7 shows.

Part II Marrying PSP to the Web

Figure 5.7
The table with
BORDER=5.

The numeric value that you specify for BORDER sets the width of the border, in pixels.

BORDER can be used to make an image appear to be inside a picture frame, as in Figure 5.8.

Figure 5.8
BORDER can be used to
simulate a picture frame
around an image.

Here's the HTML code for the table used for this example:

```
<table border="15">

<tr><td><img src="MyCat.jpg" HEIGHT="300" WIDTH="400" ALT=
"My cat"></td></tr>

</table>
```

Another TABLE attribute that often comes in handy when displaying your image is BGCOLOR. Just as you can set the background color of a Web page with the BGCOLOR attribute of the BODY tag, you can also set a background color for a table with the BGCOLOR attribute of the TABLE tag. Figure 5.9 shows a Web page that has a textured background for the main page and a table with a solid-colored background on which text is displayed.

Figure 5.9
You can use BGCOLOR
in a table.

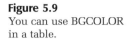

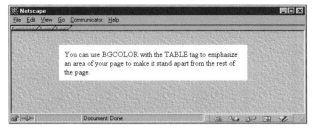

Here's the HTML code used for this example:

```
<html>
<body background="concrete.gif">
<br>
<center>
<table bgcolor="#ffffff" width="400" cellpadding="10">
<tr>
<td>
```

You can use BGCOLOR with the TABLE tag to emphasize an area of your
page to make it stand apart from the rest of the page.

```
</td>
</tr>
</table>
</center>
</body>
</html>
```

Notice how in this example the WIDTH attribute is used with the TABLE
tag to fix the width of the table to 400 pixels. We've also included the
CELLPADDING attribute in order to set a 10-pixel margin around the text
contained in the table.

For more information on creating tables, consult any general HTML guide.

A Brief Look at Frames

Another method frequently used to structure Web pages is using frames.
Frames allow you to split up the browser window into multiple areas,
each displaying a separate HTML file.

Probably the most popular use of frames is to keep a standard header or
footer on the screen for visitors exploring a Web site. Figure 5.10 shows
an example of the L.L. Bean Web page from a few years ago, where one
frame contains the main body of the page and another frame is used as a
footer. This footer contains several images that stay at the bottom of the
screen. As you surf the Web, you will probably find many sites that use
frames to keep their logo or main headline ever present. (Note, though,
that many commercial sites that used to use frames, including L.L. Bean,
no longer use frames on their sites.)

Figure 5.10
Frames keep a logo or
navigation bar always
visible throughout a
Web site.

Footer Frame

The HTML code for frames isn't complicated, but it can be tricky.
Basically, each frame is a separate page of HTML that loads a set of
images or text. Then you need another HTML file to tie the frames
together. For example, your INDEX.HTML file might look like this:

```
<html>
<frameset rows="80%,20%">
<frame src="homepage.html">
<frame src="footer.html">
</frameset>
</html>
```

Frames are defined in a special HTML file. This file doesn't have a BODY
tag, but instead has a FRAMESET tag. In our example, the index file is a
special HTML file that defines two horizontal frames, one that takes up
80 percent of the page space and one that takes up 20 percent of the
space. The source file displayed in the first frame is HOMEPAGE.HTML,
while the source file displayed in the second frame is FOOTER.HTML.
These two HTML files can be normal HTML files, or they can themselves
define other framesets.

To learn more about how to use and build frames, check out any
comprehensive reference on HTML.

CAUTION
Many Web surfers strongly dislike frames. Keep this in mind when deciding
whether or not to use frames on your own Web site.

6

Creating Transparent Images

Throughout much of this book, we've focused on the primary image types of the Web—GIF, JPEG, and PNG. Because each format offers different advantages over the others in various situations, part of the process of creating high-quality Web graphics is choosing the correct image format for the circumstances.

In general, GIF, JPEG, and PNG images share many similarities and are the three most widely accepted Web graphics formats. As you have learned, the key differences between the three formats dictate when you want to use one method over another. In this chapter, we change gears and show you how to take advantage of a powerful feature for your Web images called *transparency*. Both the GIF and PNG formats support transparency, and Paint Shop Pro enables you to exploit this useful feature.

► **What Transparent Images Are**
Learn the technical specifications for how transparent GIFs work, are saved, and are displayed by Web browsers. Understand the mechanics of how browsers treat these special types of images.

► **When to Use Transparent GIFs and PNGs**
Like most graphics features, transparent images are ideal only for certain situations. Learn to determine when creating transparent images is worth the time and effort.

► **How to Use PSP's Transparent Tools**
Paint Shop Pro has several useful tools that enable you to quickly create transparent GIF and PNG images. Understand your transparency options and how to create and modify images to use this trait.

► **How to Specify a Color to Be Transparent**
Learn how to identify and indicate that a particular color be transparent by using built-in Paint Shop Pro tools.

GIF and PNG images allow you to specify parts of an image that Web browsers will ignore and treat as **transparent**. The end result is that your Web browser displays the normal image but ignores the part(s) designated as transparent. Instead, the browser shows the Web page's background color or pattern the same way it does when you put text on a Web page. This allows more natural-looking images.

Transparent GIFs and PNGs are powerful tools in a Web developer's toolbox. Creating effective images for the World Wide Web requires that you understand and use transparent images to enhance your entire Web page experience for viewers.

What is Transparency?

It's easy to understand what transparency is by thinking of how an overhead projector works. An overhead projector takes pieces of clear plastic with writing on them and displays only the writing on a screen. Since the plastic is transparent, it isn't projected onto the screen. Transparent images work in a similar fashion. The GIF and PNG file formats allow you to specify one of the colors from a file to be transparent when shown within a Web browser. Typically, only browsers support transparency, and not other programs found on your computer.

So, instead of appearing normally, the area of specified color allows the background image or color of a Web page to be displayed. Generally, you can choose only one color to be transparent on a GIF and PNG—but with Paint Shop Pro, you have several ways you can set the transparency values.

TIP

New to Paint Shop Pro 7, you can designate multiple colors and parts of an image as transparent by using the selection tools. Paint Shop Pro essentially converts the selected area into a single color that will be transparent, but the practical applications are tremendous. This feature is covered later in this chapter in the section labeled "Advanced Transparency Options."

Often, the white background of an image is the area made transparent, so that the image lays on the Web page better. The white part of the image represents area not being used and is saved as a section of blank white.

Figure 6.1 shows an example of this phenomenon. On this Web page I have created a simple tic-tac-toe board using two repeated images—X and O. For this example, the background color of the Web page is set to grey. By setting white to be transparent, my browser ignores it in the image and the image appears to "float," or fit in with the actual Web page better.

Figure 6.1
The Os fit in much
more nicely with the
screen than the Xs do
because the background
of the Os is transparent.

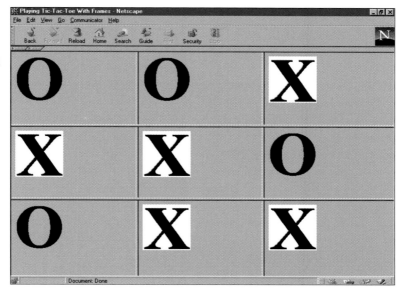

The images are nearly identical. Both are the same size in pixel height
and width and use only two colors—black and white. I used Paint Shop
Pro to create both of them. The only difference is that I instructed Paint
Shop Pro to make the white on the *O*s transparent. For the *X*s, I did not
instruct PSP to make the white transparent. As a result, the browser
ignores the white for the *O*s, but not for the *X*s.

Transparent images improve the appearance of images on your Web page.
Nontransparent images sometimes look awkward and out of place because
they force a browser to display the image as a square or rectangle—not
allowing the useless part of the image to disappear.

TIP

In general, transparent images should be investigated under two scenarios:

When you define any background color or use a background image on
your Web page. This allows your Web browser to ignore parts of an image
that are not necessary.

When your images are not perfectly rectangular (like a photograph) and
have parts that need to cut away so they look proper on a page.

The creation and use of icons on Web pages represents a common
situation for using transparency. Many people like to create their own
colorful bullets and lines instead of using standard ones available through
HTML. Web-page bullets often are round or other nonrectangular shape,
but images can be saved only as rectangles. The result is that an odd-
shaped bullet might not fit with the design of the rest of the page because

it looks like a rectangle when displayed. To compensate for this problem, icon designers make the backgrounds of their bullets transparent. Figure 6.2 shows an example of a Web page using transparent and nontransparent icons—both depicting a dollar sign. Which would you rather use?

Figure 6.2
Transparency functionality is one reason most icons and bullets are saved as GIFs instead of JPEGs.

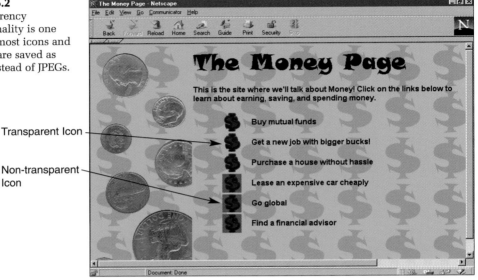

Transparent Icon

Non-transparent Icon

Because this is an essential feature, Paint Shop Pro 7 has a new feature that makes transparency even easier to use—and more powerful. Remember to design all of your images in the .PSP format. Once you are done designing the images, you can export your graphic into the GIF or PNG format and set transparency settings as part of the export process.

Creating a Simple Transparent GIF

Now that you know what transparent images are and how browsers display them, it's time to learn how to create your own. In this section you'll learn how to create a simple transparent GIF.

NOTE

I selected a GIF because they are generally easier to use when controlling transparency settings. GIFs can have only 256 unique colors, so selecting the one color to be transparent is usually straightforward. Because PNG images can use the entire 16.7-million color palette, setting transparency settings often requires expertise and finesse. That's because it can be harder to select the one correct color to be designated as transparent.

Creating a Transparent GIF from Scratch

First, I'll show you an example of how to make a simple transparent image from scratch. We'll look at how to create a transparent *X* to mate with the *O* used earlier in this chapter. I'll walk you through creating the graphic from start to finish.

1. First, start up Paint Shop Pro and choose **File** > **New** from the menu bar to bring up the **New Image** dialog box (Figure 6.3 below).

Figure 6.3
Creating transparent images is just as easy as working with any other type of GIF file.

2. For this example, in the **Im**age type drop-down list box, choose *256 Colors* (8 bit), because the GIF file type limits us to a maximum of 256 colors. GIF transparency works only within PSP when you are working with 256 colors.

CAUTION

Remember that Paint Shop Pro can reduce the number of colors to 256 when you save the image as a GIF, so if you want to take advantage of working with more colors when initially creating your image, you can. But, often you create extra work for yourself by trying to manage all those extra colors because the color reduction process can be more complicated when your goal is to produce transparent images.

3. Choose the appropriate **H**eight and **W**idth for your new image. Although transparency features work on GIFs of any size, I'll choose 100×100 for this example. Then click on the OK button to continue. A new blank image is created.

4. Click on the **Text icon** so you can add an *X* to your image.

Part II Marrying PSP to the Web

5. Click your mouse cursor in the image to bring up the **Text Entry** dialog box (Figure 6.4).

Figure 6.4
Text can be added in any font, style, and size.

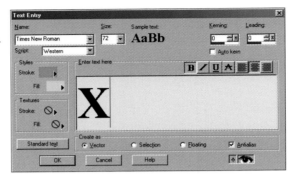

6. Choose the **Font attributes** you want your text to appear in by selecting the **N**ame, **S**ize, and attributes of the font. Now type your desired text in the **E**nter text here window. I am adding an *X* that is in Times New Roman, black, bold, and at 72 points in size. Click **OK** after making your selections. Make you sure you create the text as a ***Vector*** so you can adjust the attributes and move it around your image easily in the future.

7. Your text appears on top of your image. Move your mouse over the graphic until the pointer becomes a cross with arrows on all four points. Click your left mouse button and drag the text vector to the spot on the image where you want the text placed. You can also easily resize vector text objects by clicking on one of the edge nodes when you have the text selected. Remember, because the X is a *Vector* image, you can reselect and change it in the future, until you save it as a GIF image (upon which it loses the vector attributes). Figure 6.5 shows my newly created *X* image.

Figure 6.5
Making this simple image has been a piece of cake so far.

NOTE

This example placed the text as a vector object because, in general, vectors are easier to manipulate and edit in the future. You'll learn much more about vectors in Chapter 11, "Drawing With Vectors." Alternatively, you can select **floating** in the Text Entry dialog box and add the text as a floating selection. Floating selections are simpler to place on your image, but once you've placed it on a layer, the image becomes part of the layer. If you choose to use floating, make sure you place your text on a separate layer for easier future editing.

8. The next step is to set your transparent color. The easiest way to set a transparent color is to tell PSP to use whichever color is currently shown in the background in the Color Palette on the right-hand side of the screen. You need to ensure that the color deemed transparent is the current background color in the Color Palette. To do this, click on the **Dropper** icon from the Tool Palette.

9. Now move your mouse to anywhere in the background of your image (the white part of the image in this example) and click the *right* mouse button. The Dropper lets you select colors by pointing and clicking on them. The left mouse button controls the foreground; the right mouse button controls the background.

    Notice how in the Color Palette on the right-hand side of the screen, the background color switches and becomes whichever color you click on. For this example, my background color is white; but it would work the same if I had clicked on blue, red, green—or any other color. If I wanted to make the background color black, I would have clicked on part of the X instead.

10. Finally, you are ready to mark your transparency settings. Choose **C**olor > Set Palette Transparency to bring up the **Set Palette Transparency** dialog box (Figure 6.6). In this example, the X is a text vector and Paint Shop Pro tells you it must "flatten" your image before setting the transparency. Flattening is fine in this circumstance because you are creating a final publishable image. Be sure you save the pre-flattened image in the .PSP format first, though, so you can do future pre-flattening editing.

Figure 6.6
PSP gives you three transparency options from which to select.

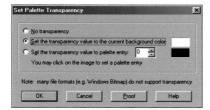

TIP

Although you are saving your image as a transparent GIF, be aware that the image will display transparent characteristics only in a Web browser that supports transparency, such as Netscape or Internet Explorer.

In Paint Shop Pro, to see how your transparency settings look, you must choose **C**olor > **V**iew Palette Transparency from the menu bar. Paint Shop Pro will make the color marked as transparent invisible—instead you will see the PSP checkerboard, which indicates a deleted or invisible area.

11. You can choose from three options: No transparency for this image; Set the current background color to be transparent; or Set a different color to be transparent (by typing in its color number, selecting the color from your current palette, or selecting the color to be transparent on the image, you can select colors in your image while this box is open).

    Select the option button labeled **Set the transparency value to the current background color**. This tells Paint Shop Pro to make a special note that the current background color (as we defined in the Color Palette during Step 9) is now the one that should be transparent for this image. For more information on the other choices in this dialog box, see "Setting the GIF Options" in the next section. Click **OK** to save your settings.

NOTE

When you edit your graphic in the future, Paint Shop Pro automatically remembers the color, by number, that you've defined as transparent.

12. Give your image a file name and save it. Now this graphic is ready to be used on a Web page with the correct color marked as transparent. Figure 6.7 shows my newly created transparent *X* on the same tic-tac-toe board Web page.

Figure 6.7
Making that X look good
wasn't too hard, was it?

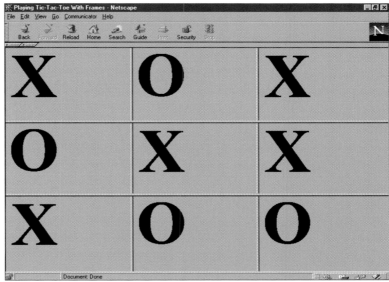

Working with Existing Images

Besides creating new images from scratch, you will often want to modify an existing image that lacks transparency by converting it to fit better on your Web page.

In general, converting an image into a transparent image follows the same process outlined above. First, you load the existing image into Paint Shop Pro. Then, using the eyedropper icon, click your *right* mouse button on the color you want to make transparent. This sets the color you select as the current background color. Finally, choose **C**olor > Set Palette **T**ransparency from the menu bar, and make sure the background color is marked as transparent.

> **NOTE**
>
> If an existing image has many intricate details, the Dropper tool can sometimes be difficult to use without a little extra help. If you have trouble selecting the correct background color, try zooming in on the picture to get additional detail. Choose **V**iew > Zoom **I**n from the Menu Bar and select a magnification from the available list. When you are finished, you can again choose **V**iew, then Zoom **O**ut.

Setting the Palette Transparency Options

When you save your transparency options, Paint Shop Pro gives you three selections to indicate which color should be transparent. I described one option earlier. Here's a brief summary of the other two options in the Set Palette Transparency dialog box:

▶ **No transparency**
As the name suggests, this option tells the image not to make a color transparent for Web browsers. This selection is often used for photographs and images with lots of colors that are saved in the GIF file format. You don't affect your image file size by ignoring transparency settings, just its appearance.

▶ **Set the transparency value to palette entry**
This selection allows you to designate any one of the colors as the transparent color by specifying its palette number, selecting it on the image or from your color palette. It's often easiest to arrange your screen so you can see your image and the Set Palette Transparency dialog box simultaneously (as shown in Figure 6.8). Then you can simply select the color in the image that should be transparent.

Figure 6.8
Selecting the transparent color from this dialog box makes transparency designation easy and straightforward.

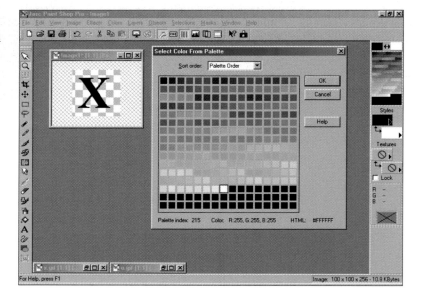

Using the GIF and PNG Optimizers

Paint Shop Pro 7 comes with two special tools that enable you to optimize your images for the Web. These two tools allow you to specify image transparency, the number of colors used in your image, image format options, and how to assess download times for this image. Called the GIF optimizer and the PNG optimizer, both tools should be used only when you've finished editing your images and are ready to publish them into the GIF or PNG format. They are both available from the **F**ile > Export in the Menu Bar.

The GIF Optimizer

To bring up the GIF optimizer, select **F**ile > Expor**t** > **G**IF Optimizer from the menu bar or click on the GIF Optimizer icon from the Web Toolbar. Figure 6.9 shows the GIF optimizer window. Notice how the window shows a before and after version of your image that depicts the options selected in the optimizer.

Figure 6.9
The GIF Optimizer.

Transparency Options, Preview Window

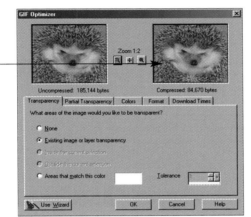

Remember that the GIF Optimizer is used to control many aspects of GIF images, not just transparency. On the transparency tab, you have five options to select from. Chapter 7, "Optimizing Web Graphics," steps you through the other tabs in the GIF Optimizer.

▶ **None**
Removes all transparency characteristics. You'll use this option most often when optimizing square/rectangular images that have no need for transparency.

▶ **Existing image or layer transparency**
Keeps the existing transparency characteristics intact. If you set transparency via the PSP Color menu bar (as we described earlier in the chapter) or you are optimizing an image someone else sent you that already has its transparency set, use this option.

▶ **Inside the current selection**
You can designate any part of an image as transparent that you have selected using the PSP tools. This is very useful when you are trying to mask out multiple parts of an image or multiple colors. Simply select the parts of the image that should be transparent and select this option.

▶ **Outside the current selection**
Similar to the previous option but creates the opposite effect. You'll use this setting when you want to add text to a Web page or have run

Part II Marrying PSP to the Web

some type of selection based filter. Paint Shop Pro will automatically make everything that is not selected transparent.

▶ **Areas that match this color**
Similar to the Set Palette Transparency dialog box (used in the simple GIF example earlier in this chapter), this option lets you pick the color to be saved as transparent. You can select your color by typing in the color's palette number, picking the color from your palette, or (most commonly) clicking on the color in the preview box with your mouse button. Paint Shop Pro will automatically identify the color for you.

Once you select your transparency option, Paint Shop Pro will show you the results in the Preview Window. Click on the **OK** button when you are finished. Paint Shop Pro will prompt you for a new file name—helping you avoid accidentally saving over your original image.

CAUTION

Paint Shop Pro lets you designate transparency via selection (inside or outside). While this may sound impossible, it isn't—but you have to use this tool carefully. Whether you select *Inside the current selection* or *Outside the current selection*, Paint Shop Pro actually converts the transparent area into a single color and marks it as transparent. Once saved, this transparent area is not recoverable—it is permanently converted into a single, uniform transparent area. The effect is identical to painting the selected area with the PSP Fill tool. You will have to open up your original image and go through the GIF Optimizer again to get different results.

NOTE

You've probably noticed that there is a Partial Transparency tab in the GIF optimizer window as well. Partial Transparency lets you designate what Paint Shop Pro should do when a color is dithered. Because dithering is the computer's way of fooling your eyes by mixing multiple colors together to create the illusion of a specific color, Paint Shop Pro wants to know how you want to handle the situation should you intend for a dithered color block to be transparent. In general, dithering and partial transparency are out of the scope of this book and not commonly used. That's because most of the time when you want to designate a color as transparent, you won't deal with dithered colors.

The PNG Optimizer

Providing you with almost identical functionality, the PNG optimizer can be accessed by selecting **F**ile > Export > **P**NG Optimizer from the menu bar or by clicking on the **PNG Optimizer** icon from the Web Toolbar. Figure 6.10 shows the PNG optimizer window.

Figure 6.10
The PNG Optimizer.

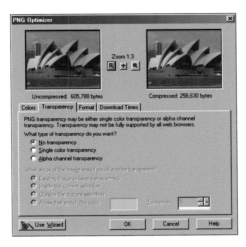

Like the GIF Optimizer, you can control many different aspects of your image from this window besides transparency. Initially, you have three options to select from:

▶ **No transparency**

Removes all transparency characteristics for this image.

▶ **Single color transparency**

Lets you access the second part of the Transparency tab by telling the PNG optimizer what part of the image is to be transparent. If selected, you have the identical four options as you did with the GIF Optimizer.

▶ **Alpha channel transparency**

The PNG graphics format supports an advanced transparency option that enables you to select multiple colors and designate them as transparent. This advanced feature requires you to learn how to set and manipulate alpha channels, which is out of the scope of this book. Be careful using this feature because few Web browsers support it—making your efforts for naught.

Once you set your transparency settings, click **OK** and PSP will prompt you to save your settings in a separate file.

More Transparent Examples

Now that you understand how transparent images work, this section shows you a few more examples of creating and using transparent GIFs within Paint Shop Pro.

A Transparent Icon

In the previous example, where I made the X image transparent, you can easily see how the background of the X was transparent. Basically, I told Paint Shop Pro not to display any of the white when putting the image on a Web page.

My next example will show you that any color, not just white, can be marked as transparent. Here's another example with a small GIF—the bullet icon used in Figure 6.2. This image is a 40×40 graphic. To build it, I used the Fill tool to paint the whole image light green. Then I added a darker green U.S. Dollar sign ($) to the small icon. Figure 6.11 shows me zoomed in 5:1 with Paint Shop Pro.

Figure 6.11
This background of this icon will become transparent in a moment.

Now I am going to make the green outside the dollar sign transparent by using the same process described earlier. Using the Dropper tool, I will select the background of my icon, then choose **Color > Set Palette Transparency**. I'll choose to make the background color transparent and then save my image. Figure 6.12 shows how the icon appears in a browser.

NOTE

It's important to point out that the graphic shown down the left-hand side of Figure 6.12 is also a transparent GIF. Created using Paint Shop Pro Tubes (the Coin Tube), this decorative graphic sets the feeling of the page. The coins were placed on an image with a white background, set to be transparent.

Figure 6.12
The same icon
displayed transparently
on a Web page.

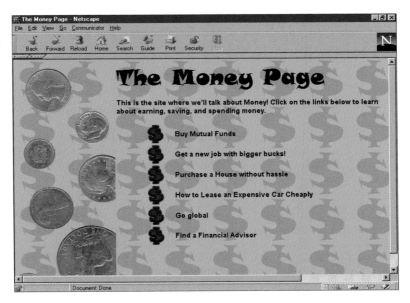

A Floating Photo

Another popular way to use the transparency feature in GIFs is to create
a "floating" photograph. Like JPEG files, GIF images can be saved only in
rectangular squares. Each file has a defined height and width, regardless
of whether you use the whole space of an image. Therefore, with an
image of a circle, your GIF file is actually still saved in a rectangular
shape, but part of the image is left blank—as unused white space.

As you've seen with other icons and images, the GIF transparency feature
is commonly used because it makes the icon appear to fit directly into
the Web page. A "floating" photograph expands that approach. Often,
you will not want to use the whole photograph for your Web page. One
useful technique is to first crop the photograph to the smallest possible
rectangular area needed and then erase the unnecessary part of the
remaining picture. You can then set the background of the photograph to
be transparent. Now, when added to a Web page, the resulting effect is a
floating photograph that appears irregularly shaped and uniquely placed
to fit the page.

Let's look at an example of this phenomenon at work. In this example,
I want to crop only the head out of a particular photograph and add it to
my home page.

Scanning the Picture

The first step is to select and scan a photograph. I'll use the scanning program that installed itself with my Umax 6450 Color Scanner. Of course, you can use any scanner and software to digitize a picture onto your computer.

TIP

You do not have to own a scanner to get digitized pictures. Digital cameras are another great source of images. For a fee, Kodak also will deliver images to you via CD, Web, or America Online when you have a roll of film developed.

If all else fails, your local Kinko's and other copy stores allow you to use scanners for a nominal fee.

Cropping the Picture

Once your image is properly scanned, open it up in Paint Shop Pro. Figure 6.13 shows my scanned photograph ready for manipulation. Remember that you can set transparent values only for images saved in the GIF file type. JPEG images tend to have smaller file sizes for photographs and use more colors, but they don't have as much flexibility and don't use the transparent options described in this chapter.

Fig 6.13
I'm ready to "float" my photograph.

Once loaded in Paint Shop Pro, the first step is to crop your photograph into the smallest rectangular area. Since GIF images must be saved as rectangles, use the Paint Shop Pro Crop tool. Click on the Crop tool icon and draw a box around the portion of your image you want to keep. Figure 6.14 shows the image with the area to be cropped marked.

Fig 6.14
I need only a small part of this image for my Web page.

My Crop Box

Then click on the **Crop Image** button in the Tool **O**ptions palette. Only the selected area will remain. Be sure to save your cropped image as a separate file so you don't overwrite your original image. Just in case, Paint Shop Pro lets you undo multiple commands, but you should save often in case you make a mistake on your image.

Sculpting Your Image

The next step in creating a floating image is to sculpt away the unnecessary parts of your newly cropped photo. Just like a sculptor, you want to whittle away the extra parts of the image so that you are left with the final image for display on your Web page. You are sculpting your image so that the unnecessary part of your Web graphic is all the same color. For this image we are sculpting around the head making the background color of the image all white so that white can be set as transparent. Sculpting around an image can be tedious and time consuming, but it is necessary if you don't want the interference from the background of your image.

PSP has many tools that are useful when you are sculpting away parts of an image. You can use your Paint Brush, Magic Wand, or Freehand Tool to effectively sculpt. For this example, we'll use the Freehand tool so you can see how it works.

You can also double click on the Background layer for the image and then click **OK** to make this a Layer and then use the Eraser tool to **Erase** the background of the image. This may be easier yet. Then go to the **C**olors menu > **D**ecrease Color Depth > **256** colors, which will give you a white background automatically.

Click on the Freehand selection tool, sometimes called the "lasso" tool, which lets you select irregularly shaped areas. Using this tool, mark the areas on the image that you want to remove from your final product. Now choose **E**dit > **C**ut from the menu bar, and Paint Shop Pro removes the selected area and replaces it with blank area. By default, your blank area is set at the background color defined in the Color Palette on the right hand side of the screen. Be careful not to select a background color that is part of the image itself. Otherwise, your Web browser might ignore parts of the image, not just the background. In general, white is an excellent color to use for transparent images.

Additionally, you may want to use the Paint Brush and Smudge tools to paint over smaller sections. The Freehand, Smudge, and Paint tools were also used to create a realistic cut-out version of this head. In particular, the Smudge tool helps soften the edges around an irregularly selected object.

CAUTION

Even the most talented sculptors don't recklessly chip and manipulate their carving. Take care to slowly cut away the unnecessary parts of the image one piece at a time. Don't rush and try to cut away the entire background part of the photo in one fell swoop. It's likely you'll accidentally cut an important part of the picture.

If it seems like this kind of detailed work on photos requires a lot of patience, it's because it does. Often professional and amateur graphics creators will spend hours sculpting and painting over detailed sections of an image to achieve the perfect effect.

You can choose to zoom in on your image so that you can sculpt in detail. To zoom in on your photograph, choose **V**iew > Zoom **In** from the menu bar. Figure 6.15 shows me whittling away part of the background wall from my photograph while zooming in for more detail. You'll find it helpful to constantly zoom in and zoom out to monitor your progress.

Fig 6.15
I zoom in considerably when sculpting my photographs.

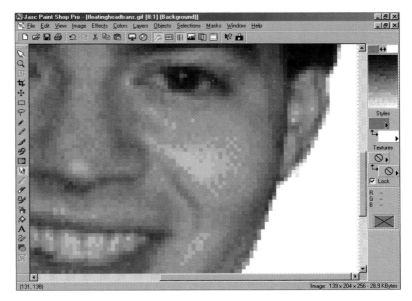

Sculpting is by far the most difficult step in creating a floating photograph for your Web page. Fortunately, Paint Shop Pro makes it easy for you to select and crop away unnecessary parts of your image. Once finished, move on to the next section. Take a look at Figure 6.16 to see how my final image looks all sculpted and ready to use.

Fig 6.16
Similar to my original image, this photograph is ready to float onto the Web.

Make sure that white is set as the current background for your graphic and then set it to be transparent. Save your image and you are complete.

Test Your Image

Once you are done creating your "floating" GIF, take a moment to test it with a Web browser. Make sure that your background color is properly identified.

Figure 6.17 shows my floating image twice—once as it should appear and once as it looks when the background transparent color isn't set right. If your image doesn't display correctly, it's likely that an incorrect color was selected to be transparent.

Fig 6.17
The floating GIF looks
slick when added to a
Web page.

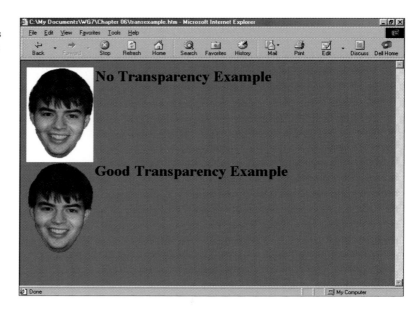

7

Optimizing
Web Graphics

As you read the first six chapters of this book, you learned how to make and edit all sorts of images for your Web pages. Whether you created a new image from scratch, used Paint Shop Pro's advanced graphics capabilities, or scanned a photograph or logo, you focused on creating and saving your images in electronic format. Learning how to create and edit good images is the important first step in adding graphics to your Web pages.

Although many individuals and companies have high-speed Internet connections, there's one important rule to keep in mind when producing Web graphics: The quicker they download, the better your site is. Since download time directly correlates to file size, it's crucial that you understand how to squeeze image file sizes to be as small as possible. However, you've got to balance your image size with image quality—a balance beam that needs to be walked very carefully.

In this chapter, you'll learn several techniques for making sure your images are small, are efficient, and take advantage of important file compression possibilities. Since visitors typically must download each image before they can see your Web page in its entirety, your site will be much quicker to explore and, consequently, more valuable when you use these techniques. Nobody wants to wait too long when visiting a Web site.

▶ **Understanding How File Size Equates to Performance**
In general, size, quality, and image format directly affect how long an image takes to download from the Web and be displayed on your computer. Learn how to balance these characteristics with one another.

▶ **Changing Image Pixel Sizing Saves Time**
By resizing, thumbnailing, and cropping your Web graphics, you can achieve significant savings in Web page download time. See how you can employ these three strategies to make your graphics more effective and efficient.

▶ **Counting the Number of Colors You Use**
Image size is highly dependent on the number of different colors used in the particular image. Learn how to control the number of colors you use in your graphics to see a dramatic difference in file size.

▶ **Understanding JPEG Compression**
Like GIFs, the JPEG file format offers special limits to control overall file size. By using JPEG compression, you can change the final file size of an image significantly without losing much image detail.

▶ **Using Interlaced and Progressive Images**
One popular way to make images appear more quickly on Web pages is by creating interlaced GIFs or progressive JPEGs. Learn how these special file options allow visitors to explore Web pages immediately.

Why Use Lean Files?

When you visit a Web page, you must wait for all the text and images to be downloaded into your Web browser. The time required for downloading to occur depends on the type and speed of Internet connection you maintain for your personal computer. High-speed Internet connections are becoming more popular, but many individuals and businesses still use a modem to browse through the Web.

Your Internet connection speed governs the rate at which graphics can be downloaded. Popular modem speeds range from 28.8 to 56.6 thousand bits-per-second (baud), but some people have DSL, cable, or even direct connections to the Internet. The faster your connection, the faster the graphics can be downloaded for viewing by visitors. Table 7.1 shows a comparison between several common connection speeds and the amount of data that can be downloaded at each speed.

Table 7.1
Download time comparison

Baud	Amount of data per minute
14,400	90K
28,800	180K
56,600	300K
DSL	10,000K
Direct Connection	60,000K

As you can see, even at the fastest modem speed, visitors will have to wait several seconds to download and see images on a large Web page. Interestingly, even with DSL and direct connections to the Internet, smaller graphics file sizes help because of the way the Internet works. Therefore, a critical task you will face when creating Web graphics is minimizing the overall file size of each image on your page. By reducing the download time, you'll have better response to your Web site from visitors who stop by, and they'll be more likely to return for another visit.

Everyone expects a few moments' wait when visiting a Web site, but nobody wants to wait 30 seconds for each page to load just to click on a hyperlink to move to another page. Visitors want to quickly see a particular page, read through it, and decide where to go next. The longer people have to wait to observe a particular page, the more likely they will click on the Stop or Back button in the Web browser and never even see your site.

For example, let's say your home page takes about 60 seconds to download and view. If ninety people visit your Web site every day, one and a half hours are spent downloading your single Web page. By finding some way to reduce the download time to 20 seconds—maybe by reducing the size or quality of an image—you can save your visitors, individually and collectively, a lot of time.

Keeping your graphics small and efficient is not only imperative but extremely challenging. Paint Shop Pro includes several methods you can use to help make your graphics small and lean.

NOTE

Besides graphics size, many other factors can affect the performance of your Web site and make your page(s) load slower. The number of simultaneous visitors to your site, the speed of your Web server, the cache settings in your Web browser, and even the overall traffic on the Internet can have a very real effect on Web site speed.

Cropping, Resizing, and Thumbnailing Images

One popular way to reduce the total download time of a Web page is to reduce the actual size, or area in pixels, of your image. You can save significant time by cropping or resizing an image so that a much smaller image is sent instead of the larger original one. Visitors can then click on a hypertext link if they want to see the larger, full-size version of the image.

This section outlines two excellent ways to reduce the size of images on your Web page. You will use these methods primarily when dealing with photographs and pictures on your Web site.

Resizing an Image

Perhaps the most common mistake Web developers make is using an image that is simply too large and unwieldy. In Figure 7.1, I created a Web page for Cary. The picture-perfect JPEG on this page is more than 50K in file size. Visitors have to wait nearly 30 seconds just to see this single picture if they are using a 28.8-baud modem.

Figure 7.1
Cary's picture is a bit too large, so let's shrink him.

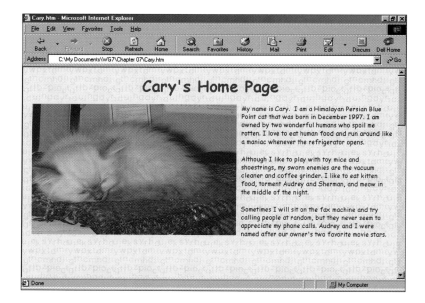

CAUTION

One major mistake that could cause even slower download times is picking the wrong image format. Figure 7.1 shows a photograph that is saved in the JPEG file format. Although 51K is large, the *identical* image is more than 100K when saved as a GIF instead. The big difference is due to the different compression techniques of the GIF and JPEG formats.

Similarly, if this image were a simple icon or headline, saving it in the JPEG format can make it unnecessarily larger because GIFs are optimized for that type of image. Make sure you always pick the proper image format, the one that's optimized for your type of Web graphic. Remember that photo and photo-like images are usually better saved as JPEGs since that format supports 16.7 million colors.

Although the image looks fine on this Web page, downloading takes too long. One way to overcome this problem is to resize the image using Paint Shop Pro. By resizing the image, you make the JPEG file size smaller because the new file will contain fewer pixel coordinates.

Originally, this image was 425 pixels wide and 284 pixels tall. I'm going to resize it to half its original size on the screen. The first step in resizing an image is loading the original in Paint Shop Pro. Once the image is opened, choose **I**mage > **R**esize from the Menu Bar to bring up the **Resize** dialog box (Figure 7.2).

Figure 7.2
Your new image can be changed to a variety of sizes.

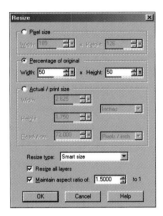

You can now choose between entering exact size coordinates or resizing the image as a percentage of the original. For this example, I am going to resize my image as 50 percent of the original. The resize dialog box, which is very useful, is described in more depth in Chapter 3, "Editing Images."

CAUTION
Make sure you don't overwrite your original image by mistake. Instead, save to a new file using the **F**ile > Save **A**s or **F**ile > Save Copy As commands. Rename your image with a similar but distinguishing descriptive name so you can easily tell the difference between the two files. For my example, I used **caryfluffybig.jpg** and **caryfluffysmall.jpg**.

Part II Marrying PSP to the Web

You can resize your graphics to nearly any size imaginable. It's helpful to evaluate several different sizes before you select the right one for your Web page. But generally you want to resize your images to be smaller than the original. Not only will that decrease your file size, but resizing an image larger than the original can cause noticeable quality degradation.

As you can imagine, the newly resized image has a significantly smaller file size. At 213×142 pixels, the new file size is only 11K, quite a difference from the original! At 11K, this image can be viewed comfortably because visitors will see it on your Web page in just about one-fifth the time required to see the original 51K image.

Figure 7.3 shows the newly redesigned Web page. I added a table, changed the way text flowed around the image, and more. You can tell that the most significant and best change comes from the resized image.

Figure 7.3
Creative use of other Web elements can make this page as attractive and useful even with a smaller image.

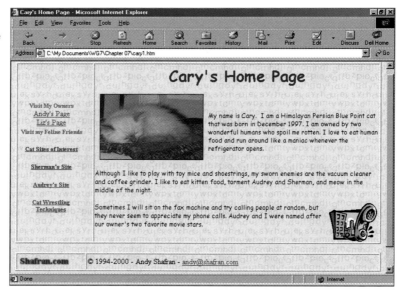

Making Thumbnails

When you resize the graphics on your Web page, you significantly reduce the time it takes visitors to browse your site. Unfortunately, resizing to a smaller image sometimes makes your graphic more difficult to see and less enjoyable for people who really want to see the full-size image. Since the image is physically smaller, your visitors have to scrutinize it more closely to notice smaller, more obscure details.

To compensate for this potential problem, many Web sites use a process called *thumbnailing*, which gives visitors the opportunity to see both the large and small versions of an image, if they so choose. Thumbnailing is a process by which you display the smaller image on your Web page but add a hyperlink to the larger, full-size graphic. This enables visitors to see the photograph in its original, larger size and form—but only when they choose to—and they know they will have to wait a few extra moments to see the image.

One site that uses thumbnailing extensively is Amazon.com, the popular Web shopping site. Publishers send Amazon large versions of their book covers so customers can see and read the entire cover. In an attempt to make each page load quicker, Amazon puts a smaller, thumbnailed version of the cover on its Web page (Figure 7.4a). If you click on the smaller cover, Amazon will display the full-size cover (Figure 7.4b).

Figure 7.4a
The smaller cover fits on the page easily, but the size makes it hard to read all the text.

Link to Image
The Mouse
Pointer

Part II Marrying PSP to the Web

Figure 7.4b
At full size, you can
see the book cover in
complete detail.

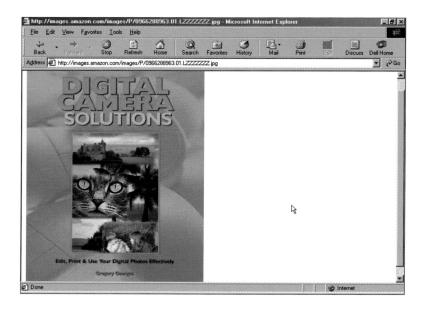

You don't have to be an Amazon.com to use thumbnailing in your site.
In fact, it's a pretty easy process. First create and edit the full-sized
image. Then, according to the steps outlined in the previous section,
make and save a smaller, resized version. For this example, I have two
files—VERYBIGCAT.JPG and VERYSMALLCAT.JPG. Notice how I named the
files accordingly. There is no doubt about which file represents the full-
size image of the cat and which is the smaller, or thumbnail-size,
version.

Normally, when adding an image to your Web page, you would use the
following line of HTML:

```
<IMG SRC="VERYSMALLCAT.JPG">
```

However, when thumbnailing, you want to link your smaller picture to
the full-size one. To accomplish this, add the <A HREF> and </A> tags
around the original image tag:

```
<A HREF="VERYBIGCAT.JPG"><IMG SRC="VERYSMALLCAT.JPG"></A>
```

This line of HTML not only tells your Web browser to display
VERYSMALLCAT.JPG as part of the Web page, but it also tells visitors they
can click on that image to download and display VERYBIGCAT.JPG. Your
Web browser adds a blue border around the image to indicate that the
smaller image links to an additional photograph. Also, your mouse
pointer transforms into a hand when placed over the linked image.

TIP

If you're like most people, you won't be building your Web pages directly in HTML. Instead, you'll use a tool like FrontPage, DreamWeaver, or HomeSite. All of these tools support thumbnailing automatically and make it very easy for you to incorporate the full-sized and smaller images in your page.

CAUTION

Many HTML tools say they will allow you to resize the appearance of an image on your Web page. This feature is not as worthwhile as it may seem. That's because the HTML editor doesn't really resize your image by making the file smaller. Instead, it simply resizes the appearance of the image. You must still download the entire full-sized image. This technique *is* very useful when you want to use the same image on your site in multiple sizes. You can create just one image and add it to multiple pages and have the browser do the resizing for you.

Cropping

Another way to reduce the size of your Web graphic is to crop it and display a small section of the original image. Image cropping has long been a tool of desktop publishers, newspaper editors, and graphic designers. Often an image includes extra, unnecessary parts that can be cut away. The resulting image is smaller and contains only the useful material.

Here's another example image continuing with the same feline trend. Figure 7.5 shows an image of Cary as a kitten. This is another good photo, but we don't need the entire image, because only part of it contains the cat. Instead, we want to crop out the non-related material. By cropping to just Cary, we get a smaller image that is much more relevant to the Web site we are creating.

Figure 7.5
Here's an image that really needs to be cropped.

Part II Marrying PSP to the Web

Paint Shop Pro has excellent built-in cropping capabilities. Using your mouse, you can simply indicate which part of the image should be saved and the extraneous parts will be discarded. To crop an image, follow these steps:

1. Load your original image in Paint Shop Pro using the **File** > **O**pen command.

2. Click the **Crop** icon from the Tool Palette. This permits you to select a rectangular area of your image to crop and save. Make sure the Tool **O**ptions palette is showing and you are in the Tool Controls tab.

3. Using your mouse, select the part of the image you want to crop. Figure 7.6 shows an area being selected within Paint Shop Pro.

Figure 7.6
I need only the cat from this photo.

The Selected Area to Crop

The Crop Image button

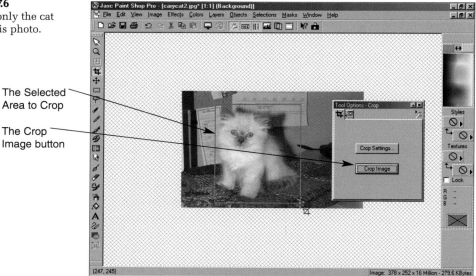

4. Double-click on the cropped area with your left mouse button or click on the **Crop Image** button on the Controls Palette. Paint Shop Pro will keep the selected area and discard the rest of the original image. Figure 7.7 shows the newly cropped area.

Figure 7.7
I'm left with the most pertinent part of the cat.

5.   Save your newly cropped image with the **File** > Save **As** command so you don't overwrite the original graphic.

For this example, the resultant cropped JPEG is only 7K, significantly smaller than the original, which was around 50K. Since we cropped the picture instead of resizing it, visitors won't have to squint to see the image, because it is the original size and detail of the photograph.

As with thumbnailed images, many Web developers also link the cropped image to the full-size one. This enables your cropped image to serve as a thumbnail so that visitors have the option of seeing the entire photo.

Consider cropping an image when using them on your Web page. Had I decided not to crop my cat picture, my visitors would have been forced to download a large image that included a lot of pointless background material.

Cropping by Selection

Instead of using the Crop tool, oftentimes you can achieve a similar effect using the Selection tool. This tool is nice because you can select rectangular or circular areas of an image, letting you create an odd-shaped final image. When you use the Selection tool, you have two options. First, you can choose Image > Crop to Selection from the Menu Bar. Paint Shop Pro crops to the smallest rectangular area possible that includes your entire selected area.

The second method comes in handy when you want to crop to a circular, elliptical, or unusually shaped image. To achieve this effect, use the Selection tool and select a circular or elliptical area. Or use the Freehand or Magic Wand tool to select another odd shaped area. But instead of cropping the image, Choose **E**dit > **C**opy from the menu bar. Then select **E**dit > **P**aste As New Image. Your image will paste with the correct shape. Finally, make the background of the image transparent, so it appears elliptical on your Web page. This method isn't exactly cropping an image, but the results are the same.

How Many Colors Are Right for a GIF Image?

The number-one way to decrease the file size of GIF images is to reduce the number of colors being used in the image. In this section, you'll learn how changing the number of colors can affect the appearance and file size of your image. Reducing the number of colors in a Web graphic offers the highest level of file compression for enhancing performance, but you can lose significant detail from your original full-color image.

How Colors Affect GIF File Size

Actually, the file size isn't as dependent on the *number* of colors used as you might think. It's really the *placement* of colors in an image that affects the GIF file size.

According to the specifications of the GIF format, an image is saved as a series of horizontal lines that go across the screen from left to right. Starting with the first pixel on the left-hand side of the screen, the image records the specifications for that particular color—let's say it's blue. Continuing to the right, one pixel at a time, the GIF assumes that it should continue using the exact same color until a different one is specified. So, if the whole line is a single shade of blue, only one color definition is needed for the whole line of that image. Often a single line of an image contains several different colors. Each time a different color needs to be displayed, that information is saved into the GIF file. Once the right-hand side of the image is reached, the GIF starts over, like a typewriter, and defines the next line (pixel by pixel) of colors in the image.

It's easy to see that when the whole image requires only one color, the file is likely to be small, because there are no color changes. The more color changes, from left to right, the larger an image. Therefore, a single-color Web graphic that is 300×300 pixels is only 1K. However, an image of the same pixel dimensions will have a dramatic increase in file size if it has several color changes on each line.

Figure 7.8 shows four 300×300 images with different file sizes, demonstrating this principle in action. Figures 7.8a and 7.8b are the exact same image except for the way the lines are turned. 7.8b is nearly twice as large as image 7.8a, even though they both have the same number of lines and colors. Similarly Figures 7.8c and 7.8d started out the same, but I added a few odd-shaped single-color shapes to the image. Figure 7.8c is only 1K, while Figure 7.8d is around 8K, even though only fourteen different colors are used in the second example.

These four images show how GIF files can vary in size.

Figure 7.8a
The horizontal stripes are smaller—only 1483 bytes.

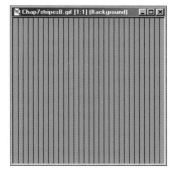

Figure 7.8b
Rotating the stripes make this image 2779 bytes.

Figure 7.8c
This single color image is very small—1K.

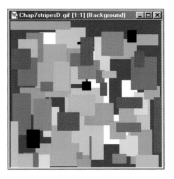

Figure 7.8d
Using only 14 colors, this image is eight times larger.

Unfortunately, this strategy only works for GIF images. JPEG files always have 16.7 million colors available and use a file structure and compression scheme different from that used for GIFs. As a result, a large GIF file that uses lots of colors will often improve significantly when converted into the JPEG file type. You'll notice this benefit particularly when working with scanned photographs for your Web page, which always use lots of colors and require a significant number of color changes.

JPEG compression is not dependent on the number of colors. Instead, JPEG files use a different form of compression that can sometimes lose detail. Usually, you'll want to save your Web graphics in both GIF and JPEG format to see which represents the best file size. Remember that file size isn't the only metric in creating Web graphics. Special features, such as transparency, interlacing, and animation, all have bearing on what file format you choose.

Part II Marrying PSP to the Web

Reducing Colors

Now that you understand the correlation between the number of colors changes and the resulting GIF file size, here's how and when colors can be manipulated to reduce your file size.

The best tool for GIF color reduction is the GIF Optimizer. The GIF Optimizer lets you see how your settings will affect the quality of your image interactively, making it easy to strike a balance between file size and image quality.

Launch the GIF Optimizer by choosing **F**ile > **E**xport > **G**IF Optimizer from the Menu Bar. Chapter 6, "Creating Transparent Images," spends time discussing the Transparency tabs within the Optimizer. In this section, we'll focus on the **Colors** tab (Figure 7.9).

Figure 7.9
The GIF Optimizer lets you easily pick the best number of colors for your image.

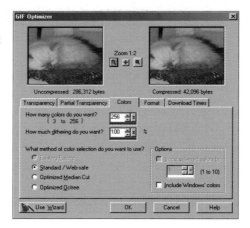

The GIF Optimizer Window

There are three major color components to the GIF Optimizer:

▶ **Selecting the Number of colors**—This is the most important setting. This setting lets you select the total number of colors used in your image, ranging from 3 to 256. The more colors you use, the better quality your final image, but also the larger your file size. You are limited to 256 colors here, because that is the maximum allowed in the GIF format.

▶ **Setting your Dithering Level**—Dithering is the process of having Paint Shop Pro alternate two different colors so that your eye is fooled into seeing a third color that isn't one of the 256 colors selected. Dithering lets Paint Shop Pro improve the quality of an image, but it makes your images larger. Dithering often doesn't work well for smaller images.

▶ **Choosing the Color Selection Method**—This setting lets you tell Paint Shop Pro how to reduce the number of colors used in your image. There are four options available:

—**Existing Palette**—This setting tells Paint Shop Pro not to make any significant changes to the palette being used in your image and to do the best job possible reducing the amount of used colors to 256 or under. This is the most useful setting when you want to convert an image with 16.7 million colors in it to a GIF.

—**Standard/Web-safe**—This tells Paint Shop Pro to use a palette optimized for Web browsers. This will guarantee your image will look the same on virtually all computers, regardless of the computer type or browser being used. Although this option sounds alluring, often this comfort level forces your image to look mediocre for everyone instead of great for the 95 percent Windows/Macintosh users out there who don't need this option as much.

—**Optimized Median Cut**—This is the best option to use when you want to experiment with under 256 colors. This option lets Paint Shop Pro always use its judgment depending on the number of colors you want to use and your dithering settings. If you want to see how your image looks at 188, 75, or 16 colors instead of 256, this is the setting to use.

▶ **Optimized Octree**—This option is another way of letting Paint Shop Pro select the best colors to use in your image, but it automatically adds 16 colors to your palette that you may or may not use in your image. You typically won't use this option.

There is one additional option you can select—**Include Windows' Colors**. This option lets you always include the 16 universal colors required by Windows to be in every color monitor. This option is not popular, because most Windows monitors support more than 16 colors nowadays.

Using the GIF Optimizer

Now that you are familiar with the options in the GIF Optimizer, this section describes how you can best use this powerful tool. Generally, you should use the GIF Optimizer as the final step in your imaging process—right before you put your graphic on your Web site.

Once you are finished editing your image, launch the **G**IF Optimizer and go to the **Colors** tab. From here it is time to select the best color settings and click on the **OK** button. Paint Shop Pro will prompt you to select a new file name for your image and save it with your selected settings. Figure 7.10 shows the same image saved at six different settings.

Here's an image of Cary saved six different ways—note the quality and file size differences.

Figure 7.10a
256 colors
100 percent dithering
Optimized Median
Cut 72K

Figure 7.10b
256 colors
0 percent dithering
Optimized Median
Cut 69 K

Figure 7.10c
256 colors
100 percent dithering
Web-safe palette
36 K

Figure 7.10d
25 colors
0 percent dithering
Optimized Median Cut
32 K

Figure 7.10e
128 colors
0 percent dithering
Optimized Median Cut
59 K

Figure 7.10f
50 colors
100 percent dithering
Optimized Median Cut
50 K

TIP

This is an excellent example of when resizing the image would help. By shrinking the image to half the original size, you don't lose any of the original image's effect. By shrinking the image and reducing the number of colors, my new image is much smaller.

Each image will require you to experiment with the Optimizer settings to achieve the best quality/size balance. But here are a few tips to always try:

▶ **Try varying numbers of colors for each image.**
I recommend creating two baseline images—one at about 20 colors and another at 256 colors. Then create images at regular intervals (such as every 50, 80, 110, 140, and 200). Then open each image within Paint Shop Pro and your Web browser to see where you can notice the quality differences. Don't forget to give each image a meaningful name so you know what settings you used.

▶ **Always try dithering values at 0, 33, 66, and 100 percent.**
Dithering often works counter to your assumptions when it comes to final image quality. Often you'll get better image quality at 0 or 33 percent dithering than you would at higher values.

▶ **Don't waste your time with Windows' colors or the Optimized Octree.**
More experimentation with the other settings will yield better results.

▶ **Don't try to squeeze too much juice from your lemon.**
Typically, you'll get 80 percent of the file size savings, at decent image quality, with just a few experiments. The difference between 12K and 13K is only an extra moment on your Web size, and in spending too much time trying to get the absolute best balance, the cost may not be worth the benefit.

▶ **If you are in a hurry, or don't want to experiment with many images, try using the GIF Optimization Wizard.**
This interesting tool asks you questions about how you'd like the final image to work and then mysteriously translates your answers into file settings. Although useful for true beginners, because you don't know the actual settings Paint Shop Pro selects for you, getting similar future results is tough. Launch the wizard by clicking on the **Use Wizard** button. Figure 7.11 shows the Wizard question that deals with image quality.

Part II Marrying PSP to the Web

Figure 7.11
The GIF Optimization Wizard lets you select image quality with your mouse.

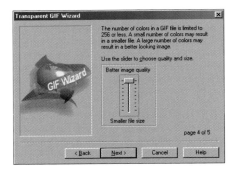

Auto-Reducing Color depth

Besides the GIF Optimizer, Paint Shop Pro has another tool that will automatically reduce the number of colors used in your image. The **Decrease Color Depth** tool lets you quickly change the number of colors used in your image from 2, to 16, to 256, to 32k, and to 64K (16.7 million colors).

Often you'll find that you can reduce the number of colors used in an image to 16 with this tool and bypass using the GIF Optimizer entirely. The first step is to get an idea of how many colors are currently being used in your GIF image. Load your GIF in Paint Shop Pro and choose **C**olors > **Co**unt Colors Used from the Menu Bar. A small dialog box will appear that will show you the unique number of colors in this image.

To reduce the number of colors in a GIF, choose **C**olors > **D**ecrease Color Depth > **16** Colors (4 bit) to bring up the Decrease Color Depth dialog box (Figure 7.12). This dialog box lets you specify exactly how you want Paint Shop Pro to mix and match hues it doesn't have in its 16-color palette. Notice that your color depth options are almost identical to those available in the GIF Optimizer—and they work the same here as well.

Figure 7.12
The Nearest Color reduction method is often best for most images.

This dialog box has many options available to you, including Palette and Reduction Method. Click **OK** to continue. Paint Shop Pro automatically interpolates your current image and displays the resulting new one to you.

Reduction Method

In the Decrease Color dialog box, you can also select a **Reduction method** for your images:

▶ **Nearest Color**—This option replaces the original colors with the closest match from the 16 new colors.

▶ **Ordered Dither**—This option only works with the **Windows** palette and is optimized for graphics that you are going to print.

▶ **Error Diffusion**—This option practices the dithering concept so that your image blends together nicely.

Usually you'll use either Nearest Color or Error Diffusion, both of which work well for reducing the number of colors in your images. In fact, you might want to save your original and reduce the number of colors twice, using each Reduction method, to see which one yields the better quality image and which the smaller file size.

Color Reduction Watchouts

Reducing the number of colors you use in your image isn't always a perfect solution. Sometimes you lose significant detail and precision from the original image. This happens primarily when a vast range of different colors is used within a single image. Matching 256 colors to a smaller color set becomes a difficult task. Paint Shop Pro does the best job it can, but you should always be careful when using either method presented in this chapter.

▶ Always make sure you save the original and don't overwrite it with a new, reduced color image.

▶ Make sure you check out the final image size within Windows Explorer. Sometimes reducing the number of colors used doesn't have any effect on the file size of your images.

▶ Be aware that bad image quality is rarely acceptable—even at the cost of a fast download.

Part II Marrying PSP to the Web

JPEG Compression

For GIF images, the best way to reduce file size is to reduce the number of colors in the graphic. As you observed, in some situations you received a huge file savings.

Similarly, the JPEG file format allows you to tweak performance and file-size metrics, but in a different manner. The JPEG file format allows you to specify how much detail/compression should be used when saving a file. The higher the compression setting, the smaller the overall file size. Of course, there's no such thing as a free lunch. By compressing JPEG images, you lose some image quality. This loss isn't usually noticeable—unless you have an extremely high-resolution image with lots of details or until the compression level is very high.

In Paint Shop Pro, JPEG image compression can be set in two ways—with the JPEG Optimizer or when you save your image. This section will cover both methods.

Using the JPEG Optimizer

The JPEG Optimizer is another tool included within Paint Shop Pro that lets you control several important settings for your images. Once you have your image open, launch the JPEG Optimizer by selecting **F**ile > Export > JPEG Optimizer from the Menu Bar (Figure 7.13).

Figure 7.13
You can control compression from the JPEG Optimizer.

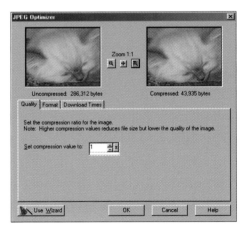

The Compression tool is on the tab labeled **Quality**. Using this tool, you can have Paint Shop Pro save your JPEG using compression levels varying from 1 percent to 100 percent. Interestingly, you'll almost always want to use JPEG compression levels of at least 60 percent unless you are creating a fine-art type of image.

Once you set your compression levels and preview your selection in this tool, click on the **OK** button to save your newly compressed JPEG image. Figure 7.14 shows the same image with different compression levels. Notice the drastic difference in file size.

JPEG compression is usually often very effective.

Figure 7.14a
1 percent compression 74 K

Figure 7.14b
60 percent compression 10 K

Figure 7.14c
80 percent compression 6 K

Figure 7.14d
95 percent compression 2 K

Much like reducing the number of colors used in GIF images, saving your JPEG at several different compression levels is a great idea. Doing so gives you the opportunity to compare the files and choose the level that has the smallest file size yet retains quality. This example alone provided nearly a 90 percent reduction in file size with no significant reduction in image quality.

Part II Marrying PSP to the Web

Optimize Your JPEG When Saving

Besides using the JPEG Optimizer, you can also set JPEG compression levels when you save your JPEG image. Open any JPEG image and choose **File > Save As** to bring up the PSP Save As dialog box. Select the **JPEG** file format and click on the **O**ptions button. From here, you can select the compression levels you want to use for this image (Figure 7.15). This method is less useful than the JPEG Optimizer, because you can't preview your settings before you select them.

Figure 7.15
JPEG compression can also be set here.

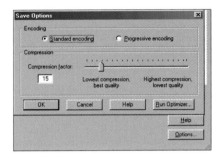

Using Interlaced and Progressive Images

Back in Chapter 4, "Making Images By Hand," you learned about interlaced GIFs and progressive JPEG graphics. You learned that interlaced GIFs display themselves in several passes, with each pass becoming more detailed and clearer.

Interlaced GIFs are nice when downloading a gigantic GIF, because you can get a general idea of what the image looks like as it is downloading—a nice feature for visitors using a slower modem. The JPEG file format allows similar functionality when saving an image in the progressive JPEG format.

Saving an image in either an interlaced or progressive format is simple. After creating your image, choose **File > Save As** to bring up the Save As dialog box. **_Interlaced_** and **_Progressive_** settings are both selected by clicking on the **O**ptions button after you have selected the file format you want to use for your graphic.

Figure 7.16 shows the GIF image options. When saving a GIF, you can choose between **Interlaced** and **Noninterlaced** image formats. Click on the proper radio button, then click **OK**. These same settings are also available on the **Format** tab in the GIF Optimizer.

Figure 7.16
Interlaced images are the way to go for larger Web graphics.

Similarly, Figure 7.17 shows the Save Options dialog box for JPEG images. With JPEGs, you can use **Standard** or **Progressive Encoding**. You can also control these settings on the Format tab in the JPEG Optimizer.

Figure 7.17
Progressively encoded JPEGs work like interlaced GIFs.

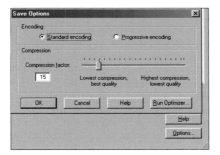

As a general rule, saving your images in Interlaced or Progressive format is useful only when dealing with images that are 10K or larger. For smaller icons, buttons, and bars, don't worry about these formats; such images are so small that they download almost instantaneously.

Saving in Interlaced or Progressive format makes your image file around 10 percent larger than the original file, but the benefit is well worth the increased file size when you are saving larger images. Allowing visitors to see a rough outline of an image as it downloads increases usability for a Web page, because visitors can start reading information on that page before the whole image is completely downloaded. Be careful not to use interlacing too much, because it can be distracting to Web page visitors. If you are worried about image performance, resizing and cropping are usually more effective.

8

Coordinating Web Graphics

Besides simply looking good, a visually unified Web site accomplishes two goals: It establishes an identity for your site that your visitors will associate with you, and it helps your visitors keep track of where they are. These are important to you, because they increase the likelihood that first-time visitors will return to your site. Ease of navigation is especially important to your visitors, because anything that helps them get around with ease will make their Web experience a more pleasant one.

A visually unified Web site is usually the result of creating a coordinated set of Web graphics that relate both to the theme of the site and to one another. This chapter shows you techniques for creating coordinated sets of Web graphics for your own use.

▶ **Thinking about Your Site's Design**
Before opening up PSP to create some nifty graphics, you need to think about your site and its design. Planning ahead can make a world of difference!

▶ **Using PSP's Effects to Create Buttons and Other Elements**
Paint Shop Pro has lots of great built-in effects that you can apply to your graphics. We'll use a few of these effects for Web graphics that are both polished and easy to make.

▶ **Putting It All Together**
And once you've thought things through and have mastered a few techniques, it's time to put everything together in your coordinated site!

Part II Marrying PSP to the Web

Unifying Your Design

The first step in creating a coordinated Web site is developing a planned look for your site that helps you achieve your goals. An artistic Web site may use images from master artists over the century as the design theme, while a comic book site might incorporate different characters throughout its site. Regardless of your design scheme, thinking about your overall goal will help you decide which Paint Shop Pro tools to use and how to best use them.

While thinking about your site, one of the first things to decide on is a color scheme, because it is one of the easiest ways to unify a site. A unified color scheme visually symbolizes that each page goes together and helps visitors know that they are still on your site as they click from one page to another. An example of this is shown in Figures 8.1 and 8.2.

Figure 8.1
On the splash page of Lori's Web Graphics, the site's color scheme and the style of the navigation buttons are introduced.

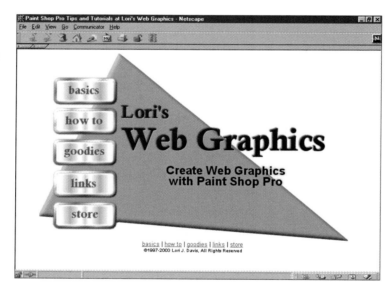

Figure 8.2
The colors, navigation buttons, and a small version of the splash page's logo are repeated on content pages.

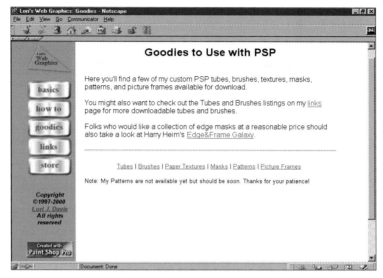

Another means of unifying your site is to have repeating design elements on your pages. On the pages shown in Figures 8.1 and 8.2, the navigation buttons are repeated and a smaller version of the splash page's logo also appears on all the content pages.

This method is also a good one to use on a site where the color scheme changes to identify different areas of the site. This is illustrated in Figures 8.3 and 8.4, where the page layout and form of the background remain the same, even though the different areas of the site have their own colors.

Figure 8.3
Each page on this site has the same style of bordered background with navigation buttons on the left.

Figure 8.4
Different content areas
are identified by
different color schemes,
while the same basic
design is repeated
throughout the site.

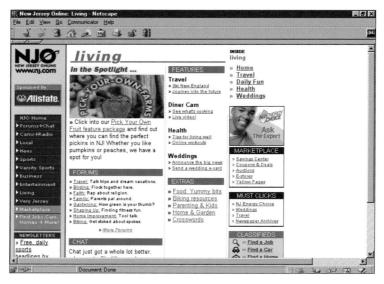

Your site should make use of one or both of these techniques, to draw it
together into a unified whole.

Besides similar design and colors, there are other ways to create a
coordinated look on your Web site:

▶ **Navigation Bars**—Many Web sites create a standard navigation bar
that appears on every page within the site. This is useful because it
always provides visitors with an easy way to get back to the main
pages on your site without having to hunt for a link. This is also
useful when other pages link to your site, because you never know
what page will be linked to.

▶ **Logo Placement**—If you have a logo, make sure you place it in the
same place on every page. This is a simple marketing task that will
help reinforce your site's brand or identity to visitors.

▶ **Coordinated Images**—When building buttons, icons, and other
graphical elements, have them relate to one another. You'll see an
example of this later in this chapter when we build a coordinated set
of graphics. A good rule of thumb is to make sure each image or
graphical element you build has to do with your site's theme. It will
make your site look more attractive and professional.

Graphical Elements for Web Pages

Before we see how you would begin in designing your own graphically coordinated Web site, let's look at how to create some of the graphical elements most commonly used on the Web. Although some of these techniques are mentioned elsewhere in this book, this section takes you through creating the most popular types of graphics you'll need when creating a coordinated Web page.

Using Text Graphics

When you add text to a Web page, you'll usually simply type it into your HTML editor and then control the font, color, size, and other general characteristics for how it should appear. Often though, you'll want to create the text in Paint Shop Pro and save it as an image. In this case, you would include it in your Web page using the IMG HTML tag. This technique has some decided advantages and disadvantages.

Advantages

▶ **You get complete control over your text appearance.**
Because HTML is a logical language, the way a page looks on your computer is not always the way it looks on other computers. The biggest issue that arises in text on the Web comes when fonts are used. If you use a fancy font on your Web site, it will not look the same on your visitors' screen unless they have *the exact same font* installed on their computer. Text saved as an image solves this problem.

▶ **You can incorporate other images as part of your text image.**
Using layers, you can easily make text appear on top of another image, if necessary, as part of your Web page. Although this is possible using advanced HTML, it can be much harder to control and is rarely worth the effort.

▶ **You can add special effects.**
When your text is an image, you can add outlines, drop shadows, or other special effects to make the text more visually stimulating.

Disadvantages

▶ **Editing the text is a two-step process.**
When you want to make a change to your image, you have to first load it in Paint Shop Pro, then make the change and save the new image. Finally, you have to reinsert the new image into your Web page.

▶ **Download times can be increased.**
Text takes virtually no time to appear on a Web page, while an image can take several seconds longer, depending on the file size.

▶ **You need to become an expert optimizer.**
You'll have to become an expert image optimizer and learn the best ways to reduce file size with text images.

Because the advantages outweigh the disadvantages in many cases, let's step through a simple example to create a textual image.

1. First, create a new image from scratch. For this example, we'll use one that is 600 pixels wide and 100 pixels tall, the perfect size for a text banner. We'll create one with a white background.

2. Next, add a phrase of text to your image using the **Text** tool (Figure 8.5). Remember to use an appropriate font and size for the text. In this case, we're going to create the text as a floating selection to add additional special effects later on. Click **OK** to add it to your image.

Figure 8.5
When adding text to this type of image, always use appropriate fonts that coordinate with the theme of your site.

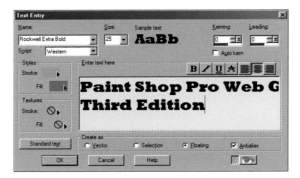

NOTE

In Figure 8.5, notice that in the Style pane the stroke for the text is set to a pale purple and the fill is set to red. This will make red letters with a pale purple outline, the outline being as wide as the Width setting already set in the Text tool's Tool Options palette.

If you want just solid-colored text with no outline, you need to set the stroke to Null. To set the stroke to Null before you click with the Text tool, set the Stroke Style swatch on the Color Palette. To set the stroke to Null after you call up the Text Entry dialog box, set the Stroke in the Styles pane of the dialog box.

3. While Paint Shop Pro has the text selected, let's add a drop shadow effect. Choose Effects > **3**D Effects > **D**rop Shadow from the Menu Bar. For this example, we'll add a light drop shadow that appears below and to the right of the text (Figure 8.6).

Figure 8.6
Drop shadow effects can vastly change the appearance of text on your page. Experiment with dark and light shadows for varying effects.

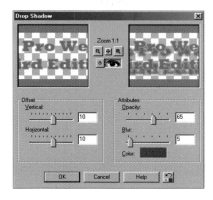

4. Figure 8.7 shows this final image that would make a great page banner. Once we send it through the GIF Optimizer, it is only 7.5K.

Figure 8.7
A more designer effect for a Web page than plain text.

Besides the Drop shadow, the Inner Bevel, Emboss, and Tile effects are great candidates for text graphics.

Creating Your Own Buttons

Buttons are extremely popular and found on virtually all Web sites with multiple pages. Buttons are graphical elements that help visitors traverse different areas of site graphically.

The Outer Bevel Button

Although the easiest way to make a button in PSP is with the Buttonize effect, this effect gives you very little control over your button's appearance. Instead, our preferred method is to use the Inner and Outer Bevel effects.

Part II Marrying PSP to the Web

The general rule when creating a button is to follow these three steps:

1. Create the button background, adjusting the colors, design, and size.

2. Use **Save Copy As** to save a copy of your blank button in PSP format. That way, when you want to create a new button, you can duplicate the blank button, ensuring that all your buttons form a perfectly matched set.

3. Add the text for your button with the Text tool. (When you're familiar with vectors, discussed in Chapter 11, "Drawing with Vectors," you'll probably want to create the text as a vector, since that allows you to easily modify the text later on. But for now, create the text as a Floating selection.) After positioning the text in the button, add any effects that you want to add to the text, and then save the button in a Web-readable format.

NOTE

Another way to create a matched set of buttons is to create the button's background on a Background layer and then add text for each button on its own individual layer. You can save the layered file in PSP format. Use the Visibility toggles to display only the text and Background for the first button, and then use one of the Export operations in the File menu to save the button in a Web-readable format. Repeat for each of the other buttons in the set.

We'll look at an example of this technique at the end of this chapter. For information on layers, see Chapter 10, "Using Layers."

By following these three steps, you'll create great looking buttons. The only tough part is creating the first button using the Bevel effects found within Paint Shop Pro. Although there are infinite ways to create great looking beveled buttons, we'll step you through one of the easiest:

1. First, create a new image the size of your standard button. To make the images appear better in the book, we'll create oversized buttons for this example, 400×200 pixels.

2. Choose **S**elections > Select **A**ll from the Menu Bar to select your entire blank image. Then choose **S**elections > **M**odify > **C**ontract to bring up the Contract Selection dialog box (Figure 8.8).

Figure 8.8
Beveled effects work better with a selection that is contracted slightly from your entire image.

3. Contract your selection about 5 percent of the overall width—for this example, 20 pixels. Figure 8.9 shows your blank image with the selection box.

Figure 8.9
The "marching ants" signify a selection on your blank image.

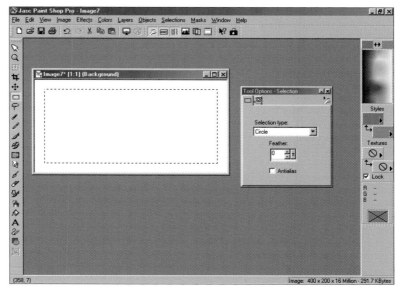

4. Now you're ready to create a cool button effect. Choose Effects > 3D Effects > Outer Bevel to bring up the Outer Bevel dialog box.

Figure 8.10
Hundreds of different button effects can be created from here.

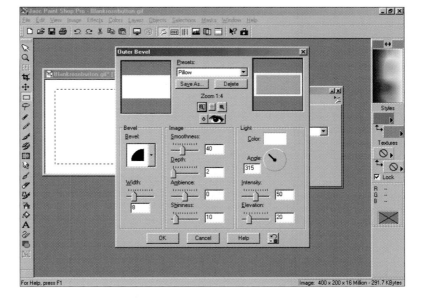

Part II Marrying PSP to the Web

5. Use the Outer Bevel presets to get some experience with how the controls affect your button's appearance. For this example, we selected the ***Pillow*** preset and then changed the default light color from white to rose. Figure 8.11 shows the resulting button from just those two changes.

Figure 8.11
Note the rounded corners and drop shadow added to this button.

6. Using the preview window, you can adjust each of the 10 settings found within the Outer Bevel dialog box. Be sure to experiment with different bevels, light angles, and light intensity. Also, use the Proof button (the eye) to see how the effect applies to your actual image while you are in the Outer Bevel dialog box.

7. Don't forget to add text to your button that fits well within the outer bevel. Figure 8.12 shows the final button with text added.

Figure 8.12
This button is ready to be recreated with different text and then added to a Web page.

8. Finally, save the button in the PSP format for future reuse, and save a Web-readable copy for your site.

NOTE

The Paint Shop Pro **B**uttonize command is useful for creating very simple buttons quickly. You can access it by choosing Effects > **3**D Effects > **B**uttonize. Figure 8.13 shows the Buttonize dialog box. Unfortunately, with Buttonize you can control only width, height, and transparency. Your color changes are limited to using your current background color.

Figure 8.13
The built-in Buttonize function is less flexible than the Outer Bevel and Inner Bevel effects.

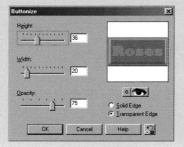

Creating Buttons with Preset Shapes

Another great way to achieve a button effect is to use the built-in Preset Shapes as your button background. Paint Shop Pro has dozens of different button shapes and colors built in as preset shapes. This is a great way to create a generic button background before you add the text on top of it. Figure 8.14 shows an oval button being added to a blank image using the Preset shape tool.

Figure 8.14
With many different button shapes and sizes, this is the quickest tool for creating basic buttons.

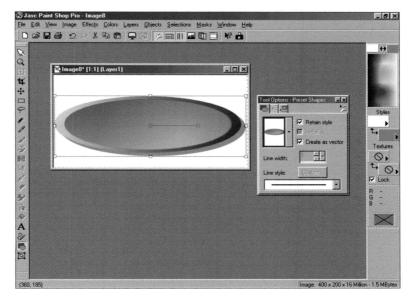

The challenge with using the preset buttons is finding one that fits well with your page concept. You'll want to explore this feature before creating buttons from scratch.

TIP

To create a perfect circle with the Ellipse preset shape, hold down the Shift key while drawing your shape. And to create a perfect square, hold down the Shift key while drawing with the Rectangle preset shape.

Here's the general rule: Any time that you want to maintain the aspect ratio of the prototype of a preset shape, draw the shape while holding down the Shift key.

Creating Your Own Separator Bars

Another graphical element that can contribute to your themed page is a divider line. With Paint Shop Pro, there are several tools which enable you to build graphical divider lines.

Using the Draw Tool

The easiest way to create a horizontal line is using the **Draw** tool. Paint Shop Pro lets you create simple solid lines and also supports 25 different line styles automatically. In the Tool Options palette, select your Line style in the drop-down menu box below the **Custom** button. Once you select a style, you can draw with that line on a blank image. Figure 8.15 shows a horizontal line using the **Whip** style.

Figure 8.15
Lines created in each style accent a Web page differently.

TIP

To create a perfectly horizontal line using the Draw tool, hold down the Shift key. With Shift down, Paint Shop Pro automatically draws a perfectly straight horizontal, vertical, or 45-degree line. Using Shift to draw a horizontal line eliminates the possibility of creating a line that looks level to your naked eye but is actually slightly off level.

Picture Tubes

Another popular way to create a graphical divider line is using Picture Tubes. Picture tubes let you create a completely unique divider line according to your own size and design specifications.

After you create a blank image, use the Picture Tube Tool Options palette to select the tube, size, and step of your divider line. Then, using your mouse, draw a horizontal line using the images from the Picture Tube. Figure 8.16 shows a Watermelon horizontal divider line made with a Picture Tube.

Figure 8.16
Picture Tubes create
colorful and unique
divider lines.

TIP
To draw a straight line using Picture tubes, click once on the left part of your image with the Picture tool and then with the Shift Key held down click a second time on the right part of your image. Paint Shop Pro will automatically draw a straight line using the tube between your two points.

Creating Bullets and Icons

Besides buttons, lines, and textual graphics, bullets and icons are also popular ways to coordinate your Web site graphically. Bullets and Icons serve the same purpose—adding a graphical design element to your page that spices up your bulleted lists or other pieces of text.

Like creating buttons, there are thousands of ways to create attractive bullets and icons. This section will step you through two of the most popular techniques.

Creating Circular Bullets

The easiest way to create a bullet is to create a circular selection and then fill in the selected area with a color or, even better, a gradient. To create a circular bullet, follow these steps:

1. Create a new image from scratch. Bullets are usually very small, so for this example, let's create one 20×20.

2. Pick the **Selection** tool. In the Tool Options Palette, change the Selection Type to be **Circle**. Make sure **Antialias** is checked. Then, using the tool, create a circular selection in your newly created image. Figure 8.17 shows the circular selection on our blank image. We've zoomed in 14x to see all the details on this image.

Part II Marrying PSP to the Web

Figure 8.17
First create a circular
selection area.

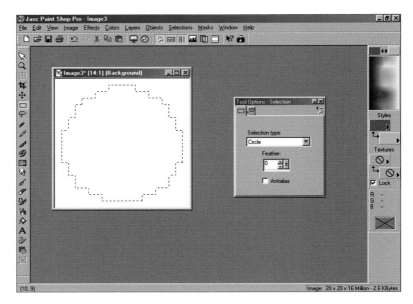

3.   Once the circular area is selected, click on the **Flood Fill** tool and
      then click anywhere within the circular selection you've just created.
      Figure 8.18 shows the filled bullet.

Figure 8.18
Our purple bullet is
complete.

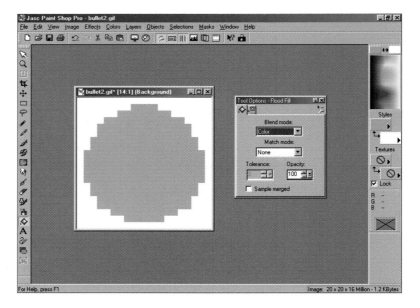

4. Besides creating a single color bullet, you can also create a gradient bullet. You can accomplish this technique using the Flood Fill as well. Simply change the paint style from the Color palette from Color to Gradient. Set the Gradient Options: Sunburst Gradient Autumn–Inverted, Horizontal and Vertical both 40. Then reapply the Flood Fill to your selected area. Figure 8.19 shows the new image.

Figure 8.19
The bullet now has a more colorful look to it.

Change paint styles by clicking here

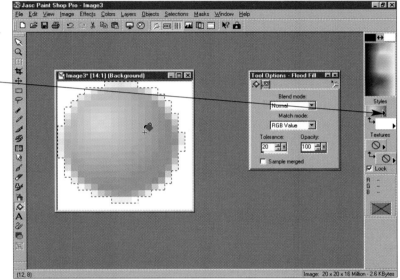

5. Finally, save your icon as a GIF. Be sure to designate your background color to be transparent so the image fits in nicely on your Web page.

Dingbat-based icons

Another popular way to create an icon is to use a special family of fonts called dingbats, or Wingdings. These special fonts display icons instead of letters and make for great iconic images:

1. Create a new image from scratch. Remember that icons should be small. For this example, create a 50×50 image.

2. Using the **Text** tool, type a few letters from the W*ingdings* font. Notice how icons appear instead of text? For this example, we'll use the Wingding snowflake, which can be created by typing in **T** in the Text Entry dialog box. Figure 8.20 shows the snowflake as a Wingding. Remember to create the text/Wingding as a floating selection.

Figure 8.20
This snowflake will
make a great icon.

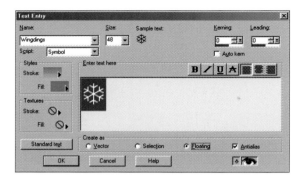

3. Place the text in your image and then save the image for future use in
    your Web site. Figure 8.21 shows an enlarged version of the final icon.

Figure 8.21
Not a bad icon for 10
seconds of work!

You can create icons using all sorts of small images besides Wingdings.
For example, in Chapter 6, "Creating Transparent Images," we created an
icon using a dollar sign ($). Clip art that comes with Microsoft Office or
free clip art Web sites also makes great Web site icons.

A Simple Example

Now let's tie together what you've what learned in this chapter. We'll do
this by creating a home page for the Web site of a fictional New England
vacation spot called the Old Leaf Inn.

Start Your Design by Thinking Things Through

Suppose that you've already worked out the basic structure of the site.
Besides the home page, there will be four other pages: One about the
great food available at the inn, one on fun things to do while staying at
the inn, one on the rates for the various rooms, and one that shows a map
of the area and provides directions and contact information.

One of the first things you'll want to settle on is the color scheme of the
site. There are only a few small pages, so having a unified color scheme is
probably the best approach here. Since the inn's name is "Old Leaf" and
the area is quite beautiful in autumn, a color scheme reflecting the
browns, yellows, and reds of New England's autumn trees would fit in
nicely. So let's begin by choosing the background color for the pages—a
pale yellow. A pale-colored background ensures that dark text will be
clearly readable, and yellow is a good background for graphical elements
that are primarily brown and red.

At this point, the home page could be partially set up with the background color and whatever you have in mind for the basic page layout, but without any graphics, as in Figure 8.22.

Figure 8.22
The site is now only in its early stages.

Now you can start to think about what graphical elements to add to the site. The site will need an eye-catching header that communicates the atmosphere of the inn. Since the header is the first element the site's visitors will see, this is a good place to begin.

Suppose the inn is old-fashioned and somewhat formal. In that case, an old-fashioned, formal font would provide a good basis for the text of the header. Browse your fonts with your font manager, if you have one, or open a file in PSP and click in the image canvas with the Text tool so you can browse your fonts in the Add Text dialog box. The font we use in this example is Bistream's Engraved Old English Bold, but if you're working through this example and don't have that font, just use a similar font that you have on hand.

You're still in the planning stages at this point—just thinking, not necessarily editing any images yet. You've got a font for your header, but you haven't yet decided what that text should look like? Should it be solid-colored? Would that emphasize the inn's formality? Should it be filled with a gradient or pattern instead? That could indicate that although the inn has a rather formal atmosphere, it also has a relaxed and playful side. Let's go with the playful angle and create a pattern that can be used to fill the text in the header.

Making the Header

In PSP, open up a new image that is 200×200 pixels. The background color isn't important, because we're going to fill every pixel of the image canvas with leaves painted on with the Picture Tube. Choose the **Picture Tube** tool, select **_Autumn Leaves_** as the tube, and set the **Scale** to 50 percent. Then fill the image canvas with leaves by clicking in it with the Picture Tube tool (Figure 8.23 shows this work in progress.) After filling the image canvas, keep the image open.

Figure 8.23
Create an image filled with leaves using the Picture Tube tool.

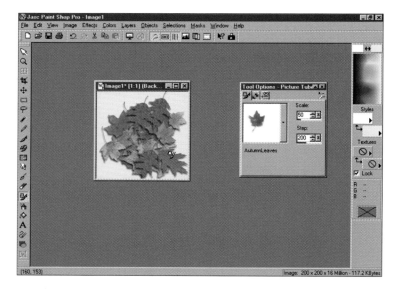

Now it's time to create your header! Set the background/fill color on the Color Palette to match the BGCOLOR setting you use on your page. Then open a new file that's as large as you want your header to be—we used 500×100 here—and for the Color, choose **_Background Color_**. Next, choose the **Text** tool and click in the lower center of the new image file. This brings up the Text Entry dialog box, shown in Figure 8.24.

Figure 8.24
Add a text selection to your header file.

In the **Text Entry** dialog box, click the **Standard Text** button to reset the options, choose the Name of your font and the Size. Select **Selection** in the Create as pane. And in the **Enter text here** pane, press the **Center** icon to center the text on the point where you clicked in your image and type the text in the large textbox. Press **OK** to make the text selection on your image.

TIP

If the selection isn't positioned exactly where you want it, chose the Mover tool and right-drag the selection marquee where you want it to be.

Let's fill the text selection with the leafy pattern you made in the first image file. Choose the **Flood Fill** tool and in its Tool Options palette, set **Blend Mode** to Normal, **Match Mode** to None, and **Opacity** to 100. Then, on the foreground/stroke swatch on the Color Palette, click and hold until the **Style** flyout menu appears. On the flyout menu, choose the **Pattern** icon (which looks like a pattern of dots). Then, click on the foreground/stroke swatch to bring up the **Pattern Picker**. Select the leafy image as your pattern by clicking the pattern preview window and clicking on the thumbnail of the leafy image file in the resulting selection menu. Click **OK**, and then click inside the text selection, as in Figure 8.25. The entire text selection is filled with leaves.

Figure 8.25
Fill the text selection with a pattern with a single click.

Part II Marrying PSP to the Web

Keep the text selection active. You can now add some interesting effects to the text. For example, you can add a bevel to the text by choosing Effects > **3D** Effects > **I**nner Bevel. The Inner bevel dialog box is shown in Figure 8.26.

Figure 8.26
You can add a bevel to your text with Inner Bevel.

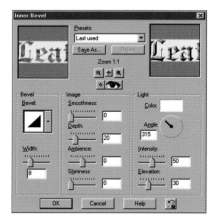

Keeping the text selection active, you can add further effects, such as a drop shadow. To add a drop shadow, choose Effects > **3D** Effects > **D**rop Shadow. Figure 8.27 shows the Drop Shadow dialog box.

Figure 8.27
And let's add a Drop Show to the beveled text.

You can now turn the text selection off. To do that, either right-click with the **Text** tool or any selection tool or choose **S**elections > Select **N**one or press **Ctrl+D**. The final header, with beveled text and a drop shadow, will look something like Figure 8.28.

Figure 8.28
The header is ready to save.

You can now save the header image, either with **S**ave or Save **A**s or **F**ile > Export. Be sure to use a Web-readable format or, if you want to work on the image some more before making a Web-readable version, use the PSP format. We saved the header as a transparent GIF, using the GIF Optimizer, available under **F**ile > Expor**t.**

CAUTION

Drop shadows on transparent GIFs look fine when you place them on Web pages with solid-colored backgrounds. But if you have a textured background on your Web page, a drop shadow can look pretty murky, since it will be made up of a blend of your drop shadow color and the image's background color. You can decrease this murkiness by using a high Opacity for Drop Shadow or by using creative workarounds. However, it might be best to avoid drop shadows on transparent GIFs that are to be displayed on a page with a textured background.

TIP

In Paint Shop Pro, you can preview your image in your Web browser by selecting **V**iew > Preview in **W**eb Browser.

Making Graphics for Navigation

You'll need a way to navigate to and from the several pages of the site. That could be accomplished by text links, buttons, or an image map. (See Chapter 12, "Splicing and Image Maps," for discussion of the creation and use of image maps.) Something that picks up the feel of the header would work well here, so let's make a set of navigation buttons that use the same leafy background and formal font of the header.

Open a new image that's the size you want for your buttons. We used 100×40 pixels. The background color doesn't matter, since you're going to fill the button with the leafy pattern. You'll be using layers, so be sure that Image type is set to 16.7 Million Colors.

Choose the Flood Fill tool and set the pattern in the Color Palette's Pattern Picker, just as you did for the header text. Fill the button with the Pattern by clicking in the image canvas with the Flood Fill tool.

Now let's make that flat patterned rectangle look more like a button. You could simply apply the Buttonize effect, but let's give ourselves a little more flexibility and use **Inner Bevel** instead. Inner Bevel needs a selection to operate on, so select the entire button image with **S**elections > Select **A**ll. Then choose Effects > 3D Effects > **I**nner Bevel. Then in the Inner Bevel dialog box, shown in Figure 8.29, select the settings you want. When the Inner Bevel effect has been added, choose **S**elections > Select **N**one.

Figure 8.29
Create a button effect
with Inner Bevel.

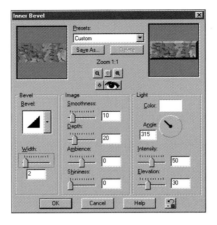

This background will be used for every button, so one of the easiest ways
to make the buttons is simply to add the text for each button on its own
individual layer. For the Food button, add a new layer by pressing the
Create Layer button on the Layer palette. Then choose the Text tool and
click on the lower center of this new layer. In the Text Entry dialog box,
choose Name of font and Size, turn the Stroke off, and select the color for
the Fill. Enter the text in the large textbox, and select Floating for Create
as. After clicking OK, you can move the floating text selection if you need
to by dragging the selection with the Text tool, as shown in Figure 8.30.

Figure 8.30
Position the
floating text.

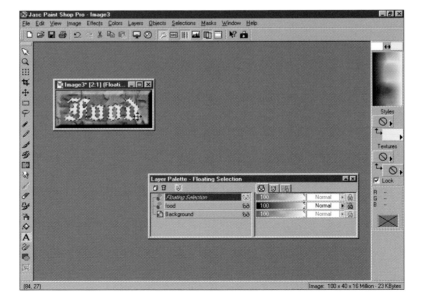

When the text is positioned correctly, right-click with the Text tool. This turns off the text selection and drops your solid-colored text onto the new layer.

At this point, you can add any effects that you want to the new text. There's no need to select the text first, because PSP treats a figure surrounded by transparency in a layer as if the figure were selected. So all you need to do is apply the effect. We applied a dark Drop Shadow to our text, to help it stand out from the background.

Repeat for each of the other buttons: Add a new layer, add and position the text, and apply any effects that you want. As you add a new layer, turn the visibility toggle off for the text layer below, so that all you see is the background and the new layer. When you've finished the text for the last button, you'll have something like what you see in Figure 8.31.

Figure 8.31
Make only the background and the text for a single button visible.

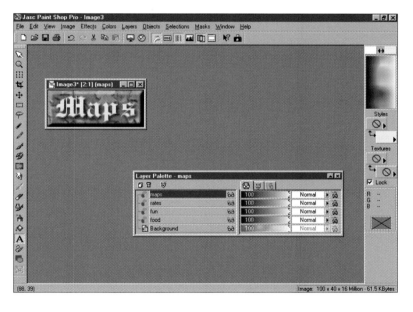

Part II Marrying PSP to the Web

You're now ready to make each individual button. With the background and the text of a single button visible, use **F**ile > Save Cop**y** As or one of the Optimizers available under **F**ile > Expor**t** to save the button. Figure 8.32 shows the Map button being created with the GIF Optimizer.

Figure 8.32
You can use the GIF Optimizer (or the JPEG or PNG Optimizer) to create the individual buttons.

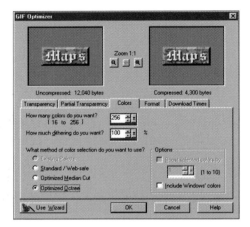

When you're done saving one button, turn the text layer off for that button and turn the text layer on for another of the buttons. Save that button and then repeat the procedure for all of the remaining buttons. Save the layered file in PSP format, just in case you ever want to add a button to this set of buttons.

Adding Accents

Graphical accents can also add a nice touch to Web sites. These might be icons or separator bars or bullets—some graphical element that is repeated on a page or across pages.

For the Old Leaf Inn site, let's create a pair of accent images that can flank the header of each of the site's pages. A good choice for an accent for this site is a single leaf, created with the Autumn Leaf Picture Tube, as shown in Figure 8.33.

Figure 8.33
Create an accent image that can be used here and there in the site.

This image is 100×100 pixels, its height matching the height of the header. It also has the same colored background as the header. A single leaf is placed in the center of the image, and the image is saved as a transparent GIF.

The image just created is for use on the left side of the banner. To make a mate that can be used on the right side of the banner, duplicate the first image by choosing **W**indow > **D**uplicate or pressing **Shift+D**. Then, make this new image the mirror image of the first image by choosing **I**mage > **M**irror. Save the mirrored image and there you are—a pair of accent images that can be used on any page of the site.

TIP

There's a good reason for making this pair of accents separate images rather than part of the header. If you plan to use these accents to surround other headers on other pages, it's much more efficient to keep the accents separate. That's because after the images load once, they're stored in your visitor's cache. Any time that the images need to be loaded again, they'll load directly from the cache rather than having to be downloaded from your server. The headers that you make for each page can therefore be smaller—and hence quicker to download—than they would be if the accents were part of each header image.

Part II Marrying PSP to the Web

The Finished Site

Now you're ready to assemble all the individual elements on your site!
Figure 8.34 shows the completed home page for the Old Leaf Inn site.

Figure 8.34
The home page of the
finished site.

The accents surrounding the header and the navigation buttons can be
used on all pages of the site, to tie the site together visually. The other
pages of the site can have their own headers, modeled on the home page's
header but using text relevant to the individual page. You might also add
some other matching accents, such as a leafy separator bar or bullets
filled with a red-yellow-brown sunburst gradient. Once you have the
basic design in place, the choices are yours!

9
Making the
Best Backgrounds

A good Web site deserves a good background. Whether you decide on a single solid color, a faded repeated logo, a textured tile, or a border, the background of your Web pages will help set your site's tone.

In this chapter, you'll learn how to create your own backgrounds. We'll cover:

▶ **Creating and Embedding Background Tiles**
You'll learn how to make seamless tiles and how to add them to your Web pages.

▶ **Creating Bordered Backgrounds**
Backgrounds with lefthand borders are very popular and can be quite elegant—and as you'll see, they're not at all difficult to make.

▶ **Using Tables with Backgrounds**
See how tables can be used to layout your Web content on a bordered background. Also see how to code tables that have their own backgrounds.

Specifying a Background Color

As you saw in Chapter 5, "Web Graphics Basics," you can set the background color for a Web page with the BGCOLOR attribute of the BODY tag. The value of BGCOLOR can be specified as a string of three pairs of hexadecimal digits and beginning with the # character, like this:

```
<body bgcolor="#fa0913">
```

Hex digits range from 0 through 9 and from A through F. A is equivalent to 10 in decimal, B is equivalent to 11, C to 12, and so on up to F, which is equivalent to 15 in decimal. The first pair of digits specify the amount of red in the color. The second pair specifies the amount of green. And the third pair specifies the amount of blue. The value of each pair ranges from 0 to 255 in decimal. In the preceding example, the amount of red is 250 (FA in hex), the amount of green is 9 (09 in hex), and the amount of blue is 19 (13 in hex).

As you may recall from Chapter 5, there are 16 standard colors that can also be specified by name, such as "red" and "green". You can refer to these colors either by name or by hex string. (See Table 5.1 for a list of the 16 standard colors along with their hexadecimal values.)

In addition to the 16 standard color names, Javascript supports an extended set of 256 color names, which can be used like the standard names. For a list of the extended color names and their hex code equivalents, check out Appendix B, "Color Values," of the *Client-side Javascript Reference* at **http://developer.netscape.com/docs/manuals/js/client/jsref**.

The BGCOLOR attribute can also be used with any of the TABLE tags. For example, to begin a table that has a background color of silver, you use HTML code like this:

```
<table bgcolor="silver">
```

Hex codes and named colors can also be used with the FONT tag to change the color of text displayed on your Web page. For example, to specify purple text, you could do this:

```
<font color="#800080">And now for some purple text.</font>
```

Or this:

```
<font color="purple">And now for some purple text.</font>
```

Creating a Simple Seamless Tile

Solid-colored Web pages are fine, but sometimes you might want to add a little more to your background—maybe some texture or a faded repeating pattern. A site for a pet shop, for example, might have a background like the one in Figure 9.1, with a faint pattern made up of paw prints.

Figure 9.1
A pet shop site might use a paw-print background.

Here's how to make a tile like this one:

1. Open a new file with a white background that is 200 pixels high by 200 pixels wide and that supports 16.7 million colors.

2. Choose the **Preset Shapes** tool and choose Ellipse as the shape. Then in the **Color Palette** set the foreground/stroke to **Null** and set the background/fill color to a pale shade of pink. In the Tool **O**ptions palette, be sure that both **Retain style** and **Create as vector** are unchecked. (If you already know how to use vectors, though, you might find it easier to work with vectors.)

3. Draw one paw print in the upper left corner of the image canvas, as in Figure 9.2. Be sure that all of the paw print falls completely within the image canvas.

Figure 9.2
Begin by drawing a paw print in the upper left.

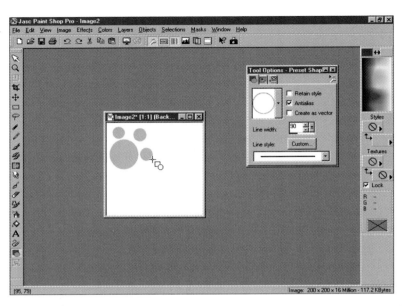

4. As shown in Figure 9.3, you can then use the **Selection** tool to select the first paw print, then copy the selection (with **E**dit > **C**opy or with **Ctrl+C**) and paste it as a new selection, (with **E**dit > **P**aste > As New **S**election or with **Ctrl+E**).

Figure 9.3
Copy the paw print to the lower right.

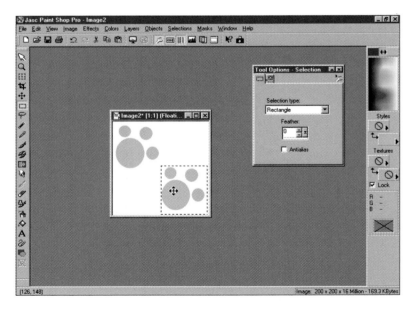

5. Choose the **Flood Fill** tool and set the foreground color on the **Color Palette** to white. Set the **Opacity** to a low value—50 percent or less—and set the **Match Mode** to **None**. Then fill the image. The result will look something like Figure 9.4.

Figure 9.4
The faded paw print tile is ready to save.

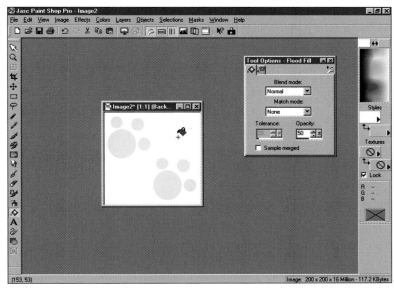

6. Save the image as a GIF, either with **File** > **S**ave or with **File** > Export > **G**IF Optimizer.

To embed this tile or any tile in a Web page, you use the BACKGROUND attribute of the BODY tag. For example, suppose the paw print file was saved as PAWS.GIF. You'd embed this tile in your HTML file like this:

```
<body background="PAWS.GIF">
```

TIP

To ensure that your page is readable even before the background tile loads, you should also set BGCOLOR to a color that matches the dominant color of your tile. For the paw print tile, you could use either this:

```
<body background="PAWS.GIF" bgcolor="#FFFFFF">
```

or this:

```
<body background="PAWS.GIF" bgcolor="white">
```

Part II Marrying PSP to the Web

You can make some interesting textured tiles using the Random Noise and Emboss effects, such as the texture shown in Figure 9.5.

Figure 9.5
A textured tile made with Random Noise and Emboss.

Here's how to make this tile:

1. Open a new 100×100 pixel image with a white background and 16.7 million colors.

2. Choose Effects > **N**oise > **A**dd to bring up the **Add Noise** dialog box (shown in Figure 9.6). Use the **R**andom setting and set the Noise to about 50 percent.

Figure 9.6
The Add Noise dialog box.

3. Choose Effects > **T**exture Effects > **E**mboss.

4. Color your tile with **C**olors > **C**olorize. The Hue setting determines the hue (which corresponds closely with the nontechnical meaning of "color"). The Saturation setting determines the saturation (the purity or vividness of the color). To make a grey tile, as in the example, simply set the Saturation to 0.

5. Save your tile as either a JPEG or a GIF. You might want to try exporting the tile as both a JPEG and a GIF, to see which one works best, by using the JPEG Optimizer and the GIF Optimizer available under **F**ile > Export.

This method produces a seamless tile because Random Noise produces a random pattern, so there is no obvious edge when the image tiles across and down the Web page. Most patterns, though, will show very obvious—and unattractive—edges. To make seamless tiles from these patterns, you'll want to try PSP's **Convert To Seamless Pattern** command.

Suppose you want to make a seamless tile from the pattern shown in Figure 9.7. In this case, use the Selection tool to define a selection inside the image, then choose **S**elections > **C**onvert to Seamless Pattern (see Figure 9.8).

Figure 9.7
The source file for a seamless tile.

Figure 9.8
Use Convert to Seamless Pattern to create a seamless tile.

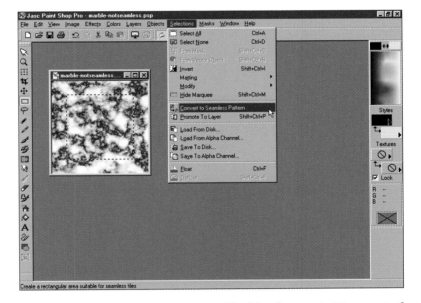

Paint Shop Pro creates a new image file, like the one in Figure 9.9, that is the size of your selection and that has edges that will tile more or less seamlessly. You can then save the new tile in a Web-readable file format. Figure 9.10 shows how our example tile looks on a Web page.

Figure 9.9
A seamless tile created with Convert to Seamless Pattern.

Part II Marrying PSP to the Web

Figure 9.10
And here's the tile used as a Web background.

This example looks pretty good, but sometimes the edges of tiles produced with this method are still somewhat noticeable. In cases like that, you'll need to do a little work by hand to get a truly seamless tile.

NOTE

If, when you try to use Convert to Seamless Pattern, you get an error message that begins "Your selection is too close to the edge of the image to complete this operation...," don't despair. Just make a new selection that begins and ends farther from the edges of your original image and then try Convert to Seamless Pattern again.

Seamless Tiles by Hand

If you're willing to put in a little work, you can make excellent seamless tiles by hand. Begin with an image such as the marble pattern we used for the Convert to Seamless Pattern example (Figure 9.7). Then create a new file that has the same dimensions as your source image, making the background of this new image file a color that contrasts significantly with the colors in your source. (You'll see why in just a minute!)

Use the Zoom tool to zoom in on the new image. That way, it will be easier to see what you're doing in the next few steps. With both the original file and the new file open, your PSP workspace will then look something like Figure 9.11.

Figure 9.11
Ready to make a
handmade seamless tile!

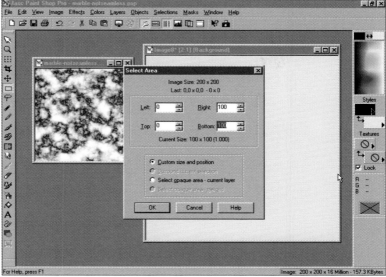

Now, make the original file the active file by clicking on its title bar. What you're about to do is to select each quadrant of the original image (the source image) and paste it into the diagonally opposite area in the new image (the target image). This will put the edges of the source image into the middle of the target image, where you can then blend the edges together.

Here's how to get those quadrants rearranged correctly:

1. First, choose the **Selection** tool, then make sure that, in the Tool **O**ptions palette, **Feather** is set to 0 and Antialias is not checked.

2. Double-click the Selection tool. This brings up the **Select Area** dialog box. With this dialog box, you can make a precise rectangular selection.

    For the first quadrant, set Left and Top to 0, and set Right and Bottom to 100. Notice that below the controls for Top and Bottom, the current size of the selection is shown. The size shown at this point is 100×100. Press **OK** and you'll get a 100×100 pixel selection in the upper left quadrant of the source image.

3. Copy the selection with **Ctrl+C**. Then click the title bar of the target file to make that image active. Paste the copied selection into the target file with **Ctrl+E**.

4. With the selection still active, position the selection by dragging it into the lower right quadrant of the target image. If you need to make precise placement adjustments, use the arrows keys with Shift depressed. Here's where that contrasting background color helps you out: Make sure that you can't see any of that background color along the edges of the image.

You'll now have something like what you see in Figure 9.12.

Figure 9.12
Place the upper left quadrant of the source in the lower right quadrant of the target.

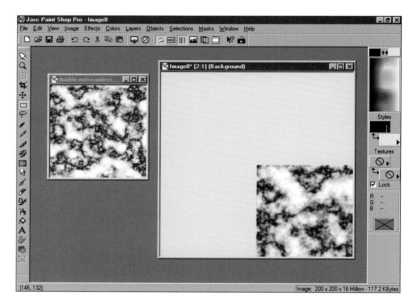

TIP

You can temporarily hide the selection marquee with **S**elections > **H**ide Marquee. This might make it easier to see how things are going when you're positioning the pasted-in selection. Just be sure when you're done to turn the marquee back on (by choosing **S**elections > **H**ide Marquee again) so that you'll again be able to see the selection marquee.

5. Repeat this procedure for the other quadrants of the source image. To select the bottom left quadrant of the source using the Select Area dialog box, set Top to 100, Bottom to 200, and Left to 0, and Right to 100. Copy this selection and paste it into the upper right quadrant of the target.

To select the top right quadrant, set Top to 0, Bottom to 100, Left to 100, and Right to 200. Copy this selection and paste it into the lower left quadrant of the target file.

To select the bottom right quadrant, set Top to 100, Bottom to 200, Left to 100, and Right to 200. Copy this selection and paste it into the upper left quadrant of the target file.

Figure 9.13 shows what the target image looks like just before you paste in the final quadrant, and Figure 9.14 shows what the image looks like when all the quadrants have been added.

Figure 9.13
Ready to paste in the final quadrant.

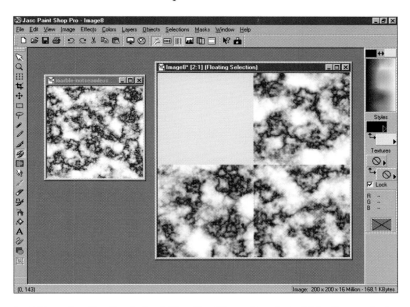

6. Now for the final step! Use the **Clone Brush** to hide those obvious seams that are now in the middle of the target image. Choose the Clone Brush and, in the Tool Options palette, set the Brush size as you like, but not too big. Set both the Hardness and the Step fairly low, and set the Opacity to 100.

   To use the Clone Brush, right-click in the area that you'd like to copy from ("clone"). Then dab along the edge line by clicking here and there. Choose a new cloning source area by right-clicking again, then dab along another part of the edge line.

   Figure 9.15 shows this work in progress. The vertical edge line in the upper half of the image has already been cloned away, and work is now beginning on cloning away the horizontal edge line on the left.

Part II Marrying PSP to the Web

Figure 9.14
The tile with all its edges moved into the center of the image.

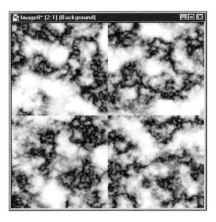

Figure 9.15
You can hide the edges with the Clone brush.

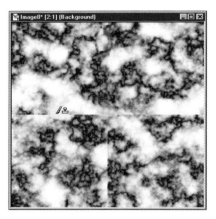

When you're done hiding the edge lines, save the tile in a Web-readable file format. Figure 9.16 shows the tile used as the background of the MarbleWorx Web page. Compare this version with the Convert as Seamless Pattern version (Figure 9.10). Do you see a difference?

Figure 9.16
The handmade tile used
as a Web background.

TIP

In addition to using the methods we've explored in this section to create seamless tiles from existing patterns or textures, you can use PSP's Kaleidoscope and Pattern effects to create abstract seamless tiles. Both of these effects are available under Effects > **R**eflection Effects.

There are also quite a few plug-in filters and tile makers available for sale or for free on the Web. For example, many of the filters included in Alien Skin's Eye Candy 4000 (**http://www.alienskin.com**), a set of commercial filters, can be set to create seamless tiles. And several of Sandy Blair's Simple Filters (available for free at **http://www.btinternet.com/~cateran/simple**) can be used to make abstract seamless tiles.

One of the Simple Filters, Half Wrap, can help you make handmade seamless tiles. This filter, and similar ones available elsewhere, automatically split your image into quadrants and rearrange them so that all the edges meet in the middle. It's then up to you to blend the edges together.

Part II Marrying PSP to the Web

Creating Bordered Backgrounds

You see them everywhere on the Web, those backgrounds that have a narrow lefthand border set off from the main text area of the page. We looked at some examples of these in Chapter 8, "Coordinating Web Graphics" (figures 8.2, 8.3, and 8.4). There's no mystery to bordered backgrounds, as you'll soon see.

Let's begin with a very simple bordered background, one which has a dark, solid-colored border that contrasts with the lighter color of the main area of the page (Figure 9.17).

Figure 9.17
A Web page with a simple bordered background.

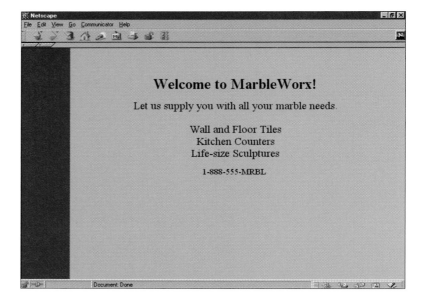

The first thing to remember when making a bordered background is that the background image must be wide enough so that it tiles vertically but not horizontally. The bordered background needs to be at least as wide as the widest browser window that your site's visitors are likely to use. With today's high-resolution monitor screens, 1600 pixels wouldn't be too wide. Figure 9.18 shows what happens when a bordered background isn't wide enough to avoid horizontal scrolling.

Figure 9.18
A bordered background that isn't wide enough to avoid horizontal tiling.

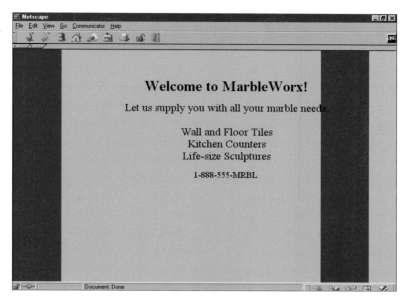

What image height to use for a bordered background is another matter entirely. You can and should keep the height of your bordered background image to a minimum. The simple bordered background in Figure 9.17 could be a single pixel high, for example (although you might instead make it 4 or 5 pixels high in order to more easily see the tile in PSP).

To make the bordered background shown in Figure 9.17, make the background color on the Color Palette a light shade of blue, then open a new image that is 1600 pixels wide and 4 pixels high, with **Background color** set to *Background Color*. Make a selection on the left side of the image, beginning at the top right corner and extending 100 pixels to the right and all the way to the bottom of the image. Choose the **Flood Fill** tool, set the foreground color on the Color Palette to dark blue, and then fill the selection. Export the image as a GIF or PNG with the GIF Optimizer or PNG Optimizer (available under **File** > Export).

Figure 9.19 shows a variation on the simple bordered background. This one starts out just like the previous example, but here you fill the selection with a linear gradient instead of a solid color.

Figure 9.19
A variation of the simple bordered background, using a gradient border.

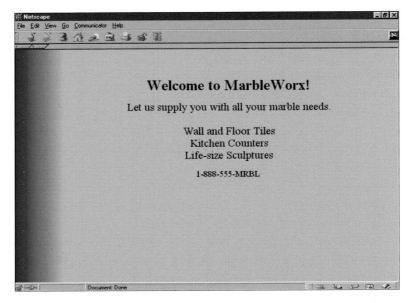

With the Flood Fill tool active, click and hold on the foreground swatch on the Color Palette and choose the **Gradient** icon. Then click on the foreground swatch to bring up the **Gradient Picker**, shown in Figure 9.20.

Figure 9.20
Choose a gradient with the Gradient Picker.

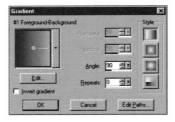

For the gradient, choose *#1 Foreground-Background* and select the *linear gradient* as the Style, and set Angle to 90. Click **OK**, and then fill the selection with the gradient.

Another variation on the simple bordered background is to add a shadow effect to the right of a solid-colored left border, as in Figure 9.21.

Part II Marrying PSP to the Web

Figure 9.21
A shadow can add depth to simple bordered background.

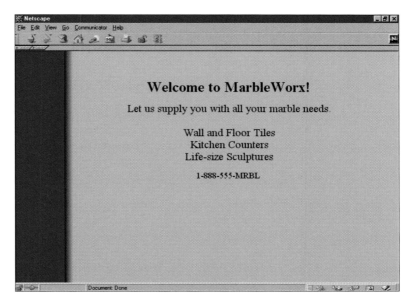

You might be tempted to use PSP's Drop Shadow effect, but resist this temptation. Drop Shadow won't extend all the way to the top and bottom edges of the image, and that produces an unattractive banding effect. Instead, make a selection that starts at the top of the image just at the right edge of the border and extends 10 or more pixels to the right and all the way to the bottom of the image. Fill this new selection with a linear gradient that goes from dark to light (in our example, from black to the light blue color of the main text area).

TIP

If you have a fancy bordered background, one whose border is a complex, multicolored texture or abstract image, you can get a nice shadow effect by using a linear gradient that goes from a dark color present in the complex border to the color of the main text area.

Fancy bordered backgrounds can be made by using a seamless tile as the left border, as in Figure 9.22. Figure 9.23 shows how this background looks on a Web page. In Chapter 10, "Using Layers," we'll look at how to make a more complex fancy bordered background.

Figure 9.22
A fancy bordered background, using a seamless tile as the border.

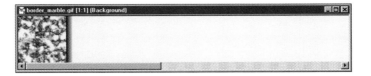

Figure 9.23
The fancy bordered
background used on
a Web page.

NOTE

When you use a seamless tile as the basis of your border in a bordered
background, the *height* of the bordered background image must match the
height of the seamless tile *exactly*. This is necessary to ensure that the
bordered background itself tiles seamlessly. Here's the best way to guarantee
that you get the right height for your image:

1. Open your seamless tile image and duplicate it with **W**indow >
   Duplicate (or simply press **Shift+D**). Close the original tile image.

2. Set the background/fill color on the Color Palette to the color that you
   want for the main text area of your bordered background.

3. With the duplicated tile the active image, choose **I**mage > Canvas Size.

4. Make sure that Center image **h**orizontally is not selected. Then set New
   width to the width that you want for your bordered background (for
   example, 1600), and be sure that New **h**eight is set to the height of your
   original image.

5. Click **OK**. Your bordered background is then ready for editing or saving!

Tables and Backgrounds

Tables and backgrounds cross paths in two ways. First, tables are needed to correctly display content on a Web page that has a bordered background. Second, tables themselves can have their own backgrounds. We'll now take a brief look at both of these topics.

Positioning Text in Columns

To position text and Web elements correctly on a page that features a bordered background, you'll need to use a table with one column for the border and another column for the main text area. Each column is defined with the TD tag, and the width of each column is defined with the WIDTH attribute. Here's an example of how the code for the page shown in Figure 9.23 might look:

```
<table cellspacing=0 cellpadding=0 border=0>
<tr>
<td width=110> </td>
<td width=520 align="center">
...
</td>
</tr>
</table>
```

Notice that the first column, which on the Web page appears to contain nothing at all except the left border, must contain something in order for the table to display correctly on the page. In the code above, this column contains code for the nonbreaking space character ( ).

In some Web browsers, simply using the WIDTH attribute in the TD tag along with some content in the column—whether text or buttons or a nonbreaking space—isn't enough to make the table display correctly. If you really want to be safe, what you'll need is a spacer image with its width set to the desired width of a column. A spacer image is just a transparent GIF that is 1 pixel high by 1 pixel wide.

To make a spacer image, open a new image that has those dimensions and that has a white background. Export that image with **File** > Export > **GIF** Optimizer. In the GIF Optimizer Wizard, set white as the transparent color. You can set the number of colors used to as low as 2. Then save the image, naming it something like SPACER.GIF. (For more information on the GIF Optimizer, see Chapter 7, "Optimizing Web Graphics.")

Part II Marrying PSP to the Web

Here's what the code for the Web page shown in Figure 9.23 would then be:

```
<table cellspacing=0 cellpadding=0 border=0>
<tr>
<td width=110><img src="SPACE.GIF" width=110></td>
<td width=520 align="center">
...
</td>
</tr>
</table>
```

Notice that here's a case where it's useful to stretch an image with the WIDTH attribute of the IMG tag. Width here is used to stretch the transparent spacer image to the width of the column.

Specifying Backgrounds for Tables

Today's Web browsers let you add a background to a table or to individual cells in a table. To do so, use the BACKGROUND attribute with the TABLE or TD tags.

Figure 9.24 shows a rather complex example of this.

Figure 9.24
A table with different backgrounds specified for specific cells.

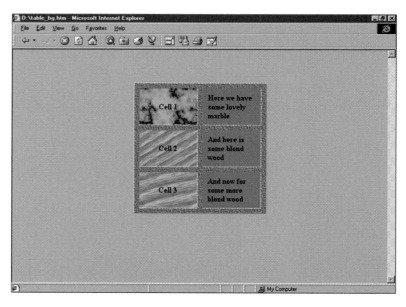

Here's the HTML code for this table:

```
<table cellpadding=10 cellspacing=10 border=1
background="tile_concrete.gif">
<tr >
<td width=100 align="center" background="tile_marble.gif">
<b>Cell 1<b>
</td>
<td width=100 bgcolor="gray">
<b>Here we have some lovely marble</b>
</td>
</tr>
<tr>
<td width=100 align="center" background="tile_wood1.gif">
<b>Cell 2</b>
</td>
<td width=100 bgcolor="gray">
<b>And here is some blond wood</b>
</td>
</tr>
<tr>
<td width=100 align="center" background="tile_wood2.gif">
<b>Cell 3<b>
</td>
<td width=100 bgcolor="gray">
<b>And now for some more blond wood</b>
</td>
</tr>
</table>
```

Be careful: You can go a little overboard with backgrounds! But used with restraint, backgrounds can add distinction and sophistication to your site.

Part III
Accelerating
Your Images

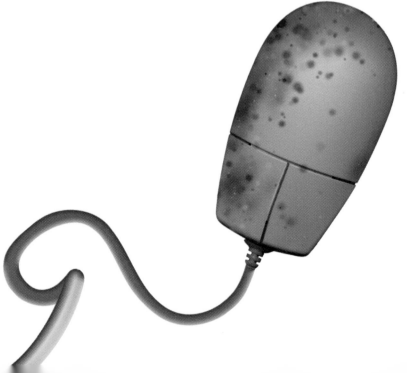

10

Using Layers

Layers let you create and manage your Web graphics in a powerful way. A layer is like a transparent sheet of acetate, with figures painted on the sheet. Several of these sheets can be stacked on top of one another, reordered, adjusted, edited separately, added, and subtracted. The image that results is a composite of all the individual sheets. This lets you work with different parts of each image individually. Although it's true that almost anything you can do with layers can also be done without them, layers make many image editing tasks a lot easier.

This chapter introduces you to Paint Shop Pro layers. You'll get a complete understanding of how they work and when to use them.

Here's what you'll learn in this chapter:

▶ **Get to Know PSP Layers**
Although powerful, layers can be confusing until you know how to recognize and use them effectively.

▶ **How to Add, Delete, and Restack Layers**
You'll often want to add and remove layers to/from your layered images.

▶ **How to Use Several Different Tools to Edit Layers**
Paint Shop Pro includes many different tools that are useful for editing layers. You'll get the rundown on how to use each of them effectively.

▶ **How to Adjust a Layer's Opacity and Blend Mode**
Since layers sit on top of one another, your final image depends on the opacity of each level.

NOTE
Only raster layers are discussed in this chapter. We'll look at vector layers in Chapter 11, "Drawing with Vectors." Another type of layer, adjustment layers, is an advanced topic that won't be discussed in this book.

Part III Accelerating Your Images

Understanding How Layers Work

Every PSP image has at least one layer. A single-layered image can be as simple as a block of solid color or as complex as images like the one in Figure 10.1.

Figure 10.1
A complex, single-layered image.

Editing the image in Figure 10.1 can be difficult. You couldn't easily blur the background or make a change to the flower's color without affecting the entire image. As a result, editing non-layered images can be tedious and difficult.

With layers, editing this image would be much easier. You can make changes to each part of the image separately. When you're finished and save the image as a GIF, JPEG, or PNG, the layers will be "flattened" into one layer automatically.

> **NOTE**
>
> While you're working on a layered image, you'll want to save the image as a .PSP file. Created by Jasc Software, this advanced format is one of the few that support layering in images, and it's optimized to work with Paint Shop Pro.
>
> When you're finished with your image, save it in a file format suitable for the Web. To do this, just choose **File** > Save **As** to save the file as a GIF, JPEG, or PNG, just as you would for any Web graphic. There's no need to merge the layers into a single layer beforehand, because Paint Shop Pro will do this automatically when you save a layered image to anything other than the PSP file format or the few other formats that support layering.

Paint Shop Pro allows you to view all of an image's layers at the same time or to hide one or more layers. Different layers can be edited independently of the others; this ability to manipulate certain parts of an image without affecting the other parts is what gives the layering its power.

Figures 10.2a, 10.2b, and 10.2c show an image with two layers—a
background and a "higher" layer. Figure 10.2a shows the image with both
layers visible. Figure 10.2b shows the same image with the background
hidden. (The checkered grid that shows behind the bee is what shows up
by default whenever PSP needs to represent an empty, or unpainted, area
of an image.) Finally, Figure 10.2c shows the same image with a Motion
Blur applied to the top layer (the bee) but with the background layer (the
clouds) unchanged.

Figure 10.2a
A two-layered image
of a bee and cloudy
background.

Figure 10.2b
The same two-layered
image with only the top
layer visible.

Figure 10.2c
The same two-layered
image with a Motion
Blur applied only to
the top layer.

Part III Accelerating Your Images

The Layer Palette

Layers are managed with the Layer Palette (Figure 10.3). To toggle the Layer Palette on and off, click the **Layers** button on the PSP Tool Bar or press the **L** key on your keyboard.

Figure 10.3
The Layer Palette for an image with two layers.

The Layer Palette has two panes. On the left are buttons for each layer, along with a **Layer Visibility Toggle**. By default, the Layer Buttons are named Background, Layer 1, Layer 2, and so on, but you can—and usually should—give your layers more meaningful names. The Layer Visibility Toggles allow you to temporarily "hide" layers so that you can see only some of your image's layers—maybe even just a single layer. Click a layer's Visibility toggle to hide that layer and click the toggle again to make the layer visible.

TIP
You can view a thumbnail of a layer, whether or not that layer is currently visible, by positioning the mouse cursor over the appropriate Layer Button. Move the mouse away from the button and the thumbnail disappears.

At the top left of the Layer Palette window are two more buttons, the **Create Layer** button and the **Delete Layer** button. Use the Create Layer button to add a new, empty layer or to make a copy of an existing layer. Use the Delete Layer button to remove an existing layer. (A third button to the right of these two buttons is the Create Mask button, but we won't be discussing masks in this book.)

In the right pane of the Layer Palette are three tabs with various controls for each layer. On the **Appearance** tab is a Layer Opacity slider, a Blend Mode selection list, and a Protect Transparency toggle for each layer. On the **Mask** tab are controls for masks. And on the **Layer Group** tab is a Layer Group toggle for each layer.

Don't let all these controls scare you away from layers. We'll look at most of them more closely later in this chapter. Once you start playing around with them, the layer controls are easy to use and remember.

Table 10.1 is a quick reminder of each control found in the Layer Palette.

Table 10.1
Quick-Reference for Layer Icons/Controls

Layer Icon	Icon Name	Description
	Create Layer Button	Press this button to add a new, empty layer.
		Drag the Layer Button of an existing layer to the Create Layer button to make a copy of an existing layer.
	Delete Layer Button	Press this button to delete the current layer.
		Alternatively, drag a Layer Button to the Delete Layer button to delete that layer.
Layer 1	Layer Button	Click on a layer button to make a layer active. Double-click on a layer button to open the Layer Properties dialog box, which is discussed in some detail later in this chapter.
		Right-click on a layer button to open a menu that contains many of the commands available in the Layers menu bar.
	Layer Visibility Toggle	Click on this button to hide and then show a specific layer.
	Protect Transparency Toggle	Turn the Protect Transparency Toggle on when you want transparent areas of a layer to remain transparent, even if you paint into those areas. Turn the toggle off when you want to paint on transparent areas of the layer.
100	Opacity Slider	Move the Opacity Slider to the left to reduce the opacity of the layer; the increased transparency will make the figures on lower layers more visible.
		Move the slider to the right to make the layer more opaque, which will make the figures on lower layers less visible.

Part III Accelerating Your Images

Table 10.1 *(continued)*
Quick-Reference for Layer Icons/Controls

Layer Icon	Icon Name	Description
Normal ▼	Blend Mode List	The Blend Mode list allows you to specify how to "blend" a particular layer with the layers beneath it.
		The blend mode determines how the layer's pixels are combined with the pixels of lower layers. For example, in a two-layered image for which Darken is the Blend Mode of the upper layer, each pixel in the upper layer is compared with the pixel in the layer beneath it, and the darker of the two pixels is what is displayed.
✖	Layer Group Toggle	Layer groups are sets of layers grouped together so they can be moved or reordered as a unit.
		When the toggle is off, it appears with the word "None". Press this button to add the layer to the first layer group (the button will be labeled "1"). Press again to add the layer to the next group, and so on. Keep pressing until the button returns to off if you want to remove a layer from a group.
ON	Layer Mask Toggle	Turn this toggle on to activate a layer mask; turn the toggle off to deactivate the mask.
		A layer mask allows you to adjust the opacity of different areas of a single layer without permanently affecting the layer. The mask can be edited or deleted, leaving the layer itself untouched. This advanced layer feature will not be detailed in this book.
⚲	Mask Link Toggle	Turn this toggle on to link a layer mask to a layer, so that the mask and layer can be moved as a unit. Turn the toggle off when you want to move the mask independently. By default, this toggle is turned on.

Naming a Layer

One way to change the name of a layer is to use the **Layer Properties** dialog box. The Layer Properties dialog box appears whenever you add a new layer to your image by clicking the Create Layer button or when you double-click on a Layer button.

Figure 10.4
The Layer Property
Dialog Box.

This dialog box has two tabs: General and Blend Ranges.

In the Layer portion of this dialog box, you'll see all the settings for the layer that you could also see in the Layer Palette itself. The Layer Properties box simplifies many of the changes that also can be made on the Layer Palette. For example, you can type in a Layer Group number instead of clicking on the Toggle button multiple times from the Layer Palette.

In addition, the Layer Properties dialog box lets you rename a layer so you can more easily recognize and use it. Giving your layers meaningful names, especially when your image includes several layers, is a good idea. That way, you don't have to remember that "Layer 1" has the cactus and "Layer 5" has the blazing sun. Instead, name your layers "Cactus" and "Blazing Sun" and leave your brain free to focus on the great image you're creating with those layers.

To rename a Layer, simply type in a new name in the **N**ame text box and click **OK** to return to the Layer Palette.

You can also rename a layer by right-clicking on the layer's **Layer** button and choosing **Rename**. Then just type in the new name that you want to give your layer and press **Enter**.

TIP
You can bypass the Layer Properties dialog box when you add a new layer by holding down the **Shift** key while you press the **Create Layer** button.

Part III Accelerating Your Images

When to Use Layering

Layers can be incredibly useful when you wish to do complex image manipulation, but you can go overboard with them. For simple operations, such as adding a solid-colored border around your image, you should probably forget about layers. But if you want to combine several image elements, and perhaps control their opacities independent of each other or apply special effects to some elements while leaving others untouched, then layers are the way to go.

You may also find layers helpful when you want to combine two or more elements but are unsure at first exactly how they should fit together. By giving each element its own layer, you can experiment with moving the elements around, positioning and repositioning each one until you've found an effect you like. You can also try out different opacities and blend modes on the separate layers.

How to Use Layers

Now that you understand how layers work and can find your way around the Layer Palette, it's time to try out this cool feature. Let's begin with an uncomplicated example. Start off with a flat digital photo, like the one in Figure 10.5. We'll add a handmade picture frame to the photo.

Figure 10.5
A photo waiting for a
picture frame.

Open your image and make sure the **Layer Palette** is open.

The first step in this example is adding a border around the image with **I**mage > Add **B**orders. Your border will be whatever color is currently set as the Background color on the Color Palette, so be sure to choose the color you want first. (We use a goldish yellow color here.) In order for later steps in this example to work correctly, choose any color other than black or white. Make your border exactly as big as you want your picture frame to be. In the example image, the Top, Bottom, Left and Right of the border are each set to 50. The result will look something like Figure 10.6.

Figure 10.6
The photo with a
border added.

Next, select the border with the Magic Wand. Choose the **Magic Wand**, and in the Tool **O**ptions palette be sure that the **Match Mode** is set to **RGB** and **Feather** is 0. Then click on the border. Keep this selection on as you do the next step.

Now, add a new layer by clicking the **Create Layer** button on the Layer Palette. With this new layer the active layer, choose the **Flood Fill** tool and set the **Style** swatch for foreground on the Color Palette to **Pattern**. Click the foreground Style swatch to call up the **Pattern Picker**, click the pattern swatch on the Pattern Picker to open the flyout menu, and select the pattern you want. (We use Craggy here.) Click **OK** and then click with the **Flood Fill** tool inside the selection. The fill will be applied to the new layer, not to your original image. The result will look something like Figure 10.7.

Figure 10.7
The beginnings of
the frame, added to its
own layer.

Part III Accelerating Your Images

For the next step, apply the **Inner Bevel** effect to the filled area of the new layer. For this step, you could leave the selection on, as you would on a flat image, but let's try out a nifty feature of layers: to apply an effect to the opaque areas of the new layer, you don't need to have those areas selected. Paint Shop Pro automatically treats any opaque areas on a layer that has transparency as if those areas were selected. So turn off the selection with **S**elections > Select **N**one and then apply **Inner Bevel** with Effects > **3**D Effects > Inner Bevel. Choose whatever settings you like for Inner Bevel and then click **OK**. The results will look something like Figure 10.8.

Figure 10.8
Inner Bevel gives the frame some depth.

Now let's try adjusting the opacity and blend mode of the frame layer. First, try adjusting the **Opacity** slider for the frame layer. Notice how this allows some of the color from the layer below to show through, as in Figure 10.9.

Figure 10.9
Lowering the opacity
of a layer lets pixels
on lower layers show
through.

Now set the Opacity slider back to 100, but select **Luminance** in the
Blend Mode selection menu. With the Luminance blend mode, only the
lightness values of the layer are applied to your image; the color is
contributed entirely by the layer below. So, in our example you get the
brightness values of the Craggy pattern but the color of the border on the
lower layer, as shown in Figure 10.10.

Figure 10.10
Blend modes affect how
the pixels on a layer are
combined with pixels
on lower layers.

Part III Accelerating Your Images

TIP

Several of the Blend Modes let you "meld" the colors and textures of two images. Experiment with Multiply, Overlay, Soft Light, and Hard Light. Each produces somewhat similar results, but all differ in their effect on brightness and contrast.

TIP

You can add a ready-made picture frame to your image using Paint Shop Pro's Picture Frame Wizard. To use the wizard, choose **I**mage > **P**icture Frame and choose the options you want in each of the wizard's dialog boxes.

Creating Your Own Layered Images

Now let's try creating a rather complex layered image completely from scratch. This example shows you why you'll want to use layered images when building most of the graphics on your Web site, so that you can edit and change them easily in the future.

This new image will be at the left edge of a border background tile for a fictional Web site called "Golden Rings." Begin by opening up a new image with the **N**ew button, then set **W**idth to 400, He**i**ght to 400, **R**esolution to 72 Pixels/inch, **B**ackground Color to Transparent, and **Image Type** to 16.7 Million Colors (24 bits).

NOTE

If Transparent isn't an available choice for **B**ackground Color, first change Image Type to 16.7 Million Colors (24 bits), and then try selecting **B**ackground Color.

Creating Interlocked Rings

Begin by creating a single round ring in the lower lefthand corner. Choose the **Preset Shapes** tool and select *Ellipse*; *deselect* **Retain style** and **Create as vector**, and set the width to whatever width you want for the rings (30 was used in our example). Then, set the stroke color in the Color Palette to a golden yellow color and the fill set to Null. To make a perfect circle, **Shift+drag** until you have a circle of about 200 pixels x 200 pixels; keep your eye on the lower left of the status bar to see the size of your shape. What you'll get as a result is something like what you see in Figure 10.11.

Figure 10.11
Draw a stroked ellipse for the first ring.

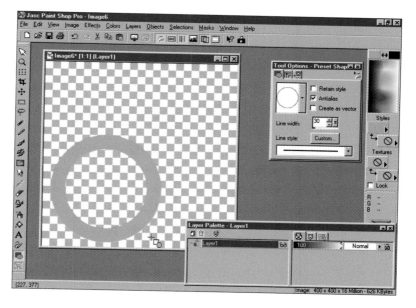

Give this layer a meaningful name, such as "Ring." Right-click on the layer's Layer button and choose **Rename**, then type the name you want and press the **Enter** key.

Next, give the ring a little depth with the Inner Bevel effect. Choose **Effects > 3D Effects > Inner Bevel**, and choose whatever settings look best to you. (We used a round bevel with the Width set to 15 and Smoothness set to 30, and with all other settings left at their defaults). Click **OK** when you have the settings you like.

Part III Accelerating Your Images

Now, make two copies of the Ring layer. Right-click on the Ring layer's Layer button and choose **Duplicate**. This creates a new layer above the Ring layer, named Copy of Ring (if the layer you just copied is named Ring). Then right-click this new layer and choose Duplicate. You get another new layer, this one named Copy of Copy of Ring. Since these names are meaningful enough, there's no need to give these layers new names. All three rings totally overlap, so you won't be able to see that there are three rings simply by looking at the image canvas. But look at the Layer Palette and you see layer buttons for all three layers.

The Copy of Ring layer is what will be the second ring. Make Copy of Ring the active layer by clicking its Layer button in the Layer Palette. Choose the **Mover tool** and then Shift-drag the ring up and to the right in the image canvas, as in Figure 10.12.

Figure 10.12
Creating the
second ring.

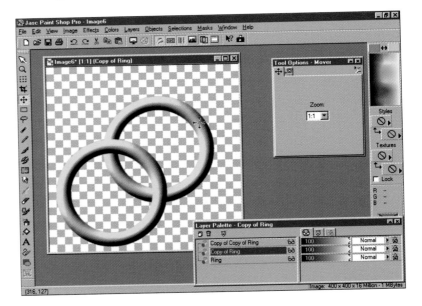

NOTE

If you simply drag with the Mover tool on a layer, then the topmost layer that has a pixel on the spot where you begin dragging will automatically become the active layer. In our ring image, that would have made the Copy of Copy of Ring layer the active layer, which isn't what you want here.

To make sure that only data on the currently active layer moves, even if what you want to move is covered up by pixels on a higher layer, use Shift-drag with the Mover tool.

Now, make the Copy of Copy of Ring layer the active layer. Choose the **Eraser** tool, and in the Tool **O**ptions palette set the brush size to about 5 to 10. Then, carefully erase where the two rings overlap on the left side. What you'll see is something like what appears in Figure 10.13, creating the appearance of interlocking by letting part of the lower layer show through.

Figure 10.13
Erasing part of the Copy of Copy of Ring layer creates the look of interlocking links.

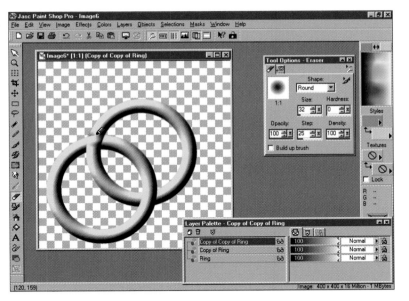

Don't worry too much about going a little too far in your erasing—the pixels on the Ring layer will show through if you overdo it a bit. Just be sure not to erase the part where the top ring overlaps the lower ring on the right.

At this point, you might want to move your rings to position them better in the image canvas. You could move each layer separately, but then they might get misaligned. An easier method, and one that keeps all the ring layers properly aligned is to use a **Layer Group**. To assign each of the ring layers to a single Layer Group, click the Layer Group tab on the Layer Palette. Then click the Layer Group button once for each layer. When you click on each button, its label changes from None to 1. Once you have all the ring layers assigned to Layer Group 1, use the Mover tool to drag the rings in place. Drag on data on one layer in the group, and all the layers move together (Figure 10.14).

Figure 10.14
You can move all the ring layers at once by first putting them in a single Layer Group.

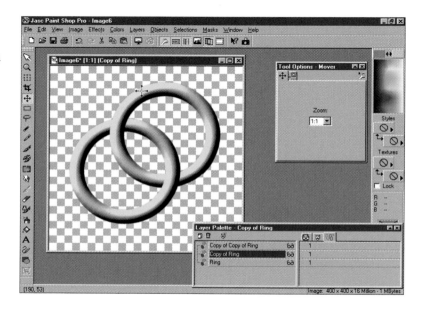

Add a Background

Suppose you want to add a textured background below the ring layers. When you add a new layer by clicking on the Layer Palette's Create Layer button, the layer gets added above the currently active layer. How can you add a layer to the bottom of the layer stack?

The answer is that you move the new layer to the bottom of the stack. So begin by adding a new layer; it doesn't matter which layer is the currently active layer. Then choose **L**ayers > Arra**n**ge > **S**end to Bottom, as shown in Figure 10.15.

Figure 10.15
Move the added layer to
the bottom of the stack
of layers.

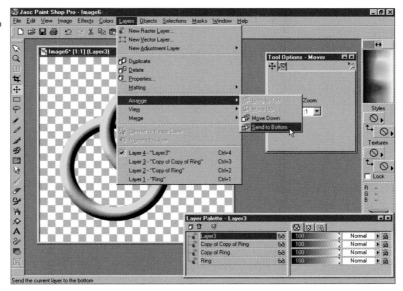

The new layer moves to the bottom of the layer stack.

Now, add a texture to the empty bottom layer. If you have an image that
tiles seamlessly, you can use that as your texture. Open the texture file,
then choose the **Flood Fill** tool. For the foreground swatch of the **Style**
section of the Color Palette, choose the **Pattern** style. Next, click the
foreground Style swatch to bring up the **Pattern Picker**. Click the pattern
swatch on the Pattern Picker and look at the top of the available pattern
list—images that are open in Paint Shop Pro appear at the top of the list.
Select your pattern image, then click **OK**. With the empty layer the active
layer, click with the **Flood Fill** tool in the image canvas to fill the empty
layer with the pattern. The result will look something like Figure 10.16.

Figure 10.16
Add a texture to the
lowest layer with the
Flood Fill tool.

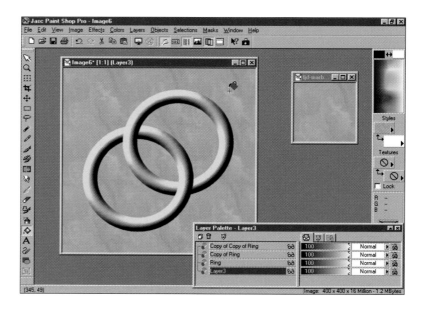

NOTE

Thousands of textures are available for download from the Web. Here are a
couple of URLs that have many textures you can use in your own Web
graphics:

> **http://www.aaabackgrounds.com/**
>
> **http://www.ecnet.net/users/gas52r0/Jay/backgrounds/main.html**
>
> **http://www.elated.com/toolbox/texturekits/**
>
> **http://infinitefish.com/texture.html**
>
> **http://www.elated.com/toolbox/texturekits/**

In addition, check out Chapter 9, "Making the Best Backgrounds," for a
step-by-step tutorial on creating your own textures.

NOTE

If you try to fill a layer but nothing seems to happen, chances are the layer
you intended to edit isn't the active layer. Make sure that the layer you want
to work on is active before you try to edit it. To make an inactive layer active,
click on its Layer button in the Layer Palette.

Final Touches

You're almost done with this advanced layered image. In this last section, you'll see how you might use the image for an element on a Web page.

Suppose you want to use this image as the basis of a border appearing on the left side of a Web page. For this, you'd use the image as the border for a bordered background tile. First, you can flatten the image, so that you're no longer working with a multiple-layer image. With all the layers visible, right-click on the Layer button of one of the layers and choose **M**erge > **M**erge All (Flatten).

CAUTION

Once you flatten an image, the separate layers cannot be retrieved. Your JPEG, GIF, or PNG will have only a single layer. If you want to keep a copy of your project with all layers intact, save a copy as a PSP file before the layers are merged.

As a general rule, always save your original image in the PSP file format, then save it as a GIF, JPEG, or PNG when you need to publish it to the Web.

The image is too large to use for a border on a Web page, but you can resize the image with **I**mage > **R**esize. Set the new size with either *Pixel size* or *Percentage of original*, as in Figure 10.17.

Figure 10.17
Resize the ring image to 100×100 pixels.

The only step left is to add a solid-colored area that will fill the body of your Web page to the right of the border. As you saw in Chapter 9, "Making the Best Backgrounds," you do this by resizing the image canvas. Set the background color on the Color Palette to the color you want; for example, a light pink is used in our example. Then choose **I**mage, >, Canvas Siz**e** and set New **w**idth to the width you think would be appropriate for the screen resolutions used by your site's users (about 1200 pixels is usually sufficient). Be sure that New he**i**ght is set to the original image height and that Center image h**o**rizontally and Center image **v**ertically are not selected. Click **OK**, and then use **F**ile > Save **A**s or one of the optimizers under **F**ile > Expor**t** to save your bordered background as a Web-ready image.

Figure 10.18 shows our example bordered background, RINGBANNER.JPG, used on a Web page.

Figure 10.18
The finished background tile used on a Web page.

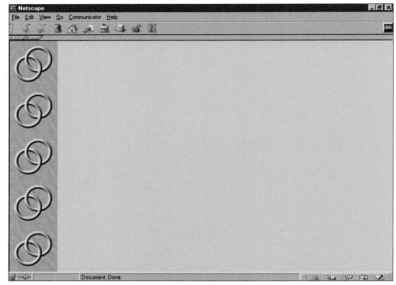

Layer Tips and Tricks

Before you leave this chapter, let's review a few points you should keep in mind when working with layers:

▶ Any greyscale or 16-million-color image can have layers added to it in an editing session, but layers can be saved only in the .PSP file format (or the PhotoShop .PSD file format).

▶ When you save your layered image to a file format that does not support layers, the file saved to disk will be flattened into a single layer. For the layered images that you create in order to make sophisticated Web graphics, save in PSP format if you want to keep a copy for future editing.

▶ Don't panic when you see how large your multi-layered PSP files are. These files contain all the layer information, which will not be saved in your Web-ready versions. The file size of your Web images will probably be *much* smaller once you save them as GIFs, JPEGs, or PNGs. For example, the Golden Ring banner created here was more than 350Kb in PSP format but became less than 10Kb when saved as a GIF using 128 colors.

▶ Spend time exploring Layer Blend modes and Opacity. These two enhancing features let you create powerful graphics with minimal effort.

11

Drawing with Vectors

The ability to draw with vectors provides an alternate method for creating graphics. For some requirements, vector objects will provide distinct advantages over the raster graphics that have been used to this point. Combining both vector and raster elements in the same image allows the best of both types to be incorporated into your Web graphics.

An image that is created and saved as raster stores information about each pixel in that image. Each pixel is assigned a color and, in some formats, transparency information. Since larger images require more pixels, the file size of these images will also be larger. In order to resize a raster image, pixels must be removed or added to the file. When removing pixels from an image, details will be lost; when adding pixels, details can become blurred. In either case the quality of the image will be degraded.

An image created with vectors stores instructions about each element in the image that define size, shape, and placement of those elements. When an image consists of elements that are repeated, or if the same image is required in many different sizes, drawing with vectors can make the task simpler.

This chapter provides information on how to incorporate vector objects into your graphics. You will learn:

▶ **Vector Basics**
What tools can be used to create vector objects, how to modify the objects and how to create preset shapes.

▶ **Creating and Using Vector Objects**
How to create simple buttons and bars for your Web pages.

▶ **Text on a Path**
Give your text more impact by having it follow a curved path.

Part III Accelerating Your Images

▶ **Logos and Banners**
Vector objects are ideal for creating logos to be used on your site or within a banner for your site. The vector definition allows them to be resized for many different applications.

Vector Basics

The ability to resize your images while maintaining their original quality makes vector drawings extremely adaptable for creating Web graphics. Beyond resizing, vector objects have many advantages over raster, including the ability to edit each object independently or as part of a group. Vector objects can be resized, deformed, or have their shape changed with no impact on other objects on the same layer; colors and patterns in the strokes and fills can be changed, added, or removed; and vector text can be edited to change the font or the characters.

New to PSP7 are commands for aligning and distributing vector objects precisely; using styles; and allowing gradients, patterns, and textures on the strokes and fills that define the vector object. Once you have created your image with vector objects, it can be saved as a preset shape to be reused in many projects.

Vector instructions include the nodes, curves, fills, size, and placement that combine to create the overall image. Nodes are the control points of the vector object; they establish the overall shape by defining the amount of curve, if any, and how the line segments on either side of the node are joined.

Due to the differences between vector and raster properties, vector objects are kept on separate layers within the PSP file. A PSP file can have many vector layers, each vector layer can have many elements, and each element is an object that can be manipulated independently of the others. Each object can be modified, moved, hidden, or deleted without modifying the other objects on the same vector layer.

Icons are used on the Layer Palette to distinguish layer types. A vector layer is identified by the red square with blue corner nodes, as shown in Figure 11.1. A vector layer will have a plus sign [+] displayed to the left of the vector layer icon, indicating that the layer contains at least one object. Clicking on the plus sign will expand the list to show each object or group of objects on the layer. Vector objects can be grouped within the layer—a group of objects is shown as a blue square over a red circle and, like the layer, will show a plus sign indicating it can be expanded and collapsed. Individual objects are identified with a curved red line and small blue circle.

Figure 11.1
Layer Palette showing
icons for vector layers.

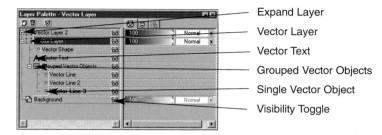

Expand Layer

Vector Layer

Vector Text

Grouped Vector Objects

Single Vector Object

Visibility Toggle

Each object on a vector layer can be hidden individually by clicking on
the **Visibility** toggle button in the Layer Palette. Hiding individual objects
or groups of objects temporarily protects them from being selected and
modified. Vector objects are also hidden to create an invisible path for
text to follow.

Within the vector layer, the elements are stacked according to the order of
the **Object** buttons within the vector layer. The element at the top of the
list is at the top of the stack, or visible in front of all other objects within
the layer. The element at the bottom of the list is at the bottom of the
stack and appears to be behind all other objects within the layer. Dragging
the Object buttons into a different order will change the stacking of the
objects, or the **Arrange** option of the Objects menu can be used to change
the relative positions.

Vector Tools

The **Text**, **Drawing**, and **Preset Shapes** tools can all be used to create
vector objects. These tools are also used on raster layers and they are used
in the same way. To create vector objects with these tools, the vector
option must be selected. Figure 11.2a shows the **Create as vector**
selection box from the Tool Options palette for the Preset Shapes tool.
The Drawing tool has the same option in a different place on its Tool
Options palette and the Text tool has the option on the Text Entry dialog
window, as shown in Figure 11.2b.

Figure 11.2a
Create as vector
option on Tool
Options palette.

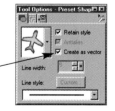

Create as
Vector Option

Part III Accelerating Your Images

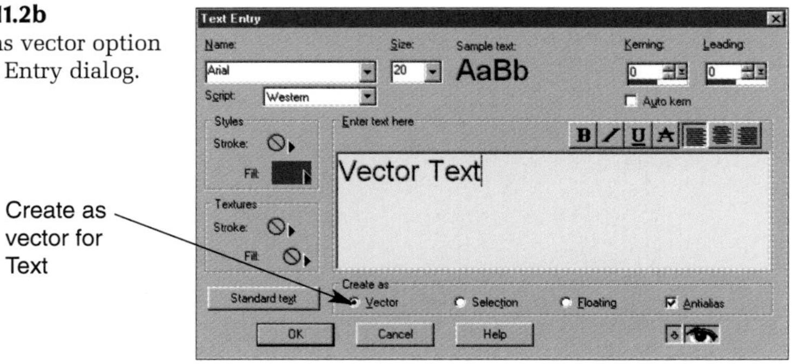

Figure 11.2b
Create as vector option
on Text Entry dialog.

Create as
vector for
Text

Modifying Vector Objects

A vector object can be modified by changing its properties, moving it, deforming it, or by modifying the shape with node edit. The **Vector Object Selection** tool is used for selecting and modifying the vector objects. This tool is only available when a vector layer is active.

Individual objects are selected either by clicking on them in the image, or by clicking on their Object button in the Layers Palette. Multiple objects can be selected by holding the Shift key while clicking on each object or button.

Groups of vector objects can be selected by using the Vector Object Selection tool to outline a rectangular section in the image. All visible objects on any vector layer will be selected if they are fully enclosed within the rectangle.

Vector Properties

Vector properties are modified by first selecting the objects with the Vector Object Selection tool. Figure 11.3a shows the first tab of the Tool Options palette and Figure 11.3b shows the Properties dialog for a Preset Shape. To edit the vector properties, click on the Properties button on the Tool Options palette or right-click on the object and choose Properties from the pop-up menu.

Figure 11.3a
Vector Object Selection
tool options.

Figure 11.3b
Vector Properties dialog
for a Preset Shape.

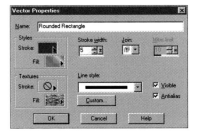

The Vector Properties dialog stores the original style and vector settings for the object and provides the ability to adjust these items after the object has been created. The Style options can be changed for Stroke and Fill types and textures. The Shape options can be modified by changing the **L**ine and **J**oin types, Stroke **w**idth, and **A**ntialias options, and the visibility toggle can also be set within this dialog. The object can be given a meaningful name in this window, making similar objects easy to identify.

TIP

To create a series of objects that are based on a single shape but have a varied color or texture, create the object only once, copy and paste it multiple times, and, for each of the copies, modify the properties as required. This saves attempting to draw the exact same shape repeatedly.

Figure 11.4 shows an image with a series of vertical dotted lines where each line has had the Stroke Style modified to different colors.

Figure 11.4
Repeated vector
line with modified
properties.

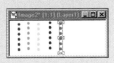

Object Alignment and Distribution

Alignment and distribution commands provide the means to space single or multiple objects evenly and precisely on the canvas and with each other instead of manually measuring and eyeing the objects. These commands are accessible through the Object Menu, the second tab on the Tool Options palette for the Vector Object Selection tool, or with a right mouse button click on the Object button in the Layer Palette.

Part III Accelerating Your Images

All of the alignment and distribution commands from the Object Menu are represented on the second tab of the Tool Options palette for the Vector Objection Selection tool, as shown in Figure 11.5.

Figure 11.5
Vector Object Selection Tool Align and Distribute Options.

Alignment refers to how objects are placed in relation to each other based on the first object selected. The first row on the Tool Options palette depicts the alignment commands. Objects may be aligned along their top, bottom, left, or right edges or on their horizontal or vertical center points. The Alignment commands are available when two or more objects have been selected.

Distribution refers either to how objects are placed in relation to the canvas or how they are placed with respect to each other. The objects are distributed between the two outside objects or, for canvas distribution, between the edges of the canvas.

The Object distribution commands are available when three or more objects have been selected. These commands are represented by the buttons on the second row of icons in Figure 11.5.

Objects can be spaced so that they are evenly distributed horizontally over the width of the canvas or evenly spaced within the selected group. Within the horizontal distribution, even spacing can be determined based on the left sides, centers, or right sides of the objects. The third row of icons, shown in Figure 11.5, represents the commands for arranging an object or group of objects in relation to the canvas. These commands are the only ones available when a single object is selected.

The final row shows the size commands as well as the grouping commands. Objects can be the same size horizontally, vertically, or both. Objects can be grouped or ungrouped to allow easier manipulation of your complex vector drawings.

Figure 11.6 shows the multiple dotted lines after using **A**lign > **T**op, **D**istribute > Horizontal Ce**n**ter and **D**istribute > Space Evenly **H**orizontal from the **O**bject Menu.

Figure 11.6
Multiple vector lines selected and aligned.

Object Deformation

A selected object or object group can be deformed by using the Vector Object Selection tool on the handles of the object boundary. There are six types of deformation: resize, rotate, change perspective, skew, shear, and distort. Figure 11.7 shows the Distort deformation on a preset star shape.

Figure 11.7
Distort deformation on preset shape.

The deformation types operate differently on vector text, lines, and shapes. Text that has been converted to curves is considered a shape and will follow the deformation options for preset shapes. A selected group of objects will be treated as text if the group includes any text objects. Table 11.1 summarizes how deformations are used with the different vector types.

Table 11.1
Deformation Controls on Vector Objects

	Shapes	**Text**	**Line**
Resize	Drag edge handles to change width or height. Change both width and height by dragging corner handles. Maintain height to width proportions by using the right mouse button.		Change line's length and angle by dragging handles. Use the right mouse button to adjust the length only. Use vector properties to change the line width.
Rotate	Drag center bar to rotate vector objects around the center point.		
Change Perspective	Ctrl + drag corner handles	Not applicable	Ctrl + drag corner handles
Skew	Shift and drag corner handles	Not applicable	Shift and drag corner handles
Shear	Shift and drag edge handles		
Distort	Shift + Ctrl + drag corner handles	Not Applicable	Shift + Ctrl + drag corner handles

Part III Accelerating Your Images

Node Edit

Node edit is available only when a single vector shape or line is selected. Start **Node Edit** from the Tool **O**ptions palette for the **Vector Object Selection** tool or by right-clicking on the object and selecting Node Edit from the pop-up menu.

When in Node Edit mode, only the shape outline is visible along with the various nodes that define the shape. Figure 11.8 shows the distorted star shape in Node Edit mode.

Figure 11.8
Node Edit mode shows only the shape outline.

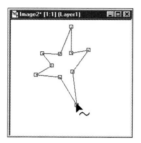

Nodes can be moved, added, or removed from the shape definition. New lines and nodes can be added by switching to the draw mode within Node Edit. Node types can be changed to treat line segments as straight lines or curves and to change how the line segments meet. To add nodes, hold the **Ctrl** key and move the cursor over the shape until it changes to show +, click on the line segment to add a node at that point. Remove nodes, and the line segments on either side, by clicking on the node and pressing **Delete** key. Right-click on the object to bring up the Node Edit menus.

Figures 11.9a and 11.9b show the star shape in Node Edit mode after moving some nodes and adding some new ones to the shape and the final shape after leaving Node Edit. To leave Node Edit, either click anywhere outside the image, right-click in the image and choose **Q**uit Node Edit, or use the quick key combination **Ctrl+Q**.

Figure 11.9a
Star shape after moving and adding nodes.

Figure 11.9b
Star shape after closing Node Edit.

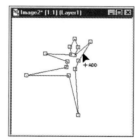

Saving Objects as Preset Shapes

Once you have created a vector object or group, export it as a Preset Shape and it will be available for any new image you create. The name of the object or group as shown in the Layers Palette will be the name shown in the Preset Shapes display.

1. Assign names to the **Vector Objects/Groups** that will be exported. Use the **Properties** adjustment to change the names or right-click on the **Object** button in the Layers Palette and choose **Rename**.

2. Select the Object(s) to be exported or make sure that none are selected if all objects are to be exported.

3. Choose File > Export > **S**hape.

4. You will be asked for a name—this will be the file name that stores all the shapes and will have a .jsl extension. Within this file all the objects will have the name from the Layers Palette.

Creating and Using Vector Objects

The next sections provide step-by-step examples for using the various vector tools to create Web graphics from simple vector objects.

Buttons and Bars from Vector Shapes

Vector shapes provide an unlimited source for unique button and bar graphics. The next two examples demonstrate how to create a simple round button and a rounded-rectangular button.

A Simple Round, Beveled Button

A simple circle with a gradient for the fill and stroke creates a practical round button. This effect works best with lighter colors, but any colors can be used.

1. Start a new image 100×100 with your choice of background color.

2. Select the **Preset Shapes** tool and set the following on the first tab of the Tool **O**ptions palette:

   —Select the preset shape **Ellipse**.

   —Ensure that **Retain style** is not checked and that Antialias and create as vector are checked.

   —Set **Line width** to 5 and **Line style** to **Solid**.

3. Set your foreground color to a medium green and the background to a light green color.

4. In the Styles palette, set both the stroke and fill styles to linear gradients, choosing the Foreground/Background gradient. Set the angle of the gradient to 45 degrees for the stroke and check the invert gradient option for the fill style. You should have the same gradient for both stroke and fill, but in opposite directions. The texture options should both be set to None.

5. Draw a circle on the canvas and a new vector layer will be created. To make a perfect circle hold the shift key down while you draw. To draw the circle from the center use the right mouse button to draw. Figure 11.10 shows the button, the Tool Options for the Shapes tool, and the Style selections to create this simple round button.

6. Name the circle shape on the Layers Palette and save your shape to the preset shapes: **F**ile > Expor**t** > **S**hape and give the shape a name.

Figure 11.10
Simple beveled buttons.

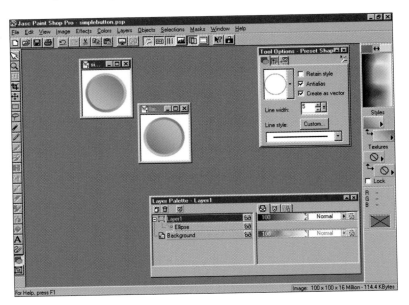

TIP
Rotating the button creates the illusion of the button being pressed. Figure 11.10 included a second copy of the round button rotated 180 degrees. The two versions could be used together to create a rollover button.

> **NOTE**
> Stroke width is a fixed size and is not adjusted automatically if the object is resized. When an object is resized, it may be necessary to change the stroke width to keep the intended proportion of stroke and fill.

A Rounded-Rectangle Button

Round buttons can be awkward to work with if you want a number of buttons with different text. The circle shape results in a lot of wasted space. A rectangle, or rounded rectangle, shape creates a more compact and versatile base for a series of buttons.

1. Start a new image 150×75 with a white background.

2. Select the **Preset Shapes** tool and on the first tab of the Tool **O**ptions palette make the following selections:

    —Select the preset shape *Rectangle*.

    —Ensure that Retain Style is not checked and that **Antialias** and **Create as vector** are checked.

    —Set **Line width** to 25 and **Line style** to Solid.

3. On the second tab of the Tool Options palette, set the **Join** to *Rounded*.

> **NOTE**
> The preset shape *Rounded Rectangle* will create rounded corners, but for small buttons the rounding is very limited. Using the *Rounded* style for **Join** creates a better rounded end for the button.

4. In the **Styles** palette, set the stroke to a **Pattern** and choose the *Finished Wood* setting. The fill setting should be set to Null and both Texture settings should be set to Null.

5. In your image, draw a very narrow rectangle, barely more than a straight horizontal line in the center of the image. The stroke width will be added to what is drawn, so care must be taken to avoid the edges.

6. To make the shape stand out from the page, a drop shadow is often used—but the drop shadow effect is not available on a vector layer. To get around this, a shadow can be added to a raster layer with a selection created from the vector object.

7. With the rounded rectangle selected, choose **S**elections > From Vector Ob**j**ect from the menu or right-click on the object and choose **Create Raster Selection**.

8. Modify the selection to remove any small gaps at the edge of the object and to create a softer edge for the shadow: Contract the selection by 2 pixels (**S**elections > **M**odify > **C**ontract), and then feather the selection by 2 pixels (**S**elections > **M**odify > **F**eather).

9. Make the background, or another raster layer, active and create the drop shadow: **E**ffects > **3**D Effects > **D**rop Shadow. Set **V**ertical and **H**orizontal Offsets to 7, **O**pacity to 55, **B**lur to 5 and **C**olor to Black. Click **OK** to add the raster drop shadow. Figure 11.11 shows the completed button.

Figure 11.11
Rounded-rectangle
button.

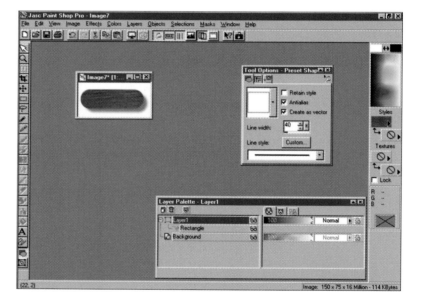

Buttons and Icons from Dingbats

Dingbats are fonts that have shapes and symbols instead of letters. Figure 11.12 shows an image created with the font Webdings. This object could be used as part of a logo or banner or as a "home" button in the common navigation for the Web site. If you do not have this font, go to **http://www.microsoft.com/OpenType/web/fonts/webdings/default.htm** to download it.

Figure 11.12
Airplane symbol button.

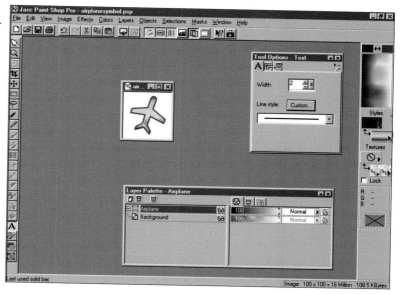

1. Open a new 100×100 image with a white background.
2. Select the **Text** tool.
3. On the first tab of the Tool **O**ptions palette, set the stroke width to 2 and line style to solid. On the second tab, set **Join** to Rounded.
4. On the **Style** palette, set the stroke to a flat color and choose a dark blue color. Set the fill to a linear gradient and choose the ***Blue Metallic*** gradient. Set the fill texture to ***Foil*** (stroke texture should be Null).
5. Click in the center of the image to bring up the **Text Entry** dialog box.
6. Select the Webdings font and enter a size of 72. Set **Create As** to vector and check the **A**ntialias option. Set the alignment to centered and make sure the other modifiers (Bold/Italic and so on) are all off.
7. Click in the text entry area. Hold down the **Alt** key and use the number pad to enter 0241 to get the airplane shape.
8. Click **OK** to finish adding the text.

Buttons and Bars from Vector Lines

Custom-defined lines can be used to make stylish bars or even buttons for your Web page.

1. Open a new image that is 500 pixels wide by 100 high.
2. Make the **Draw** tool active, set the type to ***Single Line*** and set the line Width to 20.

3.   **Create as vector** and **Antialias** should be checked. **Close path** should be unchecked.

4.   Click on the **Custom** button to define a new line style. Enter the settings as shown in Figure 11.13.

Figure 11.13
Creating a custom
Line style.

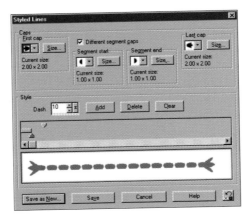

—Set the First cap and Last cap to the ***Tulip*** option and click on the size buttons for both to set them to 2×2.

—Click on Different segment caps to check it, set the segment start and end to ***round***, set the size to 1×1 for each.

—Create a dash in the line by clicking the **A**dd button and setting the **Dash** to 10. Click **A**dd again and move the **Gap** setting to 12.

—Click on the Save as New button to save the custom line style and give the line a name: Dashed Tulip. Your new custom line style will now be available from the drop-down selection list.

—Click **OK** to return to the Tool Options palette for the Draw tool.

5.   In the **Style palette**, set the stroke to a gradient fill; select the ***Ultraviolet*** gradient with a rectangular style. Set the Texture on the Stroke to the ***Brush Strokes*** texture.

6.   Draw a line in your image that will almost fill the width of your image. Keep in mind that the end caps will be added to the line you draw and may be cut off if you draw too close to the edge.

7.   Using a texture fill on the vector layer can introduce some transparency to the vector layer, allowing portions of the background to show through. Change the background layer by filling with different colors and see how it affects the look of the bar. Figure 11.14 shows the finished bar with a black background.

Figure 11.14
Completed bar with
black background.

Text on a Path

Text can have more impact when it follows a path instead of a straight line. A path can be any vector shape or line—or even other text if it has been converted to curves.

Text on a path must take into account the curve of the line. The kerning and leading properties can be used to adjust the placement of the text on the path and create better spacing. Kerning is the amount of space between the characters; increase the space by entering positive kerning values, decrease the space by entering negative kerning values. Leading is usually the space between lines of text, but when adding text to a path, this value is used to position the text relative to the path. Use positive values to place text below the path and negative values to move the text above the path.

1. Start a new image 300×150 with a white background

2. Select the **Draw** tool and create a curved vector line like the one shown in the first image of Figure 11.15. The line shown is a Beziér line with a stroke width of 10.

3. Select the **Text** tool and position it over the curved line until the cursor displays the text on a path symbol, as shown in the first image of Figure 11.15.

4. Enter properties and characters (text on a path) in the **Text Entry** dialog. Settings used here: Arial Black font, Size 20, Kerning 0, Leading 0, Create as vector, Antialias, Left Aligned, Plain color fill style.

5. The text is placed on the path along the center of the stroke width (second image in Figure 11.15). If the stroke is to remain part of the graphic, it is difficult to read the text where it overlaps the path.

NOTE

If the text does not follow the path, or if the text was added before the path, it can be applied after by selecting the text and the path and choosing **Fit Text to Path** from the **O**bjects menu.

Part III Accelerating Your Images

6. Choose the **Vector Object Selection** tool and select only the text (the path and text will both be selected after adding the text). From the Tool **O**ptions palette, click on the **Edit Text** button.

7. Change the **Leading** value to move the text above the curve: Enter -10.

8. The word "text" has a lot of space between the letters because they are on an outside curve. Use **Kerning** to bring these letters closer together. Select just the word "text" and enter -125 as the kerning value. Click on **OK**.

9. The third image of Figure 11.15 shows that the text is now above the curve and the spacing in the word "text" is improved.

Figure 11.15
Creating text on a curved path.

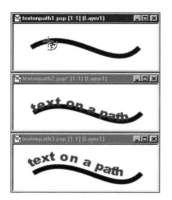

TIP

The alignment for text on a path is dependent on the *start* node. For lines, or open paths, the start point is easy to determine, but on a closed path like a circle it's not always obvious and the text may not be positioned where you want it.

To find the start point, use **Node Edit** and move the cursor over the nodes—the word *start* will be displayed with the cursor when the mouse is positioned over it.

Change the start point by breaking the path where you want the start node to be. (In Node Edit menu: **E**dit > Brea**k**, select the two nodes, **E**dit > **J**oin Select)

Creating Logos and Banners

Vectors can be combined to create complex logos that are easily incorporated into banners, buttons, and other Web graphics, because they are easily resized.

1. Create a new image 250×250 with a white background.

2. Select the **Preset Shapes** tool and choose the *Ellipse* shape with the following settings:

    —On the first tab of the Tool **O**ptions palette: Retain Style unchecked; **Antialias** and **Create as vector** checked; Line width 27, line style *Diamond.*

    —Colors on the **Styles** palette: Foreground: R0 G105 B120, Background: R168 G168 B213.

    —Styles: **Stroke Style**: Linear Gradient, Angle 0, Repeats 0, #2 Fading Foreground; **Fill Style**: Same gradient as stroke but change to *Sunburst Gradient* with Horizontal and Vertical center both set to 50.

    —Textures: **Stroke Texture:** *Tree Bark*; **Fill Texture:** *Plastic 3*.

3. Draw a circle in the center of the image—be sure to draw starting from the top left to have the Start node in the correct position. Use the **Vector** properties to adjust the line width to get even spacing of the diamond shapes around the edge.

4. Change to the **Text** tool. Click on the circle to add text on the path. In the **Text Entry** dialog box, set the following options:

    Both **Texture** options should be *None/Null*; **Stroke Style** should be *None*, **Fill Style** set to *Pattern* and choose the *Granite 2* option; **Text**: Arial Black, 20; **Kerning** 200, **Leading** 25, **Create As vector**, **Antialias**. Enter the text and click **OK**.

5. Both the circle and the text should be selected at this point. Choose **E**dit > **C**opy and then **E**dit > **P**aste > As new **V**ector Selection. Position the copy over the original.

6. The new copy of the circle can be hidden; it is required to be the path for the second copy of the text.

7. The second copy of the text should be moved below the original in the stacking order on the Layer Palette.

8. With only the second copy of the text selected, choose **Properties** and change the **Fill Style** to plain white. Move the center point of the text down slightly to expose the white at the edges of the granite filled text.

9. Select all of the vector objects, including the hidden circle, and create a group. On the second tab of the **Tool Options** palette, click on the **Group** button. In the **Layers Palette,** right click on the new group, choose ***Rename*** and name it Logo. Ensure the group is selected. Figure 11.16 shows the image and the Layer Palette at this point.

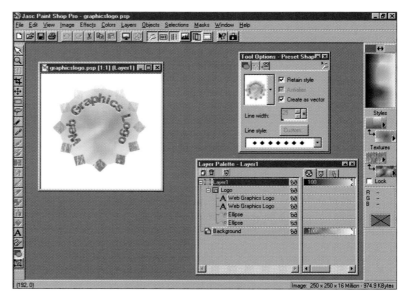

10. Export the logo as a preset shape, using **F**ile > Export > **S**hape. Enter a name for the file when prompted.

11. Make a duplicate of the image: **W**indow > **D**uplicate. In the duplicate version, select the Vector layer and choose **L**ayers > **C**onvert to Raster. This version will be used to compare resizing of the logo.

12. Create a new image 400×100 with a white background.

13. Select the **Preset Shapes** tool and choose the ***Logo*** shape that was just exported. Check the **Retain Style** option.

14. Draw a smaller version of the logo that fits into the banner image; use the **Shift** key to keep the proportions of the logo. Notice that the diamond shapes in the stroke are now too large. Adjust the stroke width to 12 by selecting the visible ellipse in the group and modifying the properties.

15. The remaining space in the image would be used for company information for the banner.

Figure 11.17 shows the banner image with two copies of the logo. On the left is the vector version from the preset shapes after modifying the stroke width; on the right is the raster version resized to fit in the banner.

The vector version has kept a better quality of the text than the raster version and is much more legible. The patterns and fills, like the stroke width, are not resized in proportion to the drawn shape, so they have a different appearance in the smaller vector object. The circle and diamond stroke kept the same pattern in the reduced raster version.

Figure 11.17
Logo graphic comparing reduced vector and raster versions.

The reduced versions of the logo show that both the vector and raster versions have advantages, but if a larger version is needed, Figure 11.18 shows that increasing the size of an image works much better with the vector format. Figure 11.18 shows portions of two images, both 600×600. The top image is the vector drawn proportionally with the Preset Shapes tool. The stroke width was modified to 85. The bottom image is the raster version of the logo resized to 300 percent of the original. The distortion and loss of detail caused by increasing the size of a raster image are readily apparent in both the background circle and the text.

Figure 11.18
Logo graphic comparing enlarged vector and raster versions.

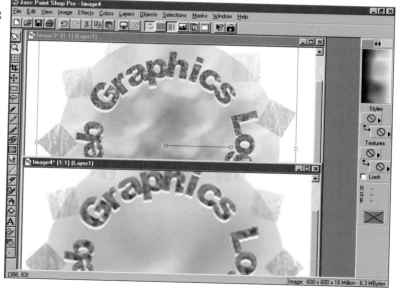

Part III Accelerating Your Images

Part IV
Powerful Web Tools

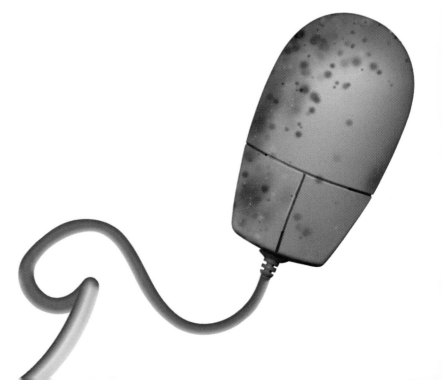

12

Image Mapping and Slicing

Images serve many purposes on your Web site—decoration, navigation, illustration, personal enjoyment, and even to improve stores. In Chapter 6, "Creating Transparent Images," you learned how PSP can be used to make many different types of effective images on your Web page. In this chapter, I'll show you how to take your images one step further and put them to work for you in your site using two techniques: *image mapping* and *image slicing.* Paint Shop Pro comes with special tools to make both powerful techniques accessible to even HTML novices.

These enhanced ways to use your Web graphics enable you to create and control the presentation of images on your Web site more easily. Using image maps, you can link different areas of a single image to different HTML files or URLs. This lets visitors to your Web page navigate from page to page by using their mouse to select different areas of an image. Similarly, image slicing lets you designate parts of an original image to link to other pages, but this technique actually splits up your original image into many smaller parts.

In this chapter, I'll describe image mapping and slicing, teach you when and how to use each technique, and provide several practical tips for mapping and slicing on your site.

▶ **Understand Mapping and Slicing**
   Although both techniques can produce similar results, they use very different methods. Learn about each technique separately.

▶ **Build a Simple Image Map for Your Web Page**
   Nothing demonstrates how easy image maps are to create as does making one on your own with Paint Shop Pro 7.

▶ **Slice an Image for Your Own Site**
   We'll take a Web graphic and run it through the Paint Shop Pro slicing tool and show you how to get great results.

What is Image Mapping and Slicing?

You are already familiar with creating and editing images from scratch and then adding them to your Web page. Using the <IMG> tag, or your favorite HTML editor, you can add any GIF, JPEG, or PNG image to a page. Of course you can include multiple images on a single Web page and link to another page just as easily. Image mapping and slicing are two enhancements that you will use to make your Web pages more graphically interactive with visitors.

How Image Maps Work

Image maps are a slightly different twist on the image linking concept. Using an image map, you can have different parts of a single image serve as links to different Web Pages. This enables you to create one great image in Paint Shop Pro and then worry about establishing the links separately. You are essentially providing your Web browser with a "map" describing where to take visitors when they click on one part of the image. Within an image, you can designate any type of shape or section of an image to link to other pages. With image mapping, you need to add only one image to achieve this effect. Figure 12.1 shows a great image map on the FamilyBeat Web page (**www.familybeat.com**). Notice how the main image on the Web page is graphically and logically divided into three sections. Clicking on each part takes you to a different part of the FamilyBeat Web site.

Figure 12.1
The FamilyBeat Web site uses an image map to link visitors graphically to areas within its Web site.

Register Button

Tour

How Image Slicing Works

Image slicing is the process of taking a single image and dividing it into several smaller images that are all optimized individually for performance. Then you add the collection of images to your Web page. When slicing an image, you create the original large image within Paint Shop Pro and then carve the different pieces of the image (each piece must be rectangular) into separate files. Paint Shop Pro remembers your slicing settings so you don't have to repeat this process when you make future changes to your original image.

Image slicing is popular because you can optimize each slice of the image to the best Web graphics format and settings. In addition, image slicing makes it easier to add special effects like rollover images to your Web page. Figure 12.2 shows the J. Jill Web site (**www.jjill.com**) with grid lines depicting each slice of the image. Even though this page looks like a single image, there are actually fourteen different images on this page.

Figure 12.2
The J. Jill Web site has perfected image slicing on its site.

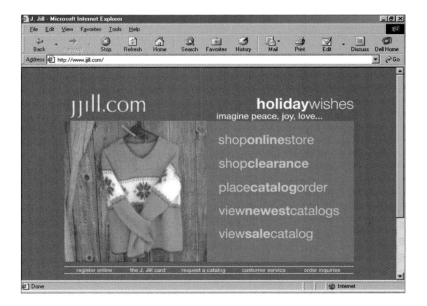

The Slicing and Mapping Process

Any image can be sliced or converted into an image map using the built-in Paint Shop Pro tools using roughly the same steps:

1. Create a plan for your Web site. The plan should describe how many pages you need to link to. This will make creating an image map or sliced image much easier, because your links will already be thought of ahead of time.

2. Create the original image within Paint Shop Pro. Save the image as a .PSP file so you can easily modify it in the future. Make sure that you create an image that clearly delineates the different sections of the image.

3. Decide whether you will use the image mapping or image slicing tools with PSP. Image maps are more flexible when your linking areas are oddly shaped, but image slicing gives you more precise control over special affects and optimization settings. Then launch the appropriate wizard in PSP (both wizards are covered in this chapter).

4. Use the mapping and slicing wizards to create the exact effects for your Web site. Then remember to save the settings for future reuse. The settings are saved as a separate file from your original and final image(s). Paint Shop Pro will save your image(s) in the GIF or JPEG format, depending on how you configure the wizard settings.

5. Add your images to your Web page. Although outside the scope of this book, you'll use the <IMG> tags if you build HTML by hand. Paint Shop Pro will build all the necessary HTML for you to copy and paste directly into your Web page. Make sure your final image(s) are saved within the same directory as your Web page.

6. Finally, finish editing your Web page and upload it so visitors can see your resulting site. Don't forget to test out every slice and section of the map to make sure all of your settings and links work properly.

Creating an Image Map

Now that you understand mapping and slicing, we'll focus on teaching you both techniques. This section steps you through the image mapping process. You'll learn how to create and select good images for mapping, how to use the built-in Paint Shop Pro mapping tools, and how to optimize your final images to load quickly within your site.

Finding a Good Image

When creating image maps, the first step is to select a good image to use. Make sure that it will be clear to visitors that they can select from several different areas on the picture to link to different items. Select definitive images with regions that are easily delineated on-screen and make sense to visitors.

Figure 12.3 shows an image created with Paint Shop Pro that will make a good image map.

Figure 12.3
Each city will take you to another page.

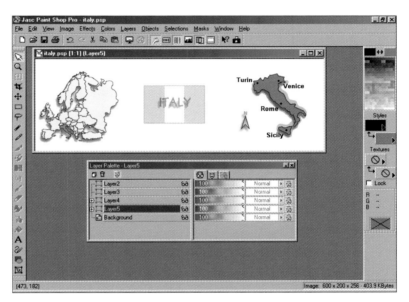

Image maps can be created from virtually any graphic that you can add to your Web page. Icons, buttons, bars, pictures, and images of all types can be sectioned out and presented as an image map for visitors. Not all images, however, make sense for use as image maps.

TIP

In general, photographs can be more difficult to turn into image maps, because they often lack clearly defined areas for the user to click. One popular technique is to take a photograph and add text on top of the image that is then turned into an image map. The text serves as an effective way for visitors coming to your Web page to know where to click. Or you can combine multiple photographs into a single image like the FamilyBeat example earlier in this chapter.

Planning the Map

Once you've selected an image, the next step is to logically divide it into different regions and define how you want the image map to work.

For the Italian sample image, Figure 12.4 shows how this will work.

Figure 12.4
Planning each link from your image map is an important step.

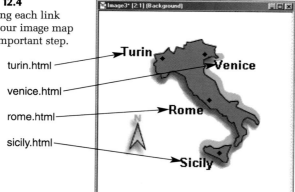

Once you have a good idea of how to divide your image map, you're ready to launch the Image Mapper tool with Paint Shop Pro.

When you create an image map, it is important to realize that you are now working with multiple Web pages. You are creating a path that visitors can use to explore the different aspects of your site. You'll have to create each page that you are linking your image map to.

Basically, you need to define each region on the image graphically and point that region to another Web page. Think of each image as a large piece of graph paper, on which you have to identify the exact X and Y coordinates for each section that links to an HTML file. For images, coordinates are measured in pixels (the dot resolution of your computer monitor). You have to specify the pixel dimensions of each section so it will properly link to an HTML file.

Fortunately, Paint Shop Pro comes with a powerful imaging mapping tool that lets you graphically select the different linking areas on an image. Launch the Image Mapper by selecting **F**ile > Expor**t** > Image **M**apper. Figure 12.5 shows the Image Mapper.

Figure 12.5
This flexible tool lets you create a great looking image map.

NOTE

Literally dozens of different programs can take care of image mapping for you automatically. In fact, many HTML editors, such as Microsoft FrontPage, Hotdog, or HoTMetaL Pro, come with this functionality built in. This chapter covers the built-in Paint Shop Pro Image Mapper, which compares favorably with the tools often built into HTML editors.

Besides the Image Mapper tool found in Paint Shop Pro, many other utilities exist to create image maps. The best stand-alone alternative is LiveImage— **http://www.liveimage.com**.

Mapping Tools

The Paint Shop Pro Image Mapper has several tools that you'll use when generating your image map. Each tool lets you modify the lines on your image in the right hand side of the window:

Arrow Tool—Use this tool to adjust the borders of a shape added to your image. When you select a shape, the nodes of the shape appear and you can adjust them with your mouse.

Mover Tool—The Mover tool lets you move shapes on your image. You can also adjust the size of a shape by moving your mouse over a shape's node and resizing it. The shape that is selected to be moved or resized is green, while the other shapes appear with red borders by default.

Polygon Tool—One of three tools used to create clickable shapes on your image. The Polygon tool lets you create uniquely shaped areas because you can have up to 127 different nodes. To use this tool, start drawing nodes on your shape to designate the clickable area. To close an area, click on the first node you drew and Paint Shop Pro will complete the shape.

Rectangle Tool—This tool lets you create clickable rectangle areas on your image. To use, click and drag your mouse across the rectangular area you want to designate as clickable.

Circle Tool—This tool lets you create circular clickable areas on your image. Similar to the rectangle tool, click and hold your mouse button while drawing the circle area on your image.

Delete Tool—Used to delete clickable areas. Use this tool carefully, because a single click anywhere with a shape removes it forever. **CTRL+Z** will undo the results of an accidental delete.

Pan Tool—This tool lets you pan the image in the preview window without zooming out, then re-zooming in again.

Setting Cell Properties

Once the object areas are created, the next step is to designate what happens when an area is clicked upon. To set your properties, use the **Arrow** tool to select the object you want to control. Then you can control three properties:

▶   **URL**—This is the URL this cell links you to when visitors click within it on a Web page.

▶ **Alt Text**—The Alt text appears instead of an image when there is a problem loading the Web page (the browser won't support the image, your Web site visitor has turned off image loading, or there is a problem with the Web server finding this image slice). Alt text also appears in most current Web browsers when you move and hold your mouse over an image or when there is a problem with the Web server displaying this image.

▶ **Target**—This property lets you configure how a link launches. You have five options:

—**top**—Opens the linked page within the same browser window, regardless of whether your Web design uses frames.

—**parent**—Opens the linked page within the window of the browser used to link to the existing page. Seldom used, it operates the same as _self if frames are not used within the Web design.

—**blank**—Brings up the link in a new browser window. Very useful when you are creating a link to another site, not just a page within your current site.

—**self**—Brings the linked page up within the same frame the link appears within. Works identically to _top if you don't use frames in your Web design. This is the default value if none is selected.

—**Named Frame**—Brings up the link in a frame that has been named directly within HTML when the web page was built. Substitute your actual frame name for "Named Frame."

CAUTION

Paint Shop Pro always sets your URL to be relative to the Web page that contains your image map. Relative addressing means that if you are linking to another page on the same site as the image map, you can simply type the file name and path of the HTML file. But if you want to link to another site, always include the **http://** or your link won't work properly.

TIP

When creating links to other sites, you'll almost always want to visit that site in your browser and then copy and paste the complete URL in this Window to avoid mistyping the URL.

The Target properties are used only if you use frames in your Web design. Frames are a way of splitting your Web browser into multiple areas, with each area displaying a separate HTML file. Before experimenting with frames, you'll want to become more proficient with HTML or your Web design application (for example, Dreamweaver).

Other Mapping Options

Besides using the slicing tools and setting the individual cell properties, you should be familiar with three other components in the Image Mapper Window:

▶ **Rollovers**—This option allows you to set up to six image rollovers for each object area. A rollover is a separate image that appears in that cell when one of six actions occur: Moving the mouse over the cell, moving the mouse out of the cell, clicking on the cell, double clicking on the cell, pushing your left mouse button down, and letting go of your left mouse button. Using rollovers with image maps is an advanced task, because it is very difficult to line up rollover images with object areas precisely. See Chapter 14 for more on rollovers in Paint Shop Pro.

▶ **Format**—Paint Shop Pro let's you designate your image as a GIF, JPEG, or PNG image from this window and launch the appropriate image optimizer.

▶ **Preview in Web Browser**—This button loads the image map in your Web browser so you can test it properly.

Save your Settings and Image Map

One of the best parts of the image mapper is how easy it is to save your results. And you can save the positions of your object areas as a separate file, enabling you to easily make changes to your image map in the future.

To save your image map, click on the **Save** button to bring up the **HTML Save As** dialog box.

For each image map, Paint Shop Pro generates an HTML file that controls exactly how your image appears. You must pick the file location and name the HTML file you want to be generated. Paint Shop Pro will create the file automatically. You will then be prompted for an image file name—this helps keep you from accidentally overwriting your original image.

You can also save your mapping settings for future use. You'll almost always want to save your image map settings, because you can reload them in the future if you need to make adjustments. Click on the **Save Settings** button to bring up the **Save Map Settings** dialog box. Paint Shop Pro will automatically add a .JMD file extension to your settings file.

Using the Mapped Image

Once you've created the image map in Paint Shop Pro, the last step is to use it on your Web site. Paint Shop Pro creates an HTML file with all of the proper codes for displaying the sliced image. Below is a sample of the code created for the Italy map:

```
<HTML>
<HEAD>
<META NAME="Author" CONTENT="Default">
<META NAME="Generator" CONTENT="Jasc Paint Shop Pro 7">
<TITLE>        </TITLE>
</HEAD>
<BODY>
<IMG NAME="italy0" SRC="italy.gif" WIDTH="600" HEIGHT="200"
BORDER="0" USEMAP="#italy">
<MAP NAME="italy">
<AREA SHAPE="rect" COORDS="417,32,470,61"
HREF="http://www.italy.com/turin.html" ALT="Visit Turin">
<AREA SHAPE="rect" COORDS="501,44,562,71"
HREF="http://www.italy.com/venice.html" ALT="Visit Venice">
<AREA SHAPE="rect" COORDS="458752,-1175584768,-34204,-
1174265489">
<AREA SHAPE="rect" COORDS="465,93,517,121"
HREF="http://www.italy.com/rome.html" ALT="Visit Rome">
<AREA SHAPE="rect" COORDS="475,145,535,179"
HREF="http://www.italy.com/sicily.html" ALT="Visit Sicily">
</MAP>
</BODY>
</HTML>
```

You can use the image map HTML code directly in your Web page by editing the HTML file PSP generated or by copying it into your own HTML editor.

Make sure that you move the image used for the image map into the same directory as the final HTML file.

A Complete Mapping Example

This section takes you through creating a complete image map from scratch using Paint Shop Pro's Image Mapper tool.

1. The first step is to create the image in Paint Shop Pro. For this example I'll use the Italy image I introduced in the previous section. Once you have the image loaded, choose **F**ile > Export > Image **M**apper from the Menu Bar. Figure 12.6 shows us ready to start.

Figure 12.6
We're ready to create an image map.

2. Add the appropriate shapes to link the image to other Web pages. For this example, I used several rectangle shapes. Figure 12.7 shows the shapes added to my image.

Figure 12.7
I've added several rectangle shapes to my image.

3. For each shape, set the appropriate **Object Properties**. Each Object links visitors to a new Web page. This step takes the longest amount of time because you have to set and check each link individually. I'm not setting rollover values in this example.

4. Preview your image map in your Web browser and experiment by clicking on each object to see if the results are correct.

5. Once you've finished setting your Object Properties, click on the **Save** button and save your HTML file and the image map.

6. The final step in this example is to edit the Web page that will contain the image map. Figure 12.8 shows the final page with the image.

Figure 12.8
This page contains one image with an image map.

Mouse Pointer, link to sicily.html

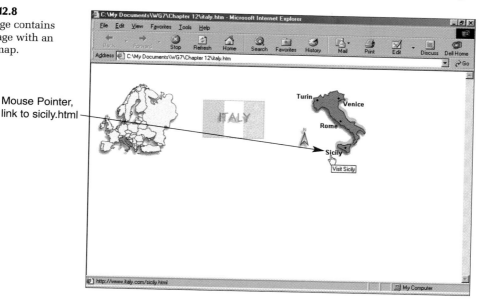

Providing a Textual Alternative

Although virtually all new Web browsers support client-side image maps, it's always a good idea to provide some sort of textual alternative. This accommodates visitors to your page who are using a browser that doesn't read client-side image maps or who don't want to wait for the entire image to download before selecting a region on the image map.

Figure 12.9 shows how the Italy home page is updated to have textual links as well as graphical ones.

Figure 12.9
This simple table provides an alternative to using my image map.

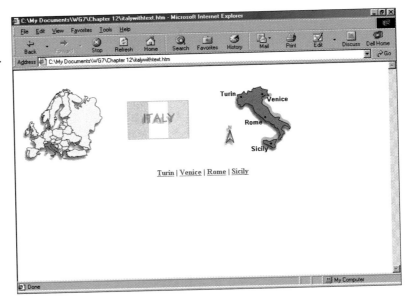

Image Map Design Tips

This section consolidates several important tips you should keep in mind when you begin using image maps in your Web pages:

▶ **Be careful of file size**—Images that are mapped tend to have larger file sizes because they usually appear larger on-screen. Make sure that your image's file size isn't outrageous (for instance, above 100K); otherwise, visitors to your Web page will become impatient. Chapter 7, "Optimizing Web Graphics," contains many tips for keeping images small and to the point.

▶ **Use interlaced or progressive images**—*Interlaced* and *progressive* images are those that load in multiple levels, starting out fuzzy and slowly becoming more detailed. Interlaced images are ideal for image maps because, as soon as visitors recognize which area they want to click, they don't have to wait for the whole image to appear.

▶ **Define mapped areas clearly**—Make sure that you use an image that makes it easy for visitors to know which sections are mapped to other HTML files. It's easy for visitors to overlook small areas (or illogical areas) on an image map.

▶ **Test your image map at least twice**—I can't stress this enough. I've seen too many image maps that haven't been tested thoroughly. Usually, some regions link properly to files, but other regions don't. Nobody enjoys using an untested image map.

Slicing an Image

This section will teach you how to slice your images with Paint Shop Pro and publish them on your Web site.

The image slicing process first requires you to create (or open) a graphic in Paint Shop. Then you launch the Image Slicing tool. From there you can decide where to make your slices and how Paint Shop Pro should handle each one. Finally, you can save the slicing results and add them to your Web page.

When Paint Shop Pro slices an image, each slice is a separate image file and an HTML file is generated so you don't have to create any complex code yourself. In fact, you simply copy the HTML and image files into your own Web site to use the sliced image immediately.

Select a Good Image for Slicing

The first step in image slicing is picking the right image to use. Most of the time you'll be creating images from scratch using Paint Shop Pro, but you can slice any image using Paint Shop Pro. Although you can slice any images, the best images are those which have clearly defined areas that link to different pages. Remember—you can slice an image only into rectangular areas. The most common use for slicing is for Web page navigation bars like the one shown in Figure 12.10.

Figure 12.10
The clearly defined use of rectangular areas makes this image a good candidate for slicing.

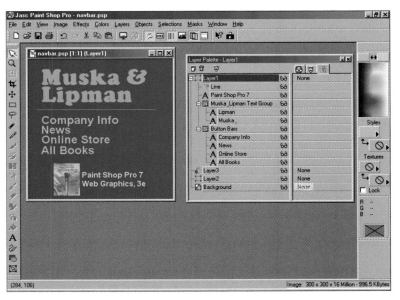

Part IV Powerful Web Tools

This figure is ideal for slicing because each area is well-defined, rectangular, and can easily take advantage of special effects like rollovers. Also, some parts of the image would be better suited saved as a JPEG while others are better optimized as a GIF.

I've created this image in Paint Shop Pro 7 and saved it as a .PSP file. Each component of the image is a separate vector, making it very easy to change in the future. Changing text, colors, or images is easy because I can use Paint Shop Pro to edit my images and then use the slicing tool to "publish" it to my Web site. Paint Shop Pro often calls each slice a *cell,* because it uses HTML tables to publish them on a Web page.

Once you've identified a good image for slicing, the next step is to launch the Paint Shop Pro Image Slicing tool. Click on the slicing icon or choose **F**ile > Expor**t** > **I**mage Slicer from the Menu Bar. Figure 12.11 shows the slicing tool.

Figure 12.11
The image slicer always shows you the current image being worked on.

Slicing Tools

The image slicer has several tools that you'll use. Each tool lets you modify the lines on your image in the right-hand side of the window:

Arrow Tool—Use this tool to select an individual cell or to move and combine slicing lines. This tool is used to set the precise locations of each slicing line. When you use the Arrow tool to move one slicing line directly on top of another slicing line, Paint Shop Pro automatically combines the two into a single line.

Grid Tool—Brings up the Grid Size dialog box when you click on your image using this tool. You use this tool to create a proportional grid of slicing lines on your image. Often, this is the first tool you'll use to add slicing lines to your image before you adjust the precise line locations with the arrow tool. You can use the grid tool recursively within cells of your image to create many grids within one another. Each cell within your grid must be at least two pixels tall and two pixels wide—Paint Shop Pro will limit the number of cells you can create based on the size of your image.

Slicer Tool—This tool lets you create slicing lines manually on your image. You can create horizontal and vertical slicing lines within a cell, multiple cells, or across the entire image.

Delete Tool—This is used to delete individual slicing lines on your image. Paint Shop Pro allows you to delete only slicing lines that are "legal." Legal slicing lines keep a section of the image intact as a square or rectangle—no L-shaped, T-Shaped or otherwise odd-shaped areas are permitted.

Pan Tool—When setting precise slicing line positions, you'll often zoom in and out your image. This tool lets you pan the image in the preview window without zooming out, then zooming in again.

Setting Cell Properties

Once the slicing lines are set, you control what happens when that cell is clicked in a Web page. To set your cell properties, use the Arrow tool to select the cell you want to control. Then you can control three properties:

▶ **URL**—This is the URL this cell links to when visitors click within it on a Web page.

▶ **Alt Text**—The Alt text appears instead of an image when there is a problem loading the Web page (the browser won't support the image, your Web site visitor has turned off image loading, or there is a problem with the Web server finding this image slice). Alt text also appears in most current Web browsers when you move and hold your mouse over an image.

▶ **Target**—This property lets you configure how a link launches. You have five options:

—**top**—Opens the linked page within the same browser window, regardless of whether your Web design uses frames.

—**parent**—Opens the linked page within the window of the browser used to link to the existing page. Seldom used, it operates the same as _self if frames are not used within the Web design.

—**blank**—Brings up the link in a new browser window. Very useful when you are creating a link to another site, not just a page within your current site.

—**self**—Brings the linked page up within the same frame the link appears within. Works identically to _top if you don't use frames in your Web design. This is the default value if none is selected.

—**Named Frame**—Brings up the link in a frame that has been named directly within HTML when the Web page was built. Substitute your actual frame name for "Named Frame."

As with the Image Mapper, Target properties are used only if you use frames in your Web design. Frames are a way of splitting your Web browser into multiple areas, with each area displaying a separate HTML file. Before experimenting with frames, you'll want to become more proficient with HTML or your Web design application.

If the **Include cell in table** checkbox is not selected, Paint Shop Pro will not store any properties for that cell.

Other Slicing Options

Besides using the slicing tools and setting the individual cell properties, you should be familiar with three other components in the Image Slicer Window:

► **Rollovers**—This option allows you to set up to six image rollovers for each cell. A rollover is a separate image that appears in that cell when one of six actions occur: Moving the mouse over the cell, moving the mouse out of the cell, clicking on the cell, double clicking on the cell, pushing your left mouse button down, and letting go of your left mouse button (See Chapter 14).

► **Format**—This is one of the advanced—and powerful—features of image slicing. You can individually save and optimize each cell within the image as a GIF, JPEG, or PNG. Since each format has its advantages, you may want to save part of the image as a JPEG while saving another part of the image as a GIF. For each cell, you can launch the Paint Shop Pro image optimizing wizards to control transparency, number of colors used, and download times. Each cell can have completely different attributes and even use different Web image formats.

CAUTION

Be careful selecting the **Apply optimization to whole image** checkbox. This checkbox *overrides* all individual cell optimization settings you have selected to order to optimize the entire image in a single step. This can have disastrous effects on a complicated sliced image where each cell is optimized for the best effects.

Another concern with optimizing each cell individually is that Paint Shop Pro might adjust the colors in each cell differently. That's because Paint Shop Pro will optimize each individual cell according to its specifications and that may change the color palette or final color appearance from one cell to another.

▶ **Preview in Web Browser**—This button loads the sliced image in your Web browser so you can test your slicing properties. For this feature to work properly, you must ensure that Paint Shop Pro can find the browser installed on your machine. Choose **File > Preferences > File** Locations from the Menu Bar and click on the **Web Browsers** tab.

Save your Settings and Sliced Image

One of the best parts of the image slicing tool is how easy it is to save your results. And you can save the positions of your slicing lines and individual cell properties as a separate file, enabling you to easily make changes to your sliced image in the future.

To save your sliced image, click on the **Save** button to bring up the **HTML Save As** dialog box (Figure 12.12).

Figure 12.12
Select where to save the HTML file and your sliced images.

For each sliced image, Paint Shop Pro generates an HTML file that controls exactly how each slice of your image appears. You must pick the file location and name the HTML file you want generated. Paint Shop Pro will then create the file and slice your image up into the appropriate cells automatically and save them in the same directory as the HTML file.

By default, each slice of your image will be named according to the cell number you created. For example, if you had an original image called **navigation.gif** and sliced it into four cells, the cells would be named **navigation_1×1.gif**, **navigation_1×2.gif**, **navigation_2×1.gif**, and **navigation_2×2.gif**. Figure 12.13 shows this example visually.

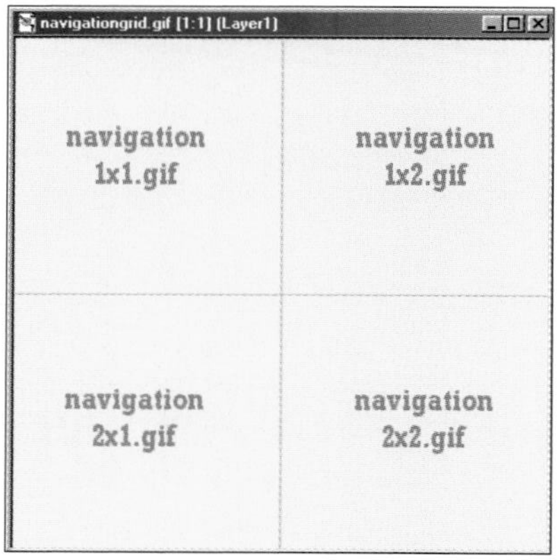

Figure 12.13
Each cell within your image is saved as a separate file.

You can also save your slicing settings for future use. You'll almost always want to save these, because you can reload them in the future if you need to make adjustments to the current image. Click on the **Save Settings** button to bring up the **Save Slice Settings** dialog box. Paint Shop Pro will automatically add a .JSD file extension to your settings file.

Using the Sliced Image

Once you've created the sliced image in Paint Shop Pro, the last step is to use it on your Web site. By default, Paint Shop Pro creates an HTML file with all of the proper codes for displaying the sliced image. Figure 12.14 shows an example of the code generated.

Figure 12.14
Creating this HTML code by hand would have been a very challenging and painstaking activity.

```
navbar.htm - Notepad
File  Edit  Search  Help

<HTML>
<HEAD>
<META NAME="Author" CONTENT="Default">
<META NAME="Generator" CONTENT="Jasc Paint Shop Pro 7">
<TITLE> </TITLE>
</HEAD>
<BODY>

<!-- Begin Table -->
<TABLE BORDER="0" CELLPADDING="0" CELLSPACING="0" WIDTH="300" HEIGHT="300">

<TR>
<TD ROWSPAN="1" COLSPAN="6" WIDTH="300" HEIGHT="19">
        <IMG NAME="navbar0" SRC="navbar_1x1.jpg" WIDTH="300" HEIGHT="19" BORDER="0"></TD>
</TR>

<TR>
<TD ROWSPAN="1" COLSPAN="1" WIDTH="27" HEIGHT="80">
        <IMG NAME="navbar1" SRC="navbar_2x1.jpg" WIDTH="27" HEIGHT="80" BORDER="0"></TD>
<TD ROWSPAN="1" COLSPAN="4" WIDTH="220" HEIGHT="80">
        <IMG NAME="navbar2" SRC="navbar_2x2.jpg" WIDTH="220" HEIGHT="80" BORDER="0"></TD>
<TD ROWSPAN="1" COLSPAN="1" WIDTH="53" HEIGHT="80">
        <IMG NAME="navbar3" SRC="navbar_2x3.jpg" WIDTH="53" HEIGHT="80" BORDER="0"></TD>
</TR>

<TR>
<TD ROWSPAN="1" COLSPAN="6" WIDTH="300" HEIGHT="21">
        <IMG NAME="navbar4" SRC="navbar_3x1.jpg" WIDTH="300" HEIGHT="21" BORDER="0"></TD>
</TR>

<TR>
<TD ROWSPAN="1" COLSPAN="6" WIDTH="300" HEIGHT="22">
        <A HREF="http://www.muskalipman.com/companyinfo.html"><IMG NAME="navbar5"
SRC="navbar_4x1.jpg" WIDTH="300" HEIGHT="22" BORDER="0" ALT="Company Info"></A></TD>
</TR>
```

You can use the sliced image in several ways, but here are the two most popular:

▶ **Load the HTML file in your favorite HTML editor**—You can add text, additional images, and all of the other Web components normally available to you. You'll do this if you are building a new page from scratch.

▶ **Load the HTML in Notepad, then select the HTML code and paste it into your editor**—You'll do this if you are adding the sliced image to an existing Web page. You will have to copy ALL of the HTML the text between the <TABLE> and </TABLE> tags.

Make sure that you move the images into the same directory as the final HTML file.

A Complete Slicing Example

Now that you understand the Image Slicing tool, I'm going to lead you through a complete example. We'll create a navigation bar for a Web page.

1. The first step is to create the image in Paint Shop Pro. For this example, I'll use the navigation bar I introduced in the previous section. Once you have the image loaded, Choose **F**ile > Export > **I**mage Slicer from the Menu Bar, Figure 12.15 shows us ready to start.

Figure 12.15
We're ready to create the sliced image.

2. Add some initial slicing lines by clicking on the **Grid** tool and clicking on the image preview window. Figure 12.16 shows the grid size dialog box. For this example, I'll enter 10×3.

Figure 12.16
I'm creating a grid with ten rows and three columns.

3. Using the **Arrow** tool, line up the precise locations of each grid line. Don't be afraid to zoom in and out to set precise locations for your lines.

4. For this example, I've also used the **Delete** and **Arrow** tools to create a box exactly around the book cover. This is because I want to save the book cover as a JPEG image—the most efficient file type for it—and the rest of the image as a GIF. Figure 12.17 shows my image with my grid lines properly set.

Figure 12.17
My seventeen cells are ready to have their individual cell properties set.

5. For each cell, set both the cell properties and the cell format. Each cell is linking visitors to a new Web page. Each cell will be optimized as a GIF image *except* for the cell with the book cover. The book cover uses many more colors than the rest of my graphic and would be better optimized as a JPEG. This step takes the longest amount of time, because you have to check and recheck your settings to ensure they are correct. I'm not setting rollover values in this example.

6. Preview your image in your Web browser and experiment by clicking on each cell to see if the results are correct.

7. Once you've finished setting your cell properties, click on the **S**ave button and save your HTML file and all of the sliced images.

8. The final step in this example is to edit the Web page that will contain the sliced image. Figure 12.18 shows the final page with the image.

Figure 12.18
The Image Slicer let you easily create this navigation bar.

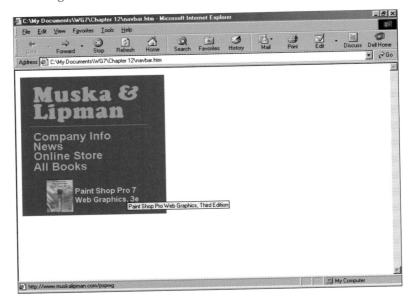

13

Animation on the Web

Normally, an image is loaded on your Web page and becomes a static part of the screen. These standard Web images are useful, but you can also create animations to drop directly into your Web page. Paint Shop Pro comes with a built-in tool to create animations—Animation Shop. This extra tool lets you "snap together" three or four images to make a simple animated graphic and helps you create complex animations with automated wizards.

This chapter describes Animation Shop and covers the best ways to build and incorporate animation into your Web tool belt. You'll learn how to create animations from scratch, how to convert static images into animated ones, and how to create those banner advertisements that are ubiquitous on the Internet—and make them attractive.

▶ **Building a GIF Animation**
Learn to quickly assemble multiple images into an animation file that you can place on your Web pages just like any other GIF.

▶ **Creating Great Banner Ads**
Animation Shop includes a Banner Ad Wizard. Learn this powerful tool and generate attractive and professional banner advertisements that adhere to Web standards.

▶ **Using Layers to Make a GIF Animation**
Learn to use layers in PSP to easily make the component images for an animation.

▶ **Optimizing GIF Animations**
Learn to use the Optimization Wizard to reduce the size of your GIF animation files—sometimes by as much as half the original size.

Understanding Web Animation

Web animation isn't exactly new technology. In fact, multi-frame animation was built into the GIF file format way back in 1989. But that functionality wasn't exposed until Web browsers became popular a few years ago. Now animation has become a very popular and easy way to enhance your Web site.

Basically, GIF animations work like flip books, where "animation" occurs as you flip rapidly through a sequence of pictures. If you've never created an animation of any kind before, you may not realize that the illusion of animation is achieved by showing several still images—called "frames"— in rapid succession. Each frame starts out as a separate file. Then, using a special tool and optimization process, these multiple files are combined into a single GIF file. You can control what appears in each frame, how long each frame appears, and how to load up the next frame in the animation. Not only are GIF animations easy to create, but they usually have reasonable file sizes—a cool animated icon can be 20KB or smaller.

Web browsers simply download the animated GIF as they would any other graphic on your Web page and show it as part of the page. You can include this animation in a Web page with the `<IMG>` tag, exactly as if the animation were an "ordinary" GIF.

GIF animations can have as many frames as you'd like, but keep in mind that each frame increases the overall file size. Often, you'll want to include a handful of frames for your animation and then have the browser continuously loop through your animation so you can get the effect of many frames without the extra download time.

TIP

There are many different ways to incorporate animation on your Web site. GIF animation is by far the most popular—and the only method covered in this book. Virtually all Web browsers support GIF animation without any problems or the need for additional configuration.

Another popular, more sophisticated, way to add animation to your Web site uses a technology called *Flash*. Flash is more of a true animation tool, with very fluid transitions. Flash animations must be created and viewed with special software. You can learn more about Flash by visiting **http://www.flash.com**.

Another way to add movement to a Web page is via Java and JavaScript. To learn more about building interactive Java animations, visit **http://gamelan.earthweb.com**, the center of all Java applets online. Similarly, a great JavaScript site is **http://javascripts.earthweb.com**.

Part IV Powerful Web Tools

Animation Shop Basics

To create animated GIFs, you must launch Animation Shop. Animation Shop integrates nicely with Paint Shop Pro, enabling you to create and edit individual frames—called "cels"—in PSP and update them automatically within Animation Shop.

The first step in building a GIF animation is to create a series of images to be displayed one after the other. Just save your images as GIFs for later assembly in Animation Shop. Figure 13.1 shows a simple set of two images that we'll use in this section to create an animation.

Figure 13.1
The original GIFs before the animation is made.

TIP

You'll find it easier to build and modify animations if you give the component images for each animation similar names. You might name the images for a dog animation dog1.gif, dog2.gif, dog3.gif, and so on. The two images in this example are named new1.gif and new2.gif.

The next step is to launch Animation Shop. You can launch it from Paint Shop Pro by selecting **File** > **J**asc Software Products > Run **A**nimation Shop. Alternatively, you can launch Animation Shop directly from your Windows Program menu. Create a new animation by selecting **File** > **N**ew from the Menu Bar. Figure 13.2 shows Animation Shop with a new animation ready to be developed.

Figure 13.2
Animation Shop is
ready to go to work.

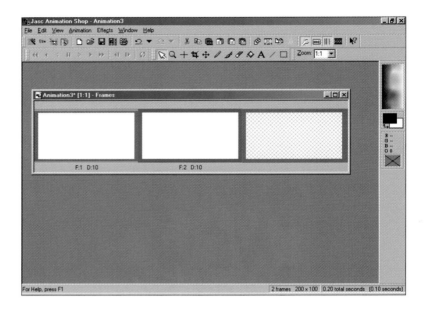

Creating with the Animation Wizard

The fastest way to create a simple GIF animation with Animation Shop is
to select **F**ile > Animation Wizard from the Menu Bar. This will start an
"interview" that leads you through several steps that will determine
automatically how to build your animation. If all of your frames are not
completed before launching the Animation Wizard, you'll be able to edit
them within Paint Shop Pro and even add new frames later on.

1   To create a new animation, select **F**ile > Animation Wizard or click
    on the **Animation Wizard** button on the Toolbar. You'll then see the
    first dialog box for the Animation Wizard (Figure 13.3), which asks
    for the dimensions of your animation. Select **S**ame size as the first
    image frame and then click **N**ext.

Figure 13.3
Step 1: in the
Animation Wizard:
Choosing the
animation size.

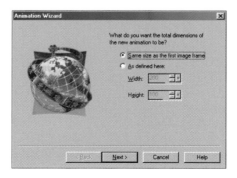

2. You're then asked to set the default canvas color for your frames (Figure 13.4), which can be either ***transparent*** or ***opaque***. For this example, we selected Opaque and chose white. When you've selected the canvas color, click **Next**.

Figure 13.4
Step 2: Picking a background color.

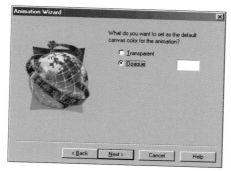

3. The next dialog box (Figure 13.5) asks how to position images in the frames and how to fill in any areas of a frame that aren't filled by an image you add to your animation. For image sets like the two in this example, all the components are the same size and each entirely fills its frame. Click **Next** to accept the defaults and continue.

Figure 13.5
Step 3: Filling in extra space.

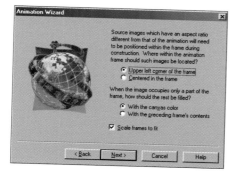

4. The next dialog box in the Animation Wizard asks how you want your animation to loop (Figure 13.6). You can have the animation loop indefinitely or loop only a specific number of times. I chose to repeat indefinitely.

NOTE
You can change the looping setting later on, after your animation is built, by selecting **Animation** > **Animation** Properties.

You can also set the **Display Time** in this dialog box. The default display time is 10/100 second. Here I chose 30/100 second. The display time is the length of time between the point at which a frame in an animation is first displayed and the point at which the next frame in the animation is displayed. When you've made your setting selections here, click **Next**.

Figure 13.6
Step 4: Play the animation once, or have it loop through?

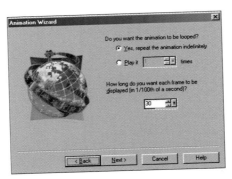

5. The next dialog box (shown in Figure 13.7) is where you add the component images to your animation. Add the first graphic by clicking the **A**dd Image button, then select and open the file from the selection list. Repeat this step for each component file.

    If you accidentally insert an incorrect file, just select that file and click the **R**emove Image button. You can select multiple files by holding down your Shift or Ctrl button when clicking on file names. When you've added all your component files, click **N**ext and then click **Finish**.

Figure 13.7
Step 5: Adding frames to your animation.

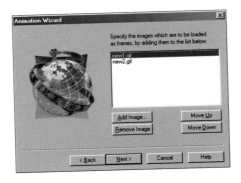

6. You'll then see a new "filmstrip," the workspace for creating your animated GIF. As shown in Figure 13.8, the filmstrip will contain each of the frames for your animation. Each frame has a label that indicates its frame number and display time.

Figure 13.8
The filmstrip provides a workspace for you to build your animated GIF.

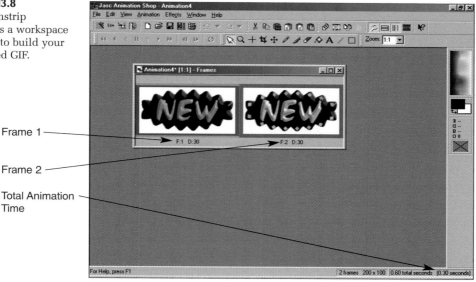

Frame 1

Frame 2

Total Animation Time

TIP
If at any point you decide you'd like to change the display time for any frame, right-click in the appropriate frame and choose **Frame Properties**. Go to the **Display Time** tab and reset the display time. Alternatively you can select **Animation > Frame Properties** from the Menu Bar.

Viewing Your Animation

Animation Shop lets you preview your newly created project two different ways. The easiest way is to choose **View > Animation** from the Menu Bar. Animation Shop will compile all of your cels and launch the animation directly. This lets you preview the actual appearance of your animation easily so you can verify the order of your frames, ensure that the proper time delays are set, and get a feeling for how the animation looks overall.

You'll also want to preview your animation within a Web browser. This lets you see how the animation will look on a Web page. Choose **View** > Preview in **W**eb Browser from the Menu Bar and you'll see the box shown in Figure 13.9.

Figure 13.9
Control how you'll preview your newly minted animation.

Leave the **Formats** setting as **Animated GIF** and make sure you select a browser in the **Web Browser** box. Although it may not be clear, iexplore.exe corresponds with Microsoft Internet Explorer. Once you've selected a browser, click on the **Preview** button. Figure 13.10 shows this animation running in Internet Explorer.

Figure 13.10
Animation Shop shows the animation and file size when previewing within a browser.

Saving Your Animation

Once your animation is created, don't forget to save it. Choose **F**ile > **S**ave from the Menu Bar to launch the Save As dialog box. Animation Shop allows you to save your animation in six different file formats:

▶ **GIF**—This is the ideal format for the Web. Animated GIFs are supported by virtually all Web browsers and this is the file format we focus on in this book.

▶ **MNG**—This is another industry standard animation format—and the one which supports the best compression levels. But because it has limited Web browser support, you'll use this format only when an animation is a work in process. When you've completed your animation, you will likely save it in another format.

▶ **FLC/FLI**—These two formats are supported by Autodesk software applications. You'll rarely save in these formats, but Animation Shop can read Autodesk animations and then let you edit them.

▶ **AVI**—This format is typically associated as the Microsoft Windows standard video format. This is a great solution when you are distributing larger animations to Windows users. The AVI format supports better transitions, but the file size is almost always larger than GIF. When you use this format, a special AVI Animation Wizard launches to configure some of the advanced settings available through this format.

▶ **ANI**—ANI is a special format that is used to create animated cursors on the Windows platform.

When you give your animation a name and click **S**ave, the Animation Optimization Wizard will be invoked (Figure 13.11). For now, accept the default settings for the Optimization Wizard by clicking on the **Next** button.

Figure 13.11
Animation quality versus file size is an important question to grapple with.

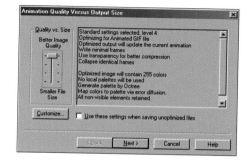

The Optimization Wizard shows you the results of your efforts, including the final file size and estimated download time for this animation. Figure 13.12 shows the Optimization Results for this simple GIF animation.

Figure 13.12
For this moving image, 11K is not too bad a file size.

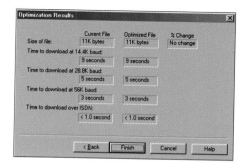

Add New Frames

If you decide that you'd like to add other frames to your animation, right-click on an existing frame and select Insert Frames > From File to bring up the **Insert Frames from Files** dialog box (Figure 13.13).

Figure 13.13
It's easy to add new frames to your animation.

You can then select the image (or series of images) that you want to add, much as you did earlier with the Animation Wizard. Set the **Insert Before** option to the frame number of the frame that should follow the newly inserted one. If you want your new frame to be the last frame in the animation, set this number to one more than the frame number of the current final frame. Set the Display Time as you like.

If you decide to delete any frames, simply right-click on the frame and select **D**elete.

Publishing Your Animation

Once your animation is complete, the final step is to add it to your Web page. Using your favorite Web page editor, make an HTML document with an IMG tag referring to the .gif file you just saved as the SRC (for example, for my "NEW" logo I might use `<IMG SRC="new-ani.gif">`). To see the results, load the document in your Web browser. Figure 13.14 shows the results of my animation efforts.

Figure 13.14
See the animation moving for real by visiting the book's home page.

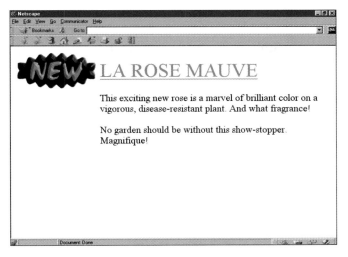

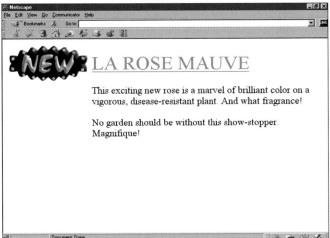

Part IV Powerful Web Tools

Using Layers to Make GIF Animations

When you are creating animations, it is very common to use the Paint Shop Pro layer tools. These tools make it easy for you to construct an image layer by layer and then convert each layer into a frame within your animation. Layering enables you to easily make changes to your entire image without building each frame individually.

We could have created each component image of the "NEW" animation in PSP as separate files, but what we did instead was create the files using PSP's layers. Layering allows you to keep various parts of an image on their own separate layers, where you can modify each independently. This makes drawing simple animations a breeze.

By way of example, let's step through how the "NEW" logo was created. To start, the button is the background layer. Then we made one version of the text for the Dark layer, then copied and edited that text layer to make the Light layer. Figures 13.15a and 13.15b show these two layers displayed separately, on top of the Button layer.

Figure 13.15a
The layered image with the Button and Dark layers visible.

Figure 13.15b
The layered image with the Button and Light layers visible.

To make the two component images for this animation, selectively hide each of the two text layers, one at a time. With the Button and the Dark layers visible, use **F**ile > Save **A**s to save these two visible layers as NEW1.GIF. Then hide the Dark layer and make the Light layer visible. Again, use **F**ile > Save **A**s to save the combined Button and Light layers as NEW2.GIF. The original file is saved in the PSP format as NEW.PSP, with all layering information for future reuse.

To make your own component GIFs with PSP's layers, you can try one of two approaches.

▶ Under one approach, you use one layer to draw your basic animated image and drag this layer to the New Layer icon in the Layers palette. Repeat as many times as you like to create multiple copies of the image. Adjust the details for each component image on each layer. Then, for the first component image, hide the layers you don't need and save what's visible. Do the same for each subsequent component image. You're then ready to assemble your component images in Animation Shop.

▶ The second approach is much like the first, except that here you draw the unchanging parts of your animation as the "lowest" layer, then draw only the changing parts on their own separate layers, one layer for each stage of movement. This approach is more common when you have multiple areas that change on different layers. Each layer represents just a single changed cell in your animation.

For more information on layers and how they work, see Chapter 10, "Using Layers."

Optimizing GIF Animations

When you save your animation as a GIF in Animation Shop, your animation will be optimized via the Optimization Wizard. The Optimization Wizard walks you through a set of dialog boxes in which you select settings to decrease animation file size. By default, the Optimization Wizard performs minimal optimization, but you can use the advanced options to control how and how much your animated GIF is optimized.

One way to reduce the size of your animated GIFs is to reduce the number of colors used in the component images. Optimization Wizard makes it easy for you to reduce the number of colors and choose the color palette for your animations.

Another way to reduce animation file size is to make transparent any part of the image that doesn't change. This reduces the size of the file because a solid region of transparency will compress much more efficiently than the same region filled with complex image data. You can readily accomplish this by setting Optimization Wizard to save only the part of the image that actually changes from one frame to the next, using only this smaller part instead of replacing the whole image in each frame.

You'll learn more about color reduction techniques in Chapter 7, "Optimizing Web Graphics," and about transparency in Chapter 6, "Creating Transparent Images."

NOTE

The entire image will show up in each frame of the filmstrip, even if you choose to replace unchanging parts with transparency.

Adjusting the Color Palette

When I created the component images for the "NEW" logo, I saved the files as GIFs, which by default have 256 colors. Animation Shop used as its palette the full 256 colors of the first component image when the "NEW" animation was saved. But this animation doesn't actually require 256 colors. So I decided to try reducing the number of colors using Animation Wizard.

I opened NEWANIMATION.GIF in Animation Shop and chose File > Optimization Wizard, which opens up a dialog box that asks which file format you want to optimize your animation for. Since we are focused on Web graphics in this book, select Animated GIF File. You can also decide whether you want to replace the current version of your animation or create a second, optimized version.

When you click the **N**ext button, you're shown the Animation Quality Versus Output Size dialog box (see Figure 13.16).

Figure 13.16
The Animation Wizard Animation Quality Versus Output Size window.

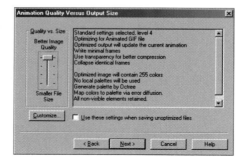

You can reduce the number of colors for your animation simply by pulling the Quality/Size Slider down, but for this example, we want to choose the specific number of colors by hand. So we clicked on the **C**ustomize button and went to the Colors tab instead (see Figure 13.17).

Figure 13.17
Tell Animation Shop how to manage colors in your final animation.

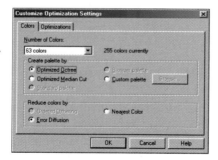

From the **N**umber of Colors list, you select the number of colors you want to use in the color palette for your animation. First, check in PSP to see how many colors the component images actually used. If you use only a handful of different colors, you can easily reduce the amount that are saved in the GIF animation.

For this example, the image quality of the animation wouldn't suffer to any noticeable degree if 63 colors was chosen. Incidentally, picking 63 colors from the Customize box corresponds exactly to the second setting from the bottom in the Animation Quality Versus Output Size dialog box.

Part IV Powerful Web Tools

TIP

Also in the Customize Optimization Settings dialog box are settings for method of palette creation and for method of color reduction. For 256-color GIFs that will be displayed on your Web pages, it's usually a good idea to see how your image appears using this palette. Since I was using fewer than 256 colors, the Browser option wasn't available to me. In this example, I picked *Optimized Octree* because it is a good general-purpose method for creating an optimized palette. Because we wanted to avoid dithering, we chose **Error Diffusion** for the color reduction method.

An animation that includes subtle gradations of color in its component images will look a lot better when dithered, although dithering creates slightly larger file sizes. For complex animations with lots of colors, try the Error Diffusion method to get approximations of all the colors, even when you use the browser-safe palette.

For most situations, though, you should use Animation Shop's nearest color algorithm to change all component images in the animation to solid, rather than dithered, colors. The colors might not look quite as pretty, but the resulting animated GIFs often come out a lot smaller and faster.

When you finish making adjustments to the color optimization settings, click **OK** to return to the Animation Quality Versus Output Size dialog box. Clicking **Next** then brings up the **Optimization Progress** window, then the **Optimization Preview** window. When the optimization finishes, you click **Next** to see what effect the optimization had on file size.

For the "NEW" logo, which started out as a 13KB file, this optimization produced a 6.5KB reduction in file size. That may not seem dramatic at first, but keep in mind that this is a 50 percent reduction in size for this image. That kind of result could translate into considerable savings with larger, more complex animations.

Mapping Identical Pixels to Transparent

Sometimes the most dramatic reduction in an animation's file size can be achieved by saving the unchanging parts of the animation once, then only rewriting pixels that change from frame to frame.

In many GIF animators, to take advantage of this file-size savings you must do all the cutting into pieces and positioning of the pieces by hand. Animation Shop makes things easy for you by doing all the work itself. All you have to do is provide all the full-frame versions of your component images and then make one selection in Optimization Wizard.

Here's an example. Suppose you have a multi-framed animation of a cartoon character that does nothing except roll its eyes. Figure 13.18 shows an example of a three-frame animation.

Figure 13.18
A multi-framed cartoon with a large unchanging area—only the eyes are animated.

To optimize this animation, fire up the **Optimization Wizard**, press the **Customize** button in the Animation Quality Versus Output Size dialog box, and click the **Optimizations** tab, shown in Figure 13.19.

Figure 13.19
The Optimizations tab of the Animation Wizard's Customize Optimization Settings window.

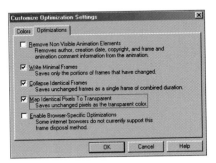

Then make sure that **Map Identical Pixels to Transparent** is selected. Make any other setting adjustments here or on the Colors tab, and run the optimization. That's all you need to do!

For this particular animation, CAT.GIF, the file size went from 15KB to about 11KB, a savings of about 23 percent. And when I also reduced the number of colors to 63, the file size dropped to 6KB—less than half the original file size. Don't be surprised if this technique provides you with similar—or even better—savings in file size.

Looping

Looping isn't directly relevant to optimization, but you should know one thing about looped animations that can affect both the quality and file size of your animated GIFs. Because of the way some browsers process and display multi-image GIF files, you will often find that the first frame of a looping animation is skipped or only half displayed, making a noticeable jerk or some other subtle-but-annoying effect.

The way to avoid this is to repeat the first image at the end of the animation. This way, the "jerk" becomes invisible because it occurs between two identical images. For example, an animation that has seven frames might contain only six different images, with the seventh being a repeat of the first.

Repeating the first image does increase the size of the GIF file, so you may be willing to tolerate a little jerkiness to keep the size down. Also, in some animations such as the "NEW" logo example, you never notice or care about the jerk anyway. So, it's a good idea to try the animation without the first image repeated to see whether you're happy with the results.

Special Animation Shop Techniques

Besides building GIF animations with layers and separate images, Animation Shop has several other innovative tools used to create cool animations for your Web site—Image Transitions, Image Effects, Text Effects, Video to Animation, and the Banner Wizard.

Each of these tools allows you to create professional looking animations quickly and automatically. In fact, you'll find yourself using these tools more regularly than most of the other Animation Shop tools when you need to create a down and dirty animation.

Image Transitions

Animation Shop comes with the ability to animate an image with any of twenty-six different transitions. By starting with an original image, you can tell PSP to build an animation that shakes, zooms, splits, blurs, explodes, dissolves, or more. Generally, you start with one or two images and then tell Animation Shop which image transition you want to apply. The image uses the technique you've selected and *transitions* itself into a second image—using from 1 to 500 frames of animation along the way. Animation Shop builds all the necessary frames automatically to achieve any of these twenty-six cool effects. I recommend it highly.

To jazz up any site in a matter of moments, open any image and select Effects > Insert Image Transition from the Menu Bar.

Figure 13.20 shows the **Insert Image Transition** dialog box that appears. This box shows the **Clock Wipe** transition being applied. Notice how Animation Shop shows the images you start and end with and builds a set of frames in between them. For the Clock Wipe transition, Animation Shop paints the new image on top of the first image as if a clock hand were sweeping away the original image.

Figure 13.20
Image Transitions are powerful and very simple to use.

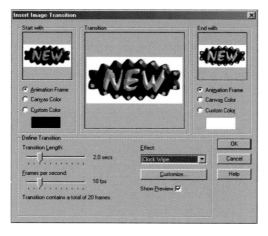

Animation Shop even shows you a live preview of the transition occurring on your image within the dialog box shown in Figure 13.20. Most of the Image Transitions can be configured by clicking on the button labeled **C**ustomize. You'll want to experiment and explore with this powerful feature. Figure 13.21 shows four frames from the animation that was created using the Clock Wipe transition.

Figure 13.21
Here are four images from the final Clock Wipe animation.

Image Effects

Similar to Image Transitions, Animation Shop also comes with twenty-one Image Effects. Effects are different because there is only a starting image—not a starting and ending image to work with. The Effect is focused on sprucing up the appearance of a specific single image and turning it into an animation.

You can apply Image Effects in two ways. The first way applies the effect to a single image or frame. In this way, Image Effects work almost identically as image transitions do. Animation Shop applies an effect on a single image and builds the animation automatically. Open an image in Animation Shop and then choose Effects > Insert Image Effects from the Menu Bar. Figure 13.22 shows the **Insert Image Effect** dialog box.

Figure 13.22
Image Effects create automated animations based on a single image.

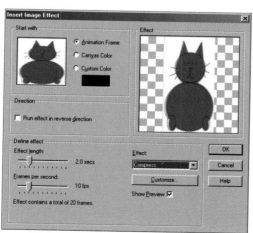

You can select effects like compress, explode, pinch, or spiral. Animation Shop will create a multi-frame animation based on the original image you opened. Like transitions, you can customize the way most image effects are applied.

The second way to apply an effect is across an entire animation. This is common when you have built a simple animation from scratch and want to add some type of final effect to it. Animation Shop applies the effect progressively in each frame of the animation you've created. It's common to build an animation from scratch, using the image transition, and then apply an image effect on the entire animation. To apply an effect to your animation, select the individual frames of your animation with your mouse, while holding down the **Shift** key. Once the entire animation is selected, choose Effects > Apply Image Effects from the Menu Bar (Figure 13.23).

Figure 13.23
Notice how the effect modifies each frame within your animation, not just the first one.

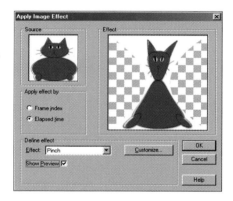

Figure 13.24 shows three frames from an animation which has had the Noise effect applied to it.

Figure 13.24
This animation effect was built after using an image transition.

Text Effects

Similar to Image Transitions and Effects, Text Effects are quick ways to build text-only animations or add textual movement to an existing animation. Text Effects don't require you to start with an original image; instead, you can just build an animation from a specific word or phrase. But you *can* start with an existing image to add animated text to it. Similar to Image Effects, you can create a text effect with a single image to build an animation from scratch, or you can add animated text to an existing animation.

The easiest way to experiment with Text Effects is with a new, blank image. Create a new file within Animation Shop and choose Effects > Insert Text Effect from the Menu Bar (Figure 13.25).

Figure 13.25
Control the color, font, size, and effect of your animated text.

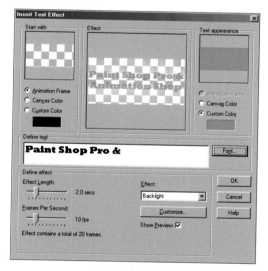

There are seven text effects you can select from: Backlight, Bouncing, Drop Shadow, Flag, Highlight, Marquee, and Wheel. Use the Font button to control specific text appearance and the Customize button to control the way animated text appears on the image.

It's common to add animated text to an existing still image. Figure 13.26 shows four frames from an animation that started with just a book cover and added text using the Marquee effect.

Figure 13.26
The text marquee added some variety to an ordinary still image.

The other way to add text animations is to add across an entire animation.

All seven text effects are available to add animated text to each frame progressively. To add a text effect to your animation, select the individual frames of your animation with your mouse, while holding down the **Shift** key. Once the entire animation is selected, choose Effects > Apply Text Effects from the Menu Bar.

Banner Wizard

Another useful animation tool is the Banner Wizard. This handy tool lets you easily create animated banner advertisements that meet industry standards. We're all familiar with banner ads—they are the commercials found on many Web pages. The most common banner ad appears at the top of a Web page and is rectangular. But there are a handful of other standard banner-size ads that you can create.

Creating banner ads used to be a painstaking process of building frames individually. Animation Shop greatly simplifies this process with the Banner Wizard.

Before you launch the Banner Wizard, you first must come up with a concept and goal for your banner advertisement. Some ads are meant to be educational—text and simple images may be enough of an enticement. Other ads require significant thought and pre-work to ensure that you have the proper graphics and have selected the best advertisement copy. To create an animated banner, follow these steps.

1. Launch the Banner Wizard by choosing **F**ile > Banner Wizard from the Menu Bar. Figure 13.27 shows the first step in this process.

Figure 13.27
Pick a background color or image for your banner advertisement.

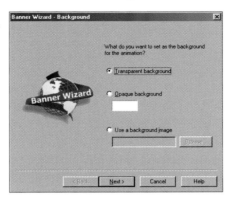

2. You can start with a simple background color or an image. If you select an image, make sure it is sized appropriately to the size of the banner ad you wish to create. For this example, we'll select an image using the Browse button—we're creating a fairly traditional banner advertisement. Then click on the **N**ext button.

3. Now you must select the size of your banner advertisement (Figure 13.28). Animation Shop lets you create advertisements in the six traditional banner ad sizes: Full Banner, Half Banner, Vertical Navbar, Vertical, Square Button, and Micro Button. The sizes are important, because if you place your advertisement on another site as a link to you, you'll have to create the *correct* banner. Some sites use only Full Banners, while others support Square, Micro, and even Vertical banner advertisements as well. You can also pick a custom-sized banner advertisement, but that typically defeats the purpose of building an animation that adheres to industry standards.

Figure 13.28
We'll pick a Full Banner for this example.

4. Next you control the animation timing. You can control animation length, number of frames, and looping properties. Select your timing options and click on the **N**ext button.

5. The Banner Wizard supports the automatic addition of text to your banner (Figure 13.29). Although sometimes convenient, we recommend that you usually skip this step and add text using the Text Effects options previously described. You'll have better controls on how text appears on your banner animation in this fashion. But, if you'd like to add text, you can add it here and control its appearance with the next three steps. You'll control the text font in Step 1, text color in Step 2, and text effect in Step 3.

Figure 13.29
You can add text to your banner automatically, but we recommend doing this as a separate step once you've finished the Banner Wizard.

6. Once you've added text to your Banner, Animation Shop creates the advertisement automatically.

Remember that this is just a starting point for you. Don't be afraid to add image or text effects, edit individual frames directly in Paint Shop Pro, or tweak the timing and looping controls for your frames. Remember to keep your eye on the animation file size and to use the Optimization Wizard when you are complete. Above all, remember that a good advertisement causes people to click on it, so create a compelling message!

Video to Animation

The final useful effect that Animation Shop lets you easily accomplish is converting a video clip into a GIF animation. You can open any .AVI file with Animation Shop and it will automatically be converted into a GIF animation format. Visitors who stop by your Web site will see only a cool-looking GIF file instead of a special video clip that sometimes requires extra software to view and extra time to download, depending on the Web browser they are using.

To convert .AVI files into animations, simply choose **File > O**pen from the Animation Shop Menu Bar. Then select a .AVI file to open and Animation shop brings up the **AVI Import Options** dialog box (Figure 13.30)

Figure 13.30
AVI files quickly convert into animation format.

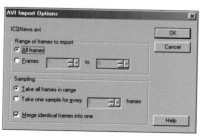

AVI files are the standard video format for Windows and are commonly used by personal video cameras that connect to your computer. Once these files are converted, you can save them as animated GIFs and use them on your Web page. Be careful, though—converted AVI clips can often be relatively large, because they tend to require a lot of individual frames to appear properly as a GIF animation.

Deciding When to Use GIF Animations

You should consider two factors when deciding whether or not to include GIF animations on your Web pages.

▶ Will the animations have a significant effect on the download time for your page?

▶ Will the animation or group of animations add to or detract from the usability and aesthetics of your page?

Animated GIFs almost always have relatively large file sizes compared to similar static Web images. So keep an eye on the file size of your animations—and make liberal use of the optimization techniques discussed in this chapter.

As for usability and aesthetics, your animated GIFs should add to the users' enjoyment of your site, not be something that drives them away. Unless the point of your site is to make users' heads spin, you'll want to keep your animations reasonably tame and the number of different animations on a page fairly small. A subtle animated logo or a few small animated attention-getters that point out new additions to your page might be a nice touch that even repeat visitors will appreciate. And a tasteful advertising banner might be fine. But a dozen harsh, clashing buttons, icons, and banners might send your visitors dashing off to someplace more serene. Visit some sites that include GIF animations and see for yourself what works and what doesn't.

To get some ideas for making your own GIF animations, you might also want to visit sites that have animation collections available for download. A place to start is **http://www.agag.com/**, home of the Animated GIF Artists Guild (Figure 13.31). The AGAG site not only has links to animated GIF collections but also tutorials and tips on making your own animated GIFs.

Figure 13.31
Learn everything about building and using great animated GIFs at the AGAG site.

14

Creating
Rollovers

This chapter introduces you to rollovers and teaches you how to make them for yourself in Paint Shop Pro.

▶ **Learn What Rollovers Are**
You see them everywhere: place your mouse over a button and the button glows. Press the button and it looks like it really has been pressed down. These are just a few examples of rollovers.

▶ **Get Acquainted with PSP's Rollover Creator**
Paint Shop Pro's Rollover Creator helps you make a JavaScript rollover even if you don't know the first thing about JavaScript!

▶ **Examine the Code that the Rollover Creator Creates**

If you're already familiar with JavaScript, you're certain to be interested in seeing the code that PSP produces. And even if you're unfamiliar with JavaScript, taking a look at the code can help you understand how and why your rollovers behave as they do.

Understanding Rollovers

A rollover is an operation that is activated by a mouse-related action performed on a link, such as positioning the mouse over a link or clicking on a link. Rollovers are coded with a scripting language, such as JavaScript, and can be applied to image links as well as text links. Table 14.1 shows the mouse-related events that can be used to trigger rollovers.

Table 14.1

Event	Description
Mouse over	Position the mouse cursor over the link.
Mouse out	Move the mouse away from the link.
Mouse click	Click on the link. That is, press the mouse button down and release.
Mouse double-click	Double-click on the link. That is, click twice in rapid succession.
Mouse down releasing.	Press the mouse button down without
Mouse up	Release the mouse button (following a mouse down).

Paint Shop Pro's Rollover Creator, available in both the Image Slicer and the Image Mapper, produces JavaScript code that you can incorporate into your own Web pages, making rollover creation a breeze even if you don't know anything about JavaScript. We'll look at a couple of examples of what you can do with rollovers and how to create them in PSP.

Creating a Simple Rollover

The simplest rollover involving images is one where one image replaces another when the mouse cursor is positioned over the original image. An example is shown in Figures 14.1 and 14.2.

Figure 14.1
Here's what you see when you first load the page.

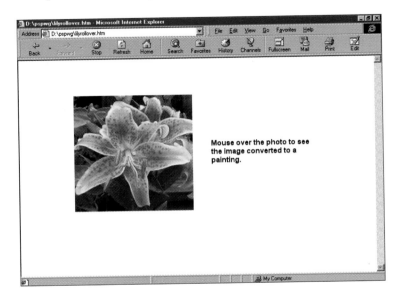

Figure 14.2
And here's what you
see when you mouse
over the image.

Making a mouse over like this in PSP is quite easy. First, make the two
versions of the image. Then in PSP open the first version—the version
that you want to be presented when your page first loads. Next, choose
File > **Export** > **Image Slicer**. You'll then see the Image Slicer dialog box,
shown in Figure 14.3.

Figure 14.3
To make a simple
rollover, open up the
Image Slicer.

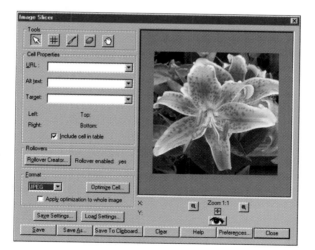

You're not actually going to slice this image, and you're also not going to provide a URL for the link associated with the rollover. What PSP will do is create a dummy link for you that will simply reload the current page and display the new image. So all you need to do in the Cell Properties pane of the **Image Slicer** dialog box is select **I**nclude cell in table.

NOTE
The link that Image Slicer creates for the rollover is needed only because the JavaScript code for the rollover is embedded as the value of an attribute of the <A> tag. For example, a mouse-over event is represented in your HTML code as the attribute onMouseOver, and the value that PSP assigns to this attribute is JavaScript code defining the action to be taken when a mouse-over event occurs.

The only other control you need to set is **Format** (which can be set to either GIF, JPEG, or PNG). Choose the format that you want for your image and then press the Optimize Cell button to optimize your image for the Web.

Now you're ready to make the rollover! Press the Rollover Creator button to bring up the **Rollover Creator** dialog box, shown in Figure 14.4.

Figure 14.4
The Rollover Creator lets you choose the rollover events you want to use and the images to use with each rollover.

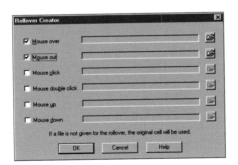

For this simple rollover, choose two events: **M**ouse over and **M**ouse out. For the Mouse over event, you need to choose the second version of your image. To do so, click the **File Open** icon to the far right of the Mouse over control. This brings up the **Select Rollover** dialog box, shown in Figure 14.5. Select the image file that you want to use for Mouse over, and then click **O**pen.

Figure 14.5
Choose the file that
you want displayed for
Mouse over.

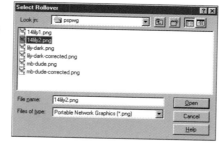

CAUTION

The dimensions of the image file you choose for a rollover should match the
dimensions of the original image file. Otherwise, the image displayed in your
rollover will be shrunk or stretched to those dimensions by the user's Web
browser.

At that point, you return to the Rollover Creator dialog box. Notice how
the path and filename for the image you just selected now show up in the
text box between the Mouse over checkbox and the **File Open** icon for
Mouse over (see Figure 14.6). Since you haven't selected a file for Mouse
out, your original file will be used for this rollover event, which occurs
when you move the mouse cursor away from the link.

Figure 14.6
The name of the file
you selected now shows
up in the Mouse over
textbox.

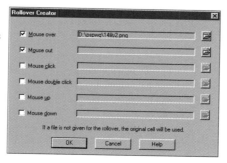

Now click **OK** to return to the Image Slicer dialog box. The only thing left to do is to save your HTML code for this rollover. Click either the **S**ave or **Save As** button. You then see the **HTML Save As** dialog box, shown in Figure 14.7. Enter a name for the HTML file that you want to save your code to and then click **S**ave.

Figure 14.7
Enter a name for the HTML file in which you want your rollover code to be saved.

Exit the Image Slicer by pressing the **Close** button. To take a look at the HTML file for your rollover, open the file with your favorite ASCII text editor or HTML editor. You can then add HTML code to this file or copy the rollover code and paste it into an existing HTML file. Figure 14.8 shows the code for our example in Lori's favorite text editor.

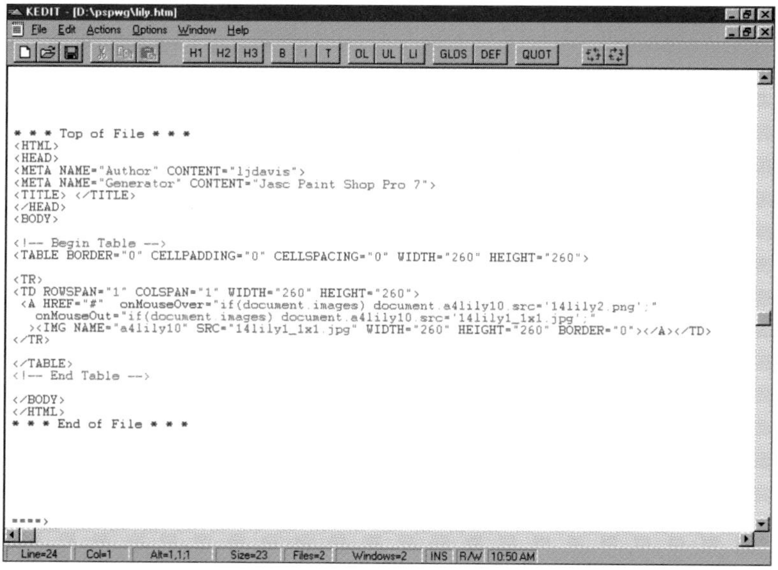

Figure 14.8
You can edit your newly created HTML file in any text editor or HTML editor.

Let's take a brief look at this code. The `<IMG>` tag is surrounded by an `<A HREF>` tag and a `</A>` end tag. The value of `HREF` is `"#"`, which means that clicking the link will simply reload the current page. The `<A HREF>` tag also contains two other attributes, `onMouseOver` and `onMouseOut`:

```
<A HREF="#"
onMouseOver="if(document.images) document.alily10.src='14lily2.png';"
onMouseOver="if(document.images) document.alily10.src='14lily1_121.png';"
>
```

For `onMouseOver`, the JavaScript code begins with `if(document.images)`, which tests to see if the user's browser is one that supports JavaScript's Image object. Don't worry if you don't know what that means. It's simply a test to make sure that the rollover code can be interpreted by the user's browser. If not, the script ends and no action is taken.

NOTE

An Image object isn't an actual image file. It's an abstract entity that JavaScript creates under certain circumstances—in particular, whenever JavaScript encounters an `IMG` tag in an HTML file. An Image object can have several properties, including a name (whose value is set with the `NAME` attribute of the `IMG` tag) and a source (whose value is set with the `SRC` attribute of the `IMG` tag).

Next comes `document.a4lily10.src='14lily2.png';` (note that the semicolon is part of the code). Notice in the `<IMG>` tag that there's a `NAME` attribute, and the value of `NAME` is `a4lily10`. The Rollover Creator automatically generated this attribute-value pair, and the value of `NAME` is what JavaScript uses to refer to the Image object. You can change what image is displayed by changing the source file for the named Image object. That's exactly what `document.a4lily10.src='14lily2.png'` does: It changes the source (`SRC`) of the Image object named `a4lily10` from `14lily1.jpg` to `14lily2.png`. When that switch is made, the displayed image changes to `14LILY2.PNG`.

For `onMouseOut`, JavaScript switches things back to the way they were originally. Here, `document.a4lily10.src='14lily1_1×1.jpg'` sets the source of the Image object named `a4lily10` to `14lily1_1×1.jpg`, the image that was originally displayed.

All rollovers work in much the same way. Each Image object that has a rollover is given a name. JavaScript then uses the name to refer to that Image object. When `.src` is tacked on to the name, JavaScript is referring to the source image associated with the Image object. Setting a new value for the Image object's source changes the image that is displayed on the Web page.

Creating a Navigation Bar with Rollovers

Now let's try something only slightly more complicated. Suppose we wanted to replace the individual buttons we used for the Old Leaf Inn site that we created in Chapter 8, "Coordinating Web Graphics," with a solid navigation bar like the one shown in Figure 14.9. This bar has four clickable areas, matching the pieces of text on the bar. When the user mouses over one of these clickable areas, the text glows. And when the user clicks on one of these areas, the relevant linked page loads.

Figure 14.9
You can create rollovers for an image bar with the Rollover Creator.

Here's how to make this image bar and its rollovers:

1. Create a new image that is as large as you want your navigation bar to be. In our example, the bar is 400×40 pixels.

2. Choose the **Picture Tube** tool and, in the Tool **O**ptions palette, set the tube to Autumn Leaves, with Scale set to 50 percent. Fill the new image with leaves. Then choose Effects > **3**D Effects > **I**nner Bevel to add a bevel to the bar. In the example here, we used the same Inner Bevel settings that were used for the header of the Old Leaf Inn Site (see Chapter 8, "Coordinating Web Graphics").

3. Add a new **Layer** to your image and then on the new layer use the **Text** tool to add the text to the bar. We used the same formal font that was used for the header of the Old Leaf Inn site.

4. Add any effects to the text that you like. For example, we used a black Drop Shadow. The result will look something like Figure 14.10.

Part IV Powerful Web Tools

Figure 14.10
First create the image for the basic navigation bar.

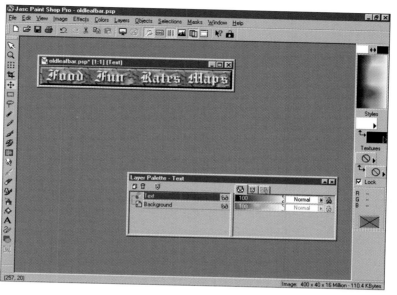

5. Save this file in PSP format, but don't close it. Instead, duplicate the file with **W**indow > **D**uplicate (or press **Shift+D**).

6. Make the text layer in the duplicated image the active layer. Modify the text in whatever way you want for Mouse over events. We added white drop shadow (with Vertical and Horizontal both set to 0) and lightened the text a bit. See Figure 14.11.

Figure 14.11
Also create a version for your rollovers.

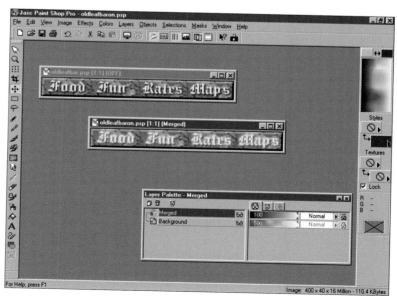

7. Save this file, giving it a name like that of the original file but with some indication that this is the Mouse-over version. In our example, we named the original file OLDLEAFBAR.PSP and the Mouse-over version OLDLEAFBARON.PSP (where "ON" indicates that this is what the buttons will look like when they're "on").

8. Now it's time to slice up that bar. Make sure OLDLEAFBARON.PSP is the active image by clicking on its title bar. Then choose **File** > Expor**t** > **I**mage Slicer to open the Image Slicer dialog box.

9. Next, click the hash mark icon. With this tool, click in the preview window. This brings up the **Grid Size** dialog box, show in Figure 14.12. For this bar, set **R**ows to 1 and **C**olumns to 4, then click **OK**.

Figure 14.12
Set the number of rows and columns in the Grid Size dialog box.

10. Now you want to save these slice settings for use later on, so click the Save Settings button. In the Save Slice Settings dialog box, enter a name for your settings file (as in Figure 14.13). Then click **S**ave.

Figure 14.13
Save your grid settings for later use.

11. Next, optimize the cells. Select Appl**y** optimization to whole image, and then click the Optimi**z**e Cell button. When the Optimization wizard opens, optimize the image. (For more information on the Optimization Wizard, see Chapter 7, "Optimizing Web Graphics.")

12. You then need to save the individual cell images sliced from OLDLEAFBARON.PSP. To do so, click the **S**ave or Save **A**s button. This saves the cells and prompts you to enter a name for your HTML file. You don't really need an HTML file associated with these images, just the images themselves, so you can enter a dummy name here.

Click **S**ave to exit the **HTML Save As** dialog box, and then click **Close** to exit the Image Slicer.

Part IV Powerful Web Tools

13. You're now done with OLDLEAFBARON.PSP and can close the file. Make OLDLEAFBAR.PSP the active file, clicking on its title bar if you need to. Then open up Image Slicer with **File** > Export > **I**mage Slicer.

14. Click the Loa**d** Settings button, and in the **Load Slice Settings** dialog box, select the settings file you just saved (see Figure 14.14). Then click the **O**pen button.

Figure 14.14
Load your previously saved Grid settings.

15. The first cell of the table is selected. Enter a URL for this cell. Set **F**ormat (GIF is used in our example) and select Appl**y** optimization to whole image. Click the Optimize Cell button. When the Optimization wizard opens, optimize the image.

16. With the first cell selected, press the Rollover Creator button. In the Rollover Creator dialog box, check **M**ouse over and **M**ouse out. For Mouse out, you want to use the original image, so there's nothing more you need to do for that event. For Mouse over, you need to select the "on" version of the Food button, so press the **File Open** icon at the far right of the Mouse over control.

17. In the **Select Rollover** dialog box, select OLDLEAFBARON_1×1.GIF, the image created from the first cell of OLDLEAFBARON.PSP when you saved the cells of that version. Press the **O**pen button to return to the Rollover Creator dialog box. The path and file id for OLDLEAFBARON_1×1.PSP now shows up in the textbox between the Mouse over checkbox and its associated **File Open** icon. Press **OK** to return to the Image Slicer dialog box.

18. With the **Arrow** tool, click the next cell to select it. Then repeat steps 15-17 for this cell, entering the URL for the Fun button and selecting OLDLEAFBARON_1×2.GIF for the Mouse over. Then repeat the same steps for the cell containing the Rates button (using OLDLEAFBARON_1×3.GIF for the Mouse over) and then for the cell containing the Maps button (using OLDLEAFBARON_1×4.GIF for the Mouse over).

19. When you're done setting the rollovers for each of the buttons on the navigation bar, press the **S**ave or Save **A**s button in the Image Slicer dialog box. In the **HTML Save As** dialog box, enter a name for your HTML file. We named ours OLDLEAFBAR-TABLE.HTM.

20. You can then open the HTML file in your favorite text editor or HTML editor. Figure 14.15 shows the HTML file in my text editor.

Figure 14.15
The HTML file contains the table for the navigation bar and its rollovers, ready to be copied and pasted into the Old Leaf Inn home page.

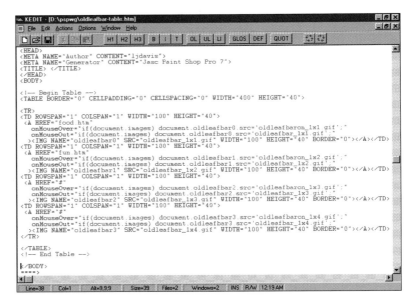

NOTE

In Figure 14.15, lines were split at the `onMouseOver` attribute so you can see all the text on each line. This does not affect how the code works, since anywhere that you have a space inside an HTML tag, you can have a linebreak instead.

More Ideas

What you've looked at so far in this chapter are pretty simple, straightforward rollovers. With a little finessing, you can also use PSP's Image Slicer and Rollover Creator to create more complex navigation controls, such as the navigation interface shown in Figure 14.16 and 14.17.

Figure 14.16
You can use the Rollover creator to make a navigation interface for a site.

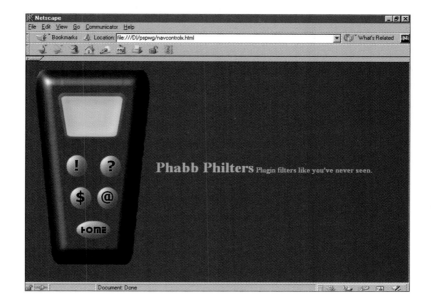

Figure 14.17
A mouse over in this navigation interface modifies not only a button but the screen as well.

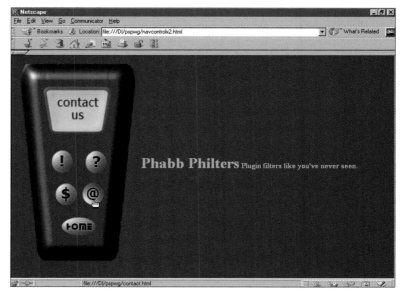

The steps for creating the navigation interface image and the rollovers for the interface are a little too long and complicated to present here. But if you're interested in seeing how such an interface can be made, head over to **http://loriweb.pair.com/interface.html**.

In addition to being available as part of the Image Slicer, the Rollover Creator is also available in PSP's Image Mapper, allowing you to create rollovers for your image maps. Be aware, though, that what gets replaced in an image map rollover isn't a small piece of a sliced image, as is the case with most Image Slicer rollovers. With Image Map rollovers, it's the whole image map that gets replaced during a rollover. Still, in certain circumstances this can come in handy.

Experiment with the Rollover Creator, both in the Image Slicer and in the Image Mapper, and see how rollovers can liven up your Web site!

Appendices

Appendix A
Resources on the Web

APPENDICES

This appendix lists all of the URLs covered in this book and many others that may be of interest to you as a reader and Paint Shop Pro user.

The most important URL for you to remember is the home page for this book, where we'll always keep an updated set of links, examples, and more. Here are some of the most important sites mentioned:

http://www.muskalipman.com/graphics
Home Page for *Creating Paint Shop Pro Web Graphics, Third Edition*

http://www.jasc.com
Jasc Software Inc. Home Page—download Paint Shop Pro here

http://www.shafran.com
Andy Shafran's Home Page

Cool Sites

There are many cool sites on the Web, and we mentioned many of them in this book. (We define a "cool" site as one that uses graphics in a creative or innovative fashion.) Here are some sites to visit:

Larger Example Sites

http://www.amazon.com
Site where you can purchase books online

http://www.yahoo.com
Yahoo! (What more needs to be said?)

http://www.cnn.com
CNN Online

http://www.llbean.com
L.L. Bean

http://www.covergirl.com
Cover Girl Makeup Home Page

Smaller Example Sites

http://www.timberwolfalaska.com
TimberWolf Gifts

http://www.siriusweb.com/BeginningExperience/
Beginning Experience Page

http://www.airplane.com
Airplane Home Page

http://www.flower.com
Flower.com

http://www.zebra.com
Zebra Softwear

http://www.thedca.org
Dalmatian Club of America

http://www.photogs.com/bwworld/index.html
Black and White World Magazine

Great Graphics Resources

This section lists many important sites that are useful when creating your own graphics. You'll find sites for scanners, graphics tools, reference information, and more.

PSP Users Groups and Newsletters

http://www.psppower.com
pspPower newsletter (really cool—and free)

http://www.pspug.org
Paint Shop Pro Users Group

http://www.pspiz.com
PSP Interactive Zone

Web Hosting Sites

http://www.register.com

Regsiter your domain name and host your site

http://www.siteamerica.com

Site America—an affordable place for Web hosting

http://wwwx.nbci.com/mywebsite/

NBCi.com (used to be Xoom.com)

http://geocities.yahoo.com

GeoCities—the original spot on the Web for free space

http://www.tripod.lycos.com/

Tripod

http://www.pair.com

Cool Development Sites

http://www.websitegarage.netscape.com

Web Site Garage

http://www.jasc.com/resources.asp

Graphic resources from Jasc

http://www.gamelan.com

Gamelan, home to Java Applets

http://www.javascripts.com

JavaScripts.com—home to thousands of JavaScript snippets

http://www.alienskin.com

Alien Skin Software

http://www.agag.com

Animated GIF Artists Guild

http://www.thepluginsite.com

Useful Sites for Digitizing Images

http://www.hp.com/peripherals.main.html
Home of HP printing and imaging products

http://www.microtekusa.com/
Home of Microtek scanners and accessories

http://www.hsdesign.com/scanning/
Sullivan's Online Scanning Resources and Tips—great place to learn some advanced scanning techniques

http://www.kodakpicturenetwork.com
Kodak Picture Network

http://www.play.com
Snappy Video Digitizer

http://www.commrex.com/scantutorial/index.html
PSP Scanning Tutorial

Graphics Collections

http://icons.simplenet.com/backgroundmain.htm
A-1 Clipart Archive

http://www.dewa.com/freeicon/
Free Icon Collection

http://www.iconbazaar.com/backgrounds/
Icon Bazaar

http://www.graphicsmaps.com
Graphic Maps—great map images for free

http://members.tripod.com/~Steffie1967/
Creative Graphics

http://www.mccannas.com/index.html
Laurie McCanna's Free Art Site

http://www.pixelfoundry.com//bgs.html
Pixel Foundry Background Archive

http://www.sru.edu/depts/ltus/images/backgr/index.htm
Slippery Rock University of Pennsylvania Background Collection

http://www.geocities.com/BourbonStreet/9584/buttonpage.html
The Button Shop

http://www.ender-design.com/rg/
Realm Graphics Library

http://www.aestheticweb.com/backgrounds/backgrounds.html
Versa-tiles Backgrounds

http://www.geocities.com/heartland/1448/
Iconz Library

http://www.nightflight.com/htdocs/tland/textures.html
Texture Land

http://infinitefish.com/texture.html
Infinite Fish Seamless Textures

http://webweaverxxi.com/wallpaper/
Wallpaper Works

http://glorianon.prohosting.com/backindex.html
Glorianon's Background World

PSP Tips and Tutorials

http://www.psppower.com/tutorials/
Tips from past issues of pspPower

http://www.geocities.com/~jburton/grab_bag_page.html
Jeff's Paint Shop Pro Tips

http://graphicssoft.about.com/compute/graphicssoft/cs/paintshoppro/index.htm
About.com's guide to Paint Shop Pro

http://psptips.com
Tips for using PSP from Abstract Dimensions

http://www.geocities.com/Heartland/Plains/9871/PSPlinks.html
Links to a wide range of tutorials. Maintained by Angela M. Cable.

http://www.apmagic.com/
APMagic

http://www.loriweb.pair.com
Lori's Web graphics

http://bysarah.com/mg/
Sarah's Making Graphics

http://www.c-gate.net/~msmith/psp.html
Marvin's Tutorials

http://members.nbci.com/psp5p/
Paint Shop Pro Papers

http://www.digital-foundry.com/index_paintshop.html
Paint Shop Pro Foundry

http://www.fortunecity.com/victorian/byzantium/260/sandbox.html
Visual Sonnets Sandbox

http://www.actden.com/grap_den/index.htm
Graphics Den

http://digitoils.com/howdo.html
Digitoils Tutorials

http://www.mardiweb.com/web/
Web Graphics on a Budget

http://members.nbci.com/fwagoner/
Wagoner Web Design

http://www.designsbydonna.com/tutorials/tutorials.html
Designs by Donna

http://members.tripod.com/~jkhart/home.html
Inside Paint Shop Pro

http://www.valsvisions.com/
Val's Visions

http://www.pspbook.com/
PSP Resources

http://desktoppublishing.com/tipspsp.html
Paint Shop Pro Tips and Techniques

http://members.aol.com/psptopten/topten.html
Tips and answers from **news: comp.graphics.apps.paint-shop.pro**

Appendix B
PSP Keyboard Shortcuts

PSP Keyboard Shortcuts

Shortcut	Function
A	Freehand Selection tool ("lasso")
B	Paintbrush tool
D	Deform tool
E	Eraser tool
F	Flood Fill tool
G	Zoom ("magnifying glass")
I	Draw tool
J	Arrow tool
K	Scratch Remover tool
M	Magic Wand tool
N	Clone Brush tool
Q	Vector Object Selection tool
R	Crop tool
S	Selection tool
U	Airbrush tool
V	Mover tool
W	Overview window
X	Text tool
Y	Dropper tool
C	Hide/Restore Color Palette
H	Hide/Restore Histogram

APPENDICES

Shortcut	Function
L	Hide/Restore Layer Palette
O	Hide/Restore Tool Options palette
P	Hide/Restore Tool Palette
T	Hide/Restore Toolbar
Tab	Hide/Restore floating palettes
Del	Clear canvas/layer
Spacebar	Step through tools
. (period)	Picture Tube
, (comma)	Color Replacer
/ (slash)	Preset Shapes
Shift+A	Full Screen Edit
Shift+B	Brightness/Contrast
Shift+C	Start Capture
Shift+D	Duplicate Window
Shift+E	Equalize (Histogram function)
Shift+G	Gamma Correction
Shift+H	Hue/Saturation/Lightness
Shift+I	Current Image Information
Shift+K	Invert Mask
Shift+L	Colorize
Shift+M	Highlight/Midtone/Shadow
Shift+O	Load Palette
Shift+P	Edit Color Palette
Shift+R	Crop to Selection
Shift+S	Resize Image
Shift+T	Stretch (Histogram function)
Shift+U	Red/Green/Blue
Shift+V	View Palette Transparency
Shift+W	New Window
Shift+Y	Hide All (Mask)
Shift+Z	Posterize
Shift+right arrow	Move selection right

Shortcut	Function
Shift+left arrow	Move selection left
Shift+up arrow	Move selection up
Shift+down arrow	Move selection down
Ctrl+right arrow	Move selection right
Ctrl+left arrow	Move selection left
Ctril+up arrow	Move selection up
Ctrl+down arrow	Move selection down
Ctrl+Shift+right arrow	Move selection right 10 pixels
Ctrl+Shift+left arrow	Move selection left 10 pixels
Ctrl+Shift+up arrow	Move selection up 10 pixels
Ctrl+Shift+down arrow	Move selection down 10 pixels
Ctrl+A	Select All
Ctrl+B	Browse
Ctrl+C	Copy
Ctrl+D	Deselect (Select none)
Ctrl+E	Paste as New Selection
Ctrl+F	Float Selection
Ctrl+G	Paste as New Vector Selection
Ctrl+H	Feather Selection
Ctrl+I	Flip Image
Ctrl+K	Edit Mask
Ctrl+L	Paste as New Layer
Ctrl+M	Mirror
Ctrl+N	New file
Ctrl+O	Open file
Ctrl+P	Print
Ctrl+R	Rotate Image
Ctrl+S	Save file
Ctrl+T	Set Transparent Color
Ctrl+V	Paste as New Image
Ctrl+W	Fit to Window
Ctrl+X	Cut

APPENDICES

Ctrl+Y	Repeat
Ctrl+Z	Undo
Ctrl+(layer number)	Select as Current Layer
Ctrl+Alt+G	Toggle Grid
Ctrl+Alt+N	Normal Viewing
Ctrl+Alt+R	Toggle Rulers
Ctrl+Alt+V	View Mask
Ctrl+Alt+Z	Redo
Ctrl+F12	Save Copy As
Ctrl+Del	Delete file
Shift+Ctrl+A	Full Screen Preview
Shift+Ctrl+B	Create Selection from Vector Object
Shift+Ctrl+C	Copy Merged Layers
Shift+Ctrl+E	Paste as Transparent Selection
Shift+Ctrl+F	Defloat Selection
Shift+Ctrl+H	Histogram Adjustment
Shift+Ctrl+I	Invert Selection
Shift+Ctrl+L	Paste Into Selection
Shift+Ctrl+M	Hide Selection Marquee
Shift+Ctrl+P	Promote Selection to Layer
Shift+Ctrl+S	Create Selection from Mask
Shift+Ctrl+T	View All Tools and Windows
Shift+Ctrl+V	Transparent Color (Selection)
Shift+Ctrl+Z	Command history
Shift+Ctrl+1	Decrease Color Depth–2 Colors
Shift+Ctrl+2	Decrease Color Depth–16 Colors
Shift+Ctrl+3	Decrease Color Depth–256 Colors
Shift+Ctrl+4	Decrease Color Depth–32K Colors
Shift+Ctrl+5	Decrease Color Depth–64K Colors
Shift+Ctrl+6	Decrease Color Depth–X Colors
Shift+Ctrl+8	Increase Color Depth–16 Colors
Shift+Ctrl+9	Increase Color Depth–256 Colors
Shift+Ctrl+0	Increase Color Depth–16.7M Colors

Shortcut	Function
Shift+Alt+D	Delete Workspace
Shift+Alt+L	Open Workspace
Shift+Alt+R	Toggle Ruler
Shift+Alt+S	Save Workspace
F5	Cycle through palette tools
F9	Cycle through active image, Tool Options window, and Histogram window
F12	Save As
Ctrl+F12	Save Copy As

Node Edit Keyboard Shortcuts

Shortcut	Function
Del	Delete
F5	Refresh
Ctrl+A	Select All
Ctrl+B	Line Before (Node Type)
Ctrl+C	Copy
Ctrl+D	Select None
Ctrl+E	Toggle between Edit and Drawing modes
Ctrl+F	Line After (Node Type)
Ctrl+J	Join selected nodes
Ctrl+K	Break the curve
Ctrl+L	Convert to Line (Node Type)
Ctrl+M	Merge
Ctrl+Q	Quit Node Edit
Ctrl+R	Reverse Contour
Ctrl+S	Symmetric (Node Type)
Ctrl+T	Smooth/Tangent (Node Type)
Ctrl+V	Paste
Ctrl+X	Cusp (Node Type)
Ctrl+Z	Undo

APPENDICES

Shortcut	Function
Shift+Ctrl+C	Close the curve
Shift+Ctrl+R	Reverse Path
Shift+Ctrl+S	Asymmetric (Node Type)
Ctrl+Alt+Z	Redo
Ctrl+1	Curve Before (Node Type)
Ctrl+2	Curve After (Node Type)

Browser Keyboard Shortcuts

Shortcut	Function
Ctrl+A	Select All
Ctrl+B	Go to new folder
Ctrl+D	Select None
Ctrl+F	Find file
Ctrl+M	Move selected image(s)
Ctrl+P	Print
Ctrl+R	Rename selected image
Ctrl+W	Fit window to thumbnails
Ctrl+Y	Copy selected image(s)
Ctrl+Del	Delete selected image(s)
Alt+F3	Find file
F3	Repeat Find
F5	Update Thumbnails
Ctrl+F5	Refresh Tree
* (on numeric keypad)	Expand selected folder
Shift+Tab	Next pane
F6	Next pane
Shift+F6	Previous Pane
Shift+I	Image Information
Alt+Enter	Image Information
Enter	Open selected image(s)
Shift+A	Full Screen Edit

Animation Shop Keyboard Shortcuts

Shortcut	Function
F1	Help Topics
F12	Save As
Ctrl+A	Select All
Ctrl+B	Browse
Ctrl+C	Copy
Ctrl+D	Select None
Ctrl+E	Paste Into Selected Frame
Ctrl+I	Flip
Ctrl+L	Paste Before Current
Ctrl+M	Mirror
Ctrl+N	New
Ctrl+O	Open
Ctrl+R	Rotate
Ctrl+S	Save
Ctrl+V	Paste As New Animation
Ctrl+X	Cut
Ctrl+Z	Undo
Shift+A	Animation Wizard
Shift+B	Banner Wizard
Shift+D	Duplicate Animation
Shift+O	Toggle Onionskin
Shift+R	Reverse Frames
Shift+S	Resize Animation
Shift+U	Export Frames to Tube
Shift+X	Export frames to PSP
Shift+Z	Optimization Wizard
Shift+Ctrl+L	Paste After Current Frame
Shift+Alt+Enter	Animation Properties
Alt+Enter	Frame Properties
Ctrl+F4	Close
Alt+F4	Exit

APPENDICES

Index

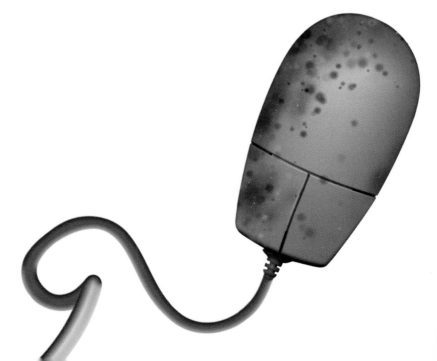

Index

Note: Italicized entries refer to illustrations, tables, figures, Tips, Notes, or Cautions.

PAINT SHOP PRO 6 POWER!

Price: $39.99
ISBN: 0-9662889-2-0
Pages: 416
Author: Lori Davis

- Full Color
- Tabbed Sections
- Technically edited by Jasc

Highlights

- Completely updated for Paint Shop Pro 6, this book is geared for PSP users who want to get the most out of their software
- Written by a well-known expert in the Paint Shop Pro field
- The focused chapters explain how to use layers, masks, animations, and filters

SCANNER SOLUTIONS

Price: $29.95
ISBN: 0-9662889-7-1
Pages: 320
Author: Winston Steward

- Full Color
- Tabbed Sections
- Index for easy use

Highlights

- Shows readers how to use their scanners for personal entertainment, in their home office, and in conjunction with the Internet
- Describes how to purchase and install scanners, specific hardware and software performance tips, and how to use the scanner as an important piece of office equipment.
- Discusses photo editing, graphic design, desktop publishing, OCR, saving and archiving, and retrieving files

GENEALOGY BASICS ONLINE

Price: $24.95
ISBN: 1-929685-00-9
Pages: 204
Author: Cherri Melton Flinn

- Glossary
- Appendix-Historical Epidemics of the Last 350 Years

Highlights

- Reviews of genealogical Web sites and tips for how to search them
- Virtual tour of courthouse and genealogy libraries nationwide
- Written in an easy step-by-step approach

DIGITAL CAMERA SOLUTIONS

Price: $29.95
ISBN: 0-9662889-6-3
Pages: 368
Author: Gregory Georges

- Full Color
- Tabbed Sections
- Index for easy use

Highlights

- Teaches readers how to edit digital images, prepare them for the Internet, and print them in a high-quality format
- Contains dozens of examples and projects to use with any type or brand of digital camera
- Focuses on mastering digital camera software and photo manipulation techniques

MUSKA & LIPMAN

Stay updated with Paint Shop Pro news, tips, and tricks. Subscribe to the free *pspPower* e-mail newsletter by visiting psppower.com

Order Form

Postal Orders:
Muska & Lipman Publishing
P.O. Box 8225
Cincinnati, Ohio 45208

Online Orders or more information:
http://www.muskalipman.com
Fax Orders:
(513) 924-9333

Title/ISBN	Price/Cost

Paint Shop Pro 6 Power!
0-9662889-2-0

Quantity _____

× $39.99

Total Cost _____

Digital Camera Solutions
0-9662889-6-3

Quantity _____

× $29.95

Total Cost _____

Title/ISBN	Price/Cost

Scanner Solutions
0-9662889-7-1

Quantity _____

× $29.95

Total Cost _____

Genealogy Basics Online
1-929685-00-9

Quantity _____

× $24.95

Total Cost _____

Ship to:

Company _____

Name _____

Address _____

City _____ State _____ Zip _____ Country _____

E-mail _____

Educational facilities, companies, and organizations interested in multiple copies of these books should contact the publisher for quantity discount information. Training manuals, CD-ROMs, electronic versions, and portions of these books are also available individually or can be tailored for specific needs.

Subtotal _____

Sales Tax _____
(please add 6% for books shipped to Ohio addresses)

Shipping _____
($5.00 for US and Canada $10.00 other countries)

TOTAL PAYMENT ENCLOSED _____

Thank you for your order.